# Recommended Short Break Holidays in Britain 2003

**Short Break Holidays throughout Britain in Recommended, Registered or otherwise Approved Establishments including Self-catering**

**Fully described and illustrated for direct booking**

**For Key to Symbols see Page 42**
**For Contents see Page 43**
**For Index of towns/counties see back of book**

plus Maps

## FALCON HOTEL

- Central London
- ★★ B&B Hotel
- Family friendly • Est. 30 years
- Tranquil position
- Set in a garden square
- 2 mins Paddington Station
- Airlines check-ins 15 mins Heathrow on Express Link

• e-mail: info@falcon-hotel.com
• website: www.falcon-hotel.com
• Tel: +44 (0) 20 7723 8603
• Fax: +44 (0) 20 7402 7009
11 Norfolk Sq., Hyde Park North, London W2 1RU

*Our guests first and always*

*Affordable prices from: Singles £35, Doubles £55*

*For latest seasonal prices please call*

- En-suite facilities
- Very clean and comfortable
- Close to tourist attractions and shops
- Triple and Family rooms
- Full freshly cooked English breakfasts

FALCON HOTEL

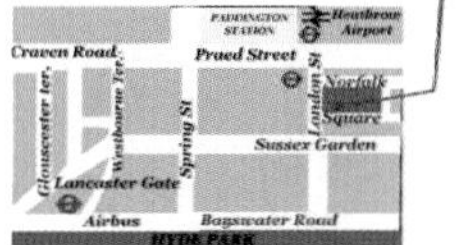


# ELIZABETH HOTEL

Quiet, convenient Townhouse overlooking the magnificent gardens of Eccleston Square. Only a short walk from Buckingham Palace and other tourist attractions. Easy access to Knightsbridge, Oxford Street and Regent Street. Extremely reasonable rates in a fantastic location. Visa, Mastercard, Switch, Delta & JCB are all accepted

37 Eccleston Square,
Victoria, London, SW1V 1PB
E-mail:info@elizabethhotel.com
Web:www.elizabethhotel.com

**info@elizabethhotel.com**

**Tel: 020 7828 6812**
**Fax: 020 7828 6814**

UNBEATABLE VALUE IN THE HEART OF LONDON, FACING HYDE PARK

## THE ELYSEE HOTEL

**25/26 CRAVEN TERRACE, LONDON W2 3EL**
**TEL: 020 7402 7633 • FAX: 020 7402 4193**
**e-mail: information@elyseehotel-london.co.uk**
**website: www.elyseehotel-london.co.uk**

Near London's famous tourist and shopping areas. Rooms with attached bath/shower and toilets. Lifts to all floors. Tea/coffee making facilities, Sky and cable TV, security safe, hairdryer. Rates include Continental breakfast. Three minutes from Lancaster Gate Underground and six minutes from Paddington Station for Heathrow Express.

**Single £50, Twin/Double £55 (for room), Family (3 persons) £75, Family (5 persons) £95**

## Gower Hotel

**129 SUSSEX GARDENS, HYDE PARK LONDON W2 2RX**

**Tel: 0207 262 2262 • Fax: 0207 262 2006**

**e-mail: gower@stavrouhotels.co.uk website: http://www.stavrouhotels.co.uk**

The Gower Hotel is a small family-run Hotel, centrally located within two minutes' walk from Paddington Station, which benefits from the Heathrow express train, "15 minutes to and from Heathrow Airport". Excellently located for sightseeing London's famous sights and shops, Hyde Park, Madame Tussaud's, Harrods, Oxford Street, Marble Arch, Buckingham Palace and many more close by. All rooms have private shower and WC, radio, TV (includes satellite and video channels), direct dial telephone and tea and coffee facilities. All recently refurbished and fully centrally heated. 24 hour reception. Private car park.

**Single Rooms from £30–£54 • Double/Twin Rooms from £26–£36**
**Triple & Family Rooms from £20–£30 • Prices are per person**

**CHILDREN HALF PRICE**
**DISCOUNTS ON LONGER STAYS.**
***Singles from £23-£34***
***Double/Twin from £30-£54***
**Triples and Family Rooms from £16pp**

## QUEENS HOTEL

33 Anson Road, Tufnell Park, London N7
Tel: 0207 607 4725 • Fax: 0207 697 9725
e-mail: queens@stavrouhotels.co.uk • website: http://www.stavrouhotels.co.uk

The Queens Hotel is a large double-fronted Victorian building standing in its own grounds five minutes' walk from Tufnell Park Station. Quietly situated with ample car parking spaces; 15 minutes to West End and close to London Zoo, Hampstead and Highgate. Two miles from Kings Cross and St Pancras stations. Many rooms en suite, TV and tea/coffee making facilities. Credit cards welcome.

***All prices include full English Breakfast plus VAT***

## Haven Hotel

**6-8 Sussex Gardens, Paddington, London W2 1UL**
**Tel: 020 7723 5481/2195 • Fax: 020 7706 4568**

Very centrally situated Bed and Breakfast. First hotel in Sussex Gardens from Edgware Road. Parking available. Reasonable rates. Major shops and attractions nearby.

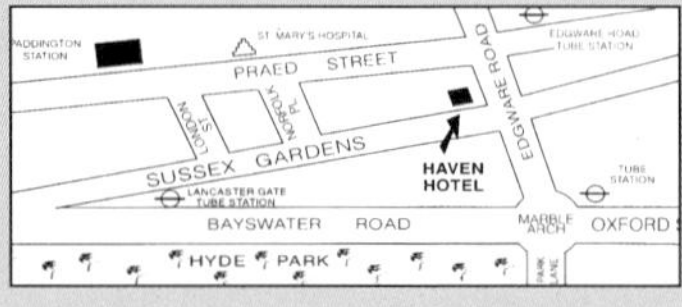


**EDGWARE ROAD, PADDINGTON, MARBLE ARCH, LANCASTER GATE**

## EUROPA HOUSE HOTEL

A small, family-run hotel since 1974, the Europa House Hotel is situated in the heart of London, in the Paddington & Hyde Park area.
Personal service of the highest standard. All rooms en suite, double, twin and family rooms available. Special rates for chidren under 10.
Five minutes from Paddington mainline and underground stations, Heathrow Airport 15 minutes away on the Heathrow to Paddington Railway link.
Marble Arch and Oxford Street within walking distance.

**151 Sussex Gardens, Hyde Park, London W2 2RY**
**Tel: 020 7723 7343 • Fax: 020 7224 9331**

E-mail: europahouse@enterprise.net • Web: www.europahousehotel.com
www.europahousehotel.org.uk www.europahousehotel.net

## Blair Victoria Hotel • Victoria • London

An impressively furnished and friendly London town house, in an excellent location for all tourist attractions.

Within easy walking distance of Buckingham Palace, St James's Park, Westminster Abbey, the Embankment and The Apollo and Palace Theatres.

***Single room from £35, twin/double from £55 including full English breakfast and VAT***

The Blair Victoria Hotel

78-84 Warwick Way, Victoria, London SW1V 1RZ

**Tel: 0207 8288603**

**Fax: 0207 976 6536**

## THE PHILADELPHIA

**19 Eliot Gardens, Newquay TR7 2QE**

**Tel: 01637 877747**

**e-mail: stay@thephiladelphia.co.uk**

**www.thephiladelphia.co.uk / www.thephiladelphia.org.uk**

Newquay's premier smoke-free guest house, recommended by Which? as one of their Top 20 Guest Houses. Quiet tree-lined avenue, award-winning gardens, car park, private patio and hot tub. Bright and spacious quality accommodation in tastefully themed rooms, all with superb en suite facilities, colour TV and complimentary beverages. Extensive choice for breakfast. Short walk to beaches, town and Trenance Gardens. Short drive to the famous Eden Project and Heligan Gardens. Special breaks in quality surroundings, relaxed and friendly atmosphere, comfort, good food and great hospitality – you'll be made very welcome at The Philadelphia.

**B&B from £25 pppn • • • Four-night Eden Break £99.**

HOTEL Victoria

NEWQUAY

## INCLUSIVE GOLF PACKAGES

*5 nights 4 rounds of golf from £265pp*

*3 nights 2 rounds of golf from £150pp*

*Courses in Newquay, Perranporth, Treloy, Lanhydrock & St. Mellion (Int.)*

- 113 en-suite rooms • 7 new luxury suites
- Unique lift through cliff to beach
- Victoria Health Club including indoor pool, spa bath, sauna & sunbeds

E.T.C. ★★★ HOTEL

East Street • Newquay • Cornwall

Tel 01637 872255 • Fax 01637 859295

For more info., take a virtual tour at: **www.hotel-victoria.co.uk**

Stunning views to coasts and moors make this very spacious house a special destination for your holiday. With the added bonus of peace, tranquillity and delicious home-made country cooking, how can you resist paying us a visit? We are well situated for the coast and moors in Devon and Cornwall, including the Eden Project. Two double and one twin room, all en suite. Games room with full-size snooker table, dining room and comfortable large conservatory with spectacular coastal views. Garden for guests' use; car parking. Non-smoking establishment. Children over 12 years welcome.

*B&B from £20, optional Evening Meal from £10 • Open February to November.*

**Whitstone, Holsworthy, Near Bude EX22 6UF • Tel: 01288 341002**

A beautiful 18th century mansion house set in acres of parkland, well situated for touring Cornwall. A health and leisure spa offers an indoor swimming pool, sauna, spa bath, new gym, beautician and masseur.

## Penventon Park Hotel

**Redruth, West Cornwall TR15 1TE**

**Telephone: 01209 20 3000 • Fax: 01209 20 3001**

**e-mail: manager@penventon.com • www.penventon.com**

The famous Dining Galleries Restaurant serves a large choice of locally caught fish, meat and home produced vegetables, with extensive à la carte menus featuring Italian, French and English dishes. Resident pianists nightly. All bedrooms are en suite, with colour television and tea and coffee making facilities.

***• Phone for details of bargain breaks***
***• Colour brochure available • AA★★★***

***"One of the most beautifully situated hotels in England"***

**Willapark Manor** is a lovely character house in a beautiful setting amidst 14 acre grounds, overlooking Bossiney Bay. Surrounded by woodland, it is secluded and has direct access to the coastal path and beach. It is a family-run hotel with a friendly and informal atmosphere, excellent cuisine and a well stocked cocktail bar. Beautifully appointed bedrooms, all en suite and with colour TV and tea/coffee making facilities. Some four-posters. A warm welcome and a memorable holiday assured.

## Willapark Manor Hotel

**Bossiney, Tintagel, Cornwall PL34 0BA**

**Tel: 01840 770782**

**www.willapark.co.uk**

**Duchy Holidays**

A selection of seaside and countryside holiday homes located throughout Cornwall. A luxury bungalow with a private swimming pool, farmhouse with fishing lake, beachside cottages, lodges and villas with swimming pools and entertainment. All properties are inspected and personally supervised. Short breaks and long weekends available from £85 (excluding school holidays).

**Duchy Holidays, 14 St Georges Hill,**
**Perranporth, Cornwall TR6 0DZ**
**Tel & Fax: 01872 572971**
**e-mail: duchy.holidays@virgin.net**
**website: www.duchyholidays.co.uk**

AA ♦♦♦♦♦ Guest Accommodation

New House Farm, Lorton, Buttermere,
near Cockermouth, Cumbria CA13 9UU
Tel: 01900 85404 • Fax: 01900 85421

Situated in the quietest and most beautiful part of the Lakes, New House Farm has 15 acres of open fields, ponds, streams and woods, which guests may wander around at leisure and there is easy access to nearby lakes and fells. All bedrooms are en suite. There is a cosy dining room and two comfortable sitting rooms with open log fires. The food served is fine traditional fare.

*Which? Hotel Guide Hotel of the Year Award Winner(Cumbria)*

e-mail: hazel@newhouse-farm.co.uk
website: www.newhouse-farm.co.uk

## The Ferndale Hotel

***Lake Road, Ambleside, Cumbria LA22 0DB***
***Tel: 015394 32207***
***e-mail: ferndalehotel@btconnect.com***
***website: www.ferndalehotel.com***

The Ferndale Hotel is a small, family-run Hotel where you will find a warm, friendly welcome and personal attention at all times. Offering excellent accommodation with good home cooked English or Vegetarian breakfast. Our 10 attractive bedrooms have all been individually decorated and furnished, each with full en suite facilities, colour television and tea/coffee making tray. Full central heating throughout, several rooms having views of the fells, and including ground floor bedrooms. The Ferndale is open all year round with a car park, is licensed, offers packed lunches, hair dryer, clothes/boot drying and ironing facilities. A wide choice of places to dine, within minutes' walking distance, ranging from excellent pub food to superb restaurants of many varied cuisines will complete your day.

English Tourism Council ♦♦♦ Guest Accommodation

Bed and Breakfast £22.00 - £26.00 pppn. Weekly £145 - £165 pp. **Please phone for brochure.**

## Clarence House *COUNTRY HOTEL & RESTAURANT*

***Skelgate, Dalton-in-Furness LA15 8BQ • 01229 462508 • Fax: 01229 467177***

***e-mail: Clarencehsehotel@aol.com • www.clarencehousehotel.com***

*This beautiful mid-Victorian mansion is set in over 3 acres of landscaped gardens. It has an enviable reputation as one of the best hotels in the area, offering excellent accommodation, fine dining, and a warm and friendly atmosphere. All 17 bedrooms have private facilities, colour TV, telephone, radio, trouser press, hairdryer and hospitality tray.*

*Throughout the year we offer Special Weekend Breaks from £95 per person per weekend, with our residents coming back time after time. At Clarence House we realise the importance of simply getting away from it all. We do hope there is a break to tempt you to come and enjoy the luxurious surroundings of Clarence House.*

## Glen Garth Hotel & Restaurant

**359 Abbey Road, Barrow-in-Furness Cumbria LA13 9JY**
**Tel: 01229 825374 • Fax: 01229 811744**

Accommodation is available in 15 comfortable en suite bedrooms (single and executive double/twin), all with TV and radio; there is a four-poster room for that special occasion. Children are welcome, and cots and high chairs can be provided. The hotel is licensed, with a popular restaurant. B&B from £25 to £35pp

*The hotel is close to historic Furness Abbey, but is only a short step away from the town centre and all its amenities, as well as the train station. The area's top tourist attraction, South Lakeland Wild Animal Park is only ¾ mile away. There is a Leisure Centre close by with sports, swimming and gym facilities, as well as an 18-hole golf course within 1 mile.*

Barrow-in-Furness is an ideal location for tourists, surrounded by beautiful beaches and within easy reach of everything the Lake District National Park has to offer. The Glen Garth Hotel is also the perfect venue for Wedding Receptions and Celebration Dinners.

## The Leathes Head Hotel and Restaurant

The Leathes Head is an eleven bedroomed hotel located in the spectacular Borrowdale Valley, set in 3 acres of secluded formal lawns and woodland, with wonderful views of the surrounding fells and Derwentwater. There are three lounges, a bar and an award winning restaurant. The menus, changed daily, put the emphasis on fresh local produce prepared by our acclaimed local chef.

• Health Club • Croquet and boules • Terrace seating • Ample parking.

**The Leathes Head Hotel**
**Borrowdale, Cumbria CA12 5UY**
**Tel: 01768 777247 • Fax: 01768 777363**
**www.leatheshead.co.uk**

## THE MANOR HOUSE GUEST HOUSE

**Oughterside, Aspatria, Cumbria CA7 2PT • Tel/Fax: 016973 22420**

We will make you very welcome at our lovely old manor farmhouse. The rooms are spacious with king-size beds, large en suite bathrooms, tea and coffee making, TV and lots of extras. The 7 acres of grounds are home to many birds, including barn owls, as well as horses, donkeys, a mule, and even sheep! Although there is easy access to the nearby Western Lakes and Solway Coast, guests enjoy the peace of our rural setting. Dogs and children welcome. B&B from £21 to £30. Dinner from £7. Special prices for longer stays. Inside bike storage. Drying facilities. Local inspection.

**e-mail: richardandjudy@themanorhouse.net**
**www.themanorhouse.net**

## *Gilpin Lodge*

★★★ HOTEL Gold GOLD AWARD

AA ★★★ RAC ★★★ Hotel

A friendly, luxurious country house hotel and restaurant with an atmosphere redolent of an elegant private house. Set in 20 acres of woodland, moors and country gardens, only 2 miles from Lake Windermere and 12 miles from the M6. All the charming bedrooms have en suite facilities; some have jacuzzis and some have four-poster beds, French windows and private patios. Dinner is the highlight of the day, with an interesting yet unpretentious style of cooking which has won many awards.

CROOK ROAD, NEAR WINDERMERE LA23 3NE
**015394 88818 FAX: 015394 88058**
**e-mail: hotel@gilpin-lodge.co.uk**
**www.gilpin-lodge.co.uk**

ETC ★★ to ★★★★★

## The Coppermines & Coniston Cottages

**50 Unique Lakeland cottages for 2-30 of quality and character in stunning mountain scenery. Log fires, exposed beams. Weekends and Short Breaks.**

**015394 41765 (24 hrs) • Mobile: 07721 584488**

**www.coppermines.co.uk Pets Very Welcome!**

***Dove Cottage, Church Lane, Mayfield, Ashbourne.***

This modernised 200-year-old cottage in Mayfield village is ideally situated for shops, pubs, busy market towns, sporting facilities, lovely Dove Valley, Alton Towers, Peaks and Staffordshire Moorlands and many other places of interest. The cottage is comfortably furnished and well-equipped with TV, fridge, automatic washing machine, gas central heating. The fenced garden overlooks farmland. Sleeps seven. Garage and parking. Children welcome. Pets by arrangement. Available for long and short lets, also mid-week bookings. Price and brochure on request. Further details from:

**Arthur Tatlow, Ashview, Ashfield Farm, Calwich, Ashbourne DE6 2EB Tel: 01335 324443 or 324279**

## Torcross Apartments

Situated directly on the beach in the unspoilt countryside of the South Hams between the blue waters of Start Bay and the Slapton Ley Nature Reserve. Seven miles to Dartmouth. Winter breaks. Central heating. Ground floor apartments and lift to all floors. In-house bar and restaurant; take-away food service. Lovely walks on coastal path.

Brochure with pleasure or visit our **website** on **www.torcross.net**

**Torcross, South Devon TQ7 2TQ Tel: 01548 580206 • Fax: 01548 580996**

**e-mail: enquiries@torcross.net**

## PRINCE HALL HOTEL

**Two Bridges, Dartmoor PL20 6SA**

**Tel: 01822 890403 • Fax: 01822 890676**

**e-mail: bookings@princehall.co.uk**

**website: www.princehall.co.uk**

The Prince Hall Hotel is a small, friendly and relaxed country house hotel, in a peaceful and secluded setting, commanding glorious views over open moorland. Nine en suite bedrooms, two with four-posters, all rooms have TV, telephone, refreshment tray. The hotel offers peaceful surroundings, attentive service, gourmet award winning food and and excellent wine list. Marvellous walks from the hotel; fishing, riding and golf nearby.

**ETC ★★, AA ★★ and Two Rosettes for Food,**

**Good Hotel Guide, 'Which?' Hotel Guide, Best Loved Hotels.**

**"Supreme Accolade 2003" Voted one of the AA top 200 hotels in Britain and Ireland**

*The English Riviera*

**ETC ★★/★★★**

## Ashfield Rise Holiday Apartments

**Ruckamore Road, Torquay, Devon TQ2 6HF**

**Tel: 01803 605156 • Fax: 01803 607373**

**e-mail: stay@ashfieldrise.co.uk**

**website: www.ashfieldrise.co.uk**

Sleep 1-8. Apartments ideal for family holidays, some with sea view. Within walking distance of the sea front, Riviera Centre and the "old world" village of Cockington. Each apartment has modern kitchen and microwave, colour TV. Children and pets welcome; cots, high chair available. Secluded garden with large car park. All linen supplied free of charge; electricity metered. Couples, families and mature singles only. Ideal for conference delegates seeking the privacy and freedom of their own apartment. Please telephone or write for our free brochure.

## *Anchorage Hotel, Babbacombe*

www.anchoragehotel.co.uk

Tel: 01803 326175, Torquay
E-mail: anchorage@aol.com

*Set in quiet Cary Park adjacent to the bowling green. All 56 bedrooms are en-suite with tea making facilities, colour TV & all non smoking. Outdoor heated pool, fully licensed. Regular entertainment, car parking & lift to most rooms.*

## Varley House, Chambercombe Park, Ilfracombe EX34 9QW

**Tel: 01271 863927 • Fax: 01271 879299 • e-mail: info@varleyhouse.co.uk • website: www.varleyhouse.co.uk**

Built at the turn of the 20th century for returning officers from the Boer War, Varley generates a feeling of warmth and relaxation, combined with an enviable position overlooking Hillsborough Nature Reserve. Winding paths lead to the Harbour and several secluded coves. Our attractive, spacious, fully en suite, non-smoking bedrooms all have colour TV, central heating, generous beverage tray, hairdryer and clock radio alarm. Superb food, beautiful surroundings and that special friendly atmosphere so essential to a relaxing holiday. Cosy separate bar. Car Park. Children over 5 years of age. Dogs by arrangement. Bed and Breakfast from £26 per person. Weekly from £170 per person. Dinner available £15.

**ETC/AA ◆◆◆◆**

## THE RISING SUN INN

**Umberleigh, Near Barnstaple, Devon EX37 9DU**

**Tel: 01769 560447 • Fax: 01769 560764**
**e-mail: risingsuninn@btinternet.com**
**website: www.risingsuninn.com**

Dating from the 13th century, the Rising Sun Inn is situated in the beautiful Taw Valley, ideal for visiting RHS Rosemoor Garden, Dartmoor, Exmoor and the North Devon coast. The inn offers traditional hospitality, excellent food and fine wines. Bedrooms are full of character and provide every modern comfort. There are nearby facilities for golf, horse riding, cycling and walking the Tarka Trail, as well as salmon fishing on the River Taw.

## SUMMERDYNE HOLIDAY APARTMENTS

Greenway Road, Chelston, Torquay TQ2 6JE
Tel: 01803 605439 • Fax: 01803 607441

★★★ SELF CATERING

Summerdyne is an elegant Victorian villa, tastefully converted into 10 spacious self-contained apartments, all comfortably furnished, centrally heated and fully equipped to a high standard. Large gardens to play in or relax. Safe off-road parking. We are close to the beach, town centre and Cockington Country Park, making Summerdyne an ideal location for families and couples alike.

Dale and Mandy Tanner, your resident hosts, will ensure you receive a very warm welcome and a pleasant stay at Summerdyne. Short Breaks from £70 per couple including central heating and bed linen. Weekly rates from £120 low season to £475 high season. Phone or e-mail for our information pack.

e-mail: stay@summerdyne.co.uk • www.summerdyne.co.uk

## CROWNDALE HOTEL 18 Bridge Road, Torquay TQ2 5BA • Tel/Fax: 01803 293068

Tom and Barbara are your friendly hosts at this 7-bedroom non-smoking hotel which is situated in a quiet, tree-lined road, but is close to all that Torquay has to offer. All our double or family rooms are en suite, well decorated and comfortable. All have central heating with thermostatic controls, colour TV, radio/alarm clock, hairdryer, and tea/coffee making facilities. There is a car park at the rear of the hotel and ground floor rooms are available.

*We welcome children and can supply a high chair, baby monitors, baby bath, changing mat and small steriliser for your convenience.*

We are open all year, take credit and debit cards and are ETC ◆◆◆◆ rated.
Please ring us to request a brochure.

## Norcliffe Hotel

★★

**Babbacombe Sea Front, Torquay TQ1 3LF**

Family-run 28-bedroom licensed hotel. All rooms have en suite facilities, colour TV, radio, tea-making facilities and telephone. Heated indoor swimming pool, sauna and games room. Ideally situated on Babbacombe Downs overlooking Lyme Bay, opposite the cliff railway down to Oddicombe Beach.

**Special Breaks, Christmas & New Year packages available**

**Tel: 01803 328456 • Fax: 01803 328023**
**www.norcliffehotel.co.uk**
**e-mail: manager@norcliffehotel.co.uk**

## THE NEW INN • High Street, Clovelly, Near Bideford EX39 5TQ

**Tel: 01237 431303 • Fax: 01237 431636** **ETC/AA ★★**

This unspoilt heritage village is filled with colourful flower-covered cottages that seem to tumble over one another down the steep and narrow cobbled street which descends towards the tiny harbour. To stay at the New Inn in the heart of the village is to wake up to the sights and sounds of a seafaring way of life that has changed little over the last hundred years. Each of the hotel bedrooms is beautifully decorated. The magic touch of a talented interior designer is to be seen everywhere. The restaurant serves local and regional specialities. **This really is a short break paradise.**

DB&B from £37.50pppn (low season, seven-night stay) to £63.00pppn (high season, one-night stay).

## Glenorleigh HOTEL

26 Cleveland Road
Torquay
Devon TQ2 5BE
Tel: 01803 292135
Fax: 01803 213717

*As featured on BBC Holiday programme*

*David & Pam Skelly*

AA ◆◆◆◆

Situated in a quiet residential area, Glenorleigh is 10 minutes' walk from both the sea front and the town centre. •Delightful en suite rooms, with your comfort in mind. •Good home cooking, both English and Continental, plenty of choice, with vegetarian options available daily. •Bar leading onto terrace overlooking Mediterranean-style garden with feature palms and heated swimming pool. •Discounts for children and Senior Citizens. •Brochures and menus available on request.

**e-mail: glenorleighhotel@btinternet.com • website: www.glenorleigh.co.uk**

# THE AVONCOURT HOTEL

**TORRS WALK AVENUE, ILFRACOMBE • TEL: 01271 862543**

**Chris and Tony welcome you to their friendly family-run hotel. The hotel is situated in a quiet private road adjacent to National Trust land. It faces south with panoramic views of town and countryside. All bedrooms are on first or ground floor and the excellent food and relaxed atmosphere will make your holiday a memorable one. The heated rooms are en suite with tea/coffee making facilities and colour TV. There is also a cosy licensed bar and a TV lounge. Ample parking.**

# Axevale Caravan Park

**Colyford Road, Seaton EX12 2DF • Tel: 0800 0688816**

A quiet, family-run park with 68 modern and luxury caravans for hire. The park overlooks the delightful River Axe Valley, and is just a 10 minute walk from the town with its wonderfully long, award-winning beach. Children will love our extensive play area, with its sand pit, paddling pool, swings and slide. Laundry facilities are provided and there is a wide selection of goods on sale in the park shop which is open every day. All of our caravans have a shower, toilet, fridge and TV. Also, with no clubhouse, a relaxing atmosphere is ensured. Prices from £75 per week; reductions for three or fewer persons early/late season.

**website: www.axevale.co.uk**

# THE CROWN *hospitality since 1760*

**Lynton's Original & Historic Coaching Inn**

**Market Street, Lynton, North Devon EX35 6AG**

**Tel: 01598 752253 • Fax: 01598 753311 • www.thecrown-lynton.co.uk**

Nestling in the heart of Exmoor National Park Conservation Area, this Old Village Inn is privately owned, family-managed and continually striving to maintain the reputation it has achieved during its present ownership.

The ambience of The Crown is enhanced by the high standard of hospitality, comfortable lounge bar, bustling bar/restaurant and covered terrace. Non-smoking areas include the hotel dining room and library.

We offer an extensive menu using fresh local produce, when available, prepared on the premises by a team of young but experienced chefs, complemented by genuinely friendly and efficient front of house staff.

**Tariff Examples:**
WINTER: 3 nights Dinner, Bed & Breakfast from £130pp
SUMMER: 3 nights Dinner, Bed & Breakfast from £180pp

# LAMBSCOMBE FARM

Medieval farmhouse and luxury barn conversions around cobbled courtyard overlooking wooded valley full of wildlife. Set in 6 secluded acres with stream, large children's play/picnic area, games room. Every home comfort including log fires and some en suite bathrooms. All inclusive rates. Open all year. Sleep 2-14.

**TWO NIGHT BREAKS AVAILABLE**

English Tourism Council ★★★★ SELF CATERING

Brenda and Richard Boulter • Tel: 01598 740558
Lamscombe Farm, North Molton, South Molton, Devon EX36 3JT
e-mail: richardboulter@supanet.com • website: www.lambscombefarm.co.uk

The beautiful 14th century Courtyard at Dartington Hall is the perfect place to relax. Set amidst 1000 acres of farmland and ancient deer park, there are many walks for you to enjoy, through the woodlands, along the River Dart and in the magnificent gardens surrounding the Hall.

*Dartington Hall is also an ideal base from which to explore Devon and Cornwall, including Dartmoor, the coast, Eden Project and National Trust properties.*

**SPECIAL BREAK OFFER**

**£49.50pppn for Bed, Breakfast and Dinner in our award-winning White Hart Bar & Restaurant.**

**STAY 5 NIGHTS FOR THE PRICE OF 4!**

*Min. stay 2 nights. Subject to availability*

## The White Hart Bar & Restaurant

**Located within the Courtyard, the White Hart Bar offers mouthwatering meals, freshly prepared using the finest local ingredients, including organic produce from Dartington Hall's own market garden.**

*Open for lunch and dinner.*

Dartington Hall, Totnes, South Devon TQ9 6EL

Accommodation and Conference enquiries: 01803 847147

Bar and Restaurant reservations: 01803 847111

www.dartingtonhall.com

*Rosette Award for Food – Which? Guide to Country Pubs • 'Pick of the Pubs' recommended – AA Pub Guide 2002 • As featured on Carlton TV's 'Taste of the West' • Gold, Silver & Bronze medals - South Hams Festival 2002.*

## GET AWAY FROM IT ALL

There will always be times when you wish there was somewhere you could go to get away from it all, relax in beautiful surroundings, and sample delicious food.

THE CHERRYBROOK HOTEL

IS AN IDEAL CHOICE – WARMEST WELCOME

Set in the heart of Dartmoor National Park, Cherrybrook is an excellent base for walking, touring or simply enjoying the breathtaking scenery.

*To find out more, telephone or fax Margaret or Andy Duncan on:* **01822 880260**

♦♦♦♦

CHERRYBROOK HOTEL, TWO BRIDGES, YELVERTON, DEVON PL20 6SP

www.cherrybrook-hotel.co.uk • e-mail: info@cherrybrook-hotel.co.uk

♦♦♦♦

## Hoops Inn

**Horns Cross, Near Clovelly, Bideford, Devon EX39 5DL**

**Tel: 01237 451222 • Fax: 01237 451247**
**e-mail: sales@hoopsinn.co.uk**
**website: www.hoopsinn.co.uk**

This lovingly cared for, picturebook thatched country inn blends 13th century charm with 21st century luxury and extends a warm welcome to its guests. Relax by one of the open log fires to soak up the olde worlde atmosphere while enjoying a real ale or wine before dining on the best of local fish, game or meat. All bedrooms are en suite, individually furnished and well appointed. Special golfing breaks available. The Hoops is a splendid base for a combined sea, country or touring holiday, with historic gardens, houses, and the world-famous fishing village of Clovelly on the doorstep, and Dartmoor and Exmoor within easy reach. RAC ★★ 3 Restaurant Ribbons

GEORGIAN COUNTRY COTTAGES

## Glebe House Cottages

**Seven cottages beautifully converted from the original Coach House, Stables and Barns of a Listed Georgian rectory set in five acres of lawns and woodland.**

** Sleeps 2-12 * Four-poster beds * Double sized spa baths * En suite facilities * Games Room * Laundry Room * Children's play area * Barbecue * Cellar Bar and Restaurant serving superb home-cooked food * 10 minutes' drive from sandy beaches * Open all year. * Tariff includes CH, electricity, TV and all bed linen * Cots, high chairs and baby monitors provided free of charge. * Special Tariff for couples (and for those with babies under two).*

**Glebe House, Bridgerule, Holsworthy, Devon EX22 7EW • Tel: 01288 381272**
**e-mail: fhg@glebehousecottages.co.uk • website: www.glebehousecottages.co.uk**

## THE LORD HALDON COUNTRY HOUSE HOTEL

The Lord Haldon Country House Hotel is the perfect venue for a quiet get-away break with your beloved pet. Acres of private grounds, mile of driveway for exercise, and animals are welcome in guests' bedrooms by arrangement. The hotel stands in its own grounds, four miles south west of Exeter, set 400 feet above sea level above the Haldon Hills. It is family-run by the Preece family, owners for over 21 years. The hotel is AA*** recognised with 2 Red Rosettes for its restaurant, which is open seven days a week, lunch times and evenings. There is also an intimate Lounge Bar which serves bar food. The Lord Haldon is the only hotel in Devon that is a member of Relais du Silence, an independent hotel consortium dedicated to fine food, service, peace and quiet. For further information about how you can enjoy the finest part of Devon, please telephone 01392 832483 for a free hotel brochure.

★★★ HOTEL

**Dunchideock, Near Exeter**
**Devon EX6 7YF**
**Tel: 01392 832483**
**Fax: 01392 833765**
E-mail: enquiries@lordhaldonhotel.co.uk
website: www.lordhaldonhotel.co.uk

AA ★★★

## Parks Hotel

Rathmore Road, Torquay TQ2 6NZ
Tel: 01803 292420
Booking enquiries – Freephone 08000 191799
www.parks-hotel.co.uk • enquiries@parks-hotel.co.uk

A delightful, tastefully furnished hotel standing in its own grounds, situated in the parks surrounding the famouse Torre Abbey. The position is QUIET and on the LEVEL, 400 yards to the seafront, 300 yards to the Conference/Leisure Centre, and 300 yards to the rail station.

- All bedrooms en suite, with colour TV and tea/coffee making
- Full central heating • Licensed bar • Ample private parking
- Heated and secluded outdoor pool • Special breaks

***B&B from £21 to £28pppn***

## Newbarn Farm Cottages

★★★★ SELF CATERING

**Totnes Road, Paignton, Devon TQ4 7PT**

**Tel: 01803 553602 • Fax: 01803 553637**

Six luxury cottages graded to 4 stars by the English Tourism Council. Exceptionally well equipped and sleeping 2-12 people. Glorious hilltop views of the South Devon countryside extending all the way to Dartmoor. 3 miles to the nearest beach. Perfectly situated for the many tourist attractions in the Torbay and South Hams areas. Very peaceful and relaxing setting. Use of large indoor swimming pool, gymnasium, sauna & solarium (adjacent property ½ mile). On site 6 coarse fishing lakes, large games room, skittle alley. 40 acres of private pastures and woodland to roam. Dogs welcome in two of the cottages.

*Visit our website www.newbarnfarm.com*

## Publisher's Note

While every effort is made to ensure accuracy, we regret that FHG Publications cannot accept responsibility for errors, omissions or misrepresentations in our entries or any consequences thereof. Prices in particular should be checked because we go to press early. We will follow up complaints but cannot act as arbiters or agents for either party.

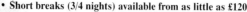

Standing in its own grounds of six acres in the heart of the country, The Compass Inn has easy access to the M4 and M5; Heathrow 1¼ hours by car. Ideally situated for visiting Bath, Bristol, Wells and the Cotswolds; easy access to the Wye Valley and the Royal Forest of Dean.

**LEISURE ACTIVITIES** which can be arranged locally include clay pigeon shooting, hot-air ballooning and horse riding.

*All guest rooms are en suite, with colour TV, direct-dial telephone and tea/coffee making • Restaurant and buffet open daily • Bars offer a choice of real ales and a range of country wines • Unique enclosed Orangery • Pleasant lawns and gardens.*

## The Compass Inn

**Tormarton, Near**
**Badminton GL9 1JB**
**Tel: 01454 218242**
**Fax: 01454 218741**

## Bells Hotel

**Lords Hill, Coleford, Gloucestershire GL16 8BE**
**Tel: 01594 832583 • Fax: 01594 832584**
**e-mail: enquiries@bells-hotel.co.uk**
**website: www.bellshotel.co.uk**

- ♦ Visit the beautiful Forest of Dean & Wye Valley
- ♦ 52 bedroom family-run Hotel established 1971
- ♦ Bar & Restaurant open all day ♦ Large car park
- ♦ 18-hole golf course, tennis court and bowling green all on site

**Bed & Breakfast from £35 per room**
**Half Board Breaks from £40pppn including Half Board and complimentary Golf**
**January to March – no single room supplement**

## • Court Farm •

### Randwick, Stroud, Gloucestershire GL6 6HH

Tel: 01453 764210

Fax: 01453 766428

A 17th century beamed farmhouse, with large, en suite bedrooms, on a small farm in the middle of the village of Ranswick. We have a large, pretty garden for guests to enjoy.

From the Cotswold escarpment there are beautiful views over the Stroud valleys and the Severn Vale with deciduous National Trust woods above the village.

Two village pubs can provide meals. Convenient overnight stop or a good base for longer visits.

Tourist attractions include: Westonbirt Arboretum, Slimbridge Wildfowl Trust, Berkeley Castle, Gloucester Cathedral and Docks.

We can arrange and advise on a wide range of walks, in and around the Stroud valleys.

Evening meals can be provided, children and pets welcome.

*• Non-smoking • Please call for a brochure •*

E-mail: JohnETaylor@courfarm.freeserve.co.uk

## Busketts Lawn Hotel

*Woodlands, New Forest,*
*Near Southampton*
*Hampshire SO40 7GL*
*Tel: 023 8029 2272/3417*
*Fax: 023 8029 2487*

enquiries@buskettslawnhotel.co.uk
www.buskettslawnhotel.co.uk

**ETC/AA/RAC ★★**

***SPECIAL SHORT BREAKS AVAILABLE ALL YEAR ROUND***

The Comfort and Charm of a family-run Country House Hotel yet only 15 minutes to Southampton City Centre.

***FIRST-CLASS ACCOMMODATION***

All rooms en suite, colour TV, radio,telephone, tea-making facilities, mini-fridge,hairdryer and trouser press.

***SUPERB FOOD AND PERSONAL, FRIENDLY SERVICE***

Pool Heated in Season. Putting. Mini Football Pitch. Croquet.

***CHILDREN AND PETS WELCOME***

***Colour Brochure on request***

## The Woodlands Lodge Hotel

**Bartley Road, Woodlands, New Forest, Hampshire SO40 7GN**
**Reservations: (023) 80 292257 • Fax: (023) 80 293090**
**e-mail: reception@woodlands-lodge.co.uk**
**website: www.woodlands-lodge.co.uk**

The Woodlands Lodge Hotel is a luxuriously restored Georgian Country House, set within the beautiful New Forest, yet only 15 minutes from Southampton. Our attractive gardens have direct access to the forest and are ideal for romantic walks. Golf, fishing and horse riding are available nearby and the hotel is perfectly situated for touring the area. Come and unwind from the stress of everyday life and enjoy pure luxury without ostentation.

★★★

*All bedrooms enjoy full en suite facilities of whirlpool bath and separate shower and have king sized beds and a full range of amenities. The quality four-course menu is changed daily to make use of local produce and is complemented by an interesting wine list. The service is friendly, efficient and informal.*

**Woodlands Lodge – where a warm welcome awaits you.**

## WHITE ROSE HOTEL

**Village Centre, Sway, Near Lymington SO41 6BA**
**Tel: 01590 682754 • Fax: 01590 682955**

An elegant Edwardian country house set on the fringe of the New Forest, the family-run White Rose stands in five acres of delightful grounds with an open air swimming pool. The hotel has thoughtfully planned accommodation on two floors linked by a lift. Guest rooms have en suite facilities, colour television, direct-dial telephone incorporating alarm call and baby listening features, and tea and coffee-making facilities. A most attractive lounge bar enjoys panoramic views over the gardens and is the ideal setting for an aperitif prior to consideration of a noteworthy à la carte and table d'hôte selection in the restaurant, vegetarian and special diets being willingly catered for.

AA ★★

**Short Break details on request**

# FHG

## Visit the FHG website

**www.holidayguides.com**

**for details of the wide choice of accommodation featured in the full range of FHG titles**

# BELMONT LODGE & GOLF

## BELMONT, HEREFORD HR2 9SA

**Tel: 01432 352666**

Belmont is situated along the beautiful River Wye, yet conveniently located just a few minutes' drive from the historic Cathedral City of Hereford - what better place to stay or play?

The lodge offers 30 purpose-built hotel rooms with splendid views over the golf course and river. Whatever the standard of your golf, you will enjoy the 18 hole 6511 yard Par 72 Belmont Golf Course and its picture postcard scenery. A warm, friendly, personal service awaits you from our team of dedicated staff whose aim is to provide you with quality service - Hotel, Golf, Meetings & Functions, Fishing, Food & Drink - all at affordable prices.

**e-mail: info@belmont-hereford.co.uk**
**website: www.belmont-hereford.co.uk**

# THE BOWENS

**COUNTRY HOUSE**

**Fownhope, Herefordshire HR1 4PS**

**Tel and Fax: 01432 860430**

ETC/AA ◆◆◆◆

Delightful Georgian house with full central heating set in the peaceful Wye Valley village of Fownhope, midway between Hereford and Ross-on-Wye on the B4224. Perfect centre for walking and touring (Wye Valley, Welsh Marches, Malverns, Brecon Beacons), Black-and-White Villages. 10 comfortable, well-appointed bedrooms (4 on the ground floor), all with full en suite facilities, TV, telephone and tea trays. Superb home-cooked meals, vegetarians welcome. Fully licensed bar and good wine list. Large attractive garden with putting green and grass tennis court (summer months only). Ample private parking.

**2 nights B&B £65pp. DB&B package available. Open all year.**

**E-mail: Thebowenshotel@aol.com Web: www.Thebowenshotel.co.uk**

# LAKE HOTEL

**Shore Road, Lower Bonchurch, Isle of Wight PO38 1RF • 01983 852613**

This lovely country house hotel is set in a beautiful quiet two-acre garden on the seaward side of the "olde worlde" seaside village of Bonchurch. Run by the same family for over 35 years, the hotel offers first class food and service, all in a relaxed and friendly atmosphere. All rooms are en suite with complimentary tea/coffee facilities and TV.

***We can offer an Isle of Wight car ferry inclusive price of just £165.00 for four nights' half board during March/April/May and October, and we really do believe that you will not find better value on our beautiful island.***

**e-mail: fhg@lakehotel.co.uk**
**website: www.lakehotel.co.uk**

# Somerville Hotel

- 7 en suite bedrooms with TV, beverage trays, heating, power showers etc
- Licensed bar and non-smoking lounge
- Off-road parking

- Relaxing "home from home" atmosphere
- Good food
- Ferries arranged
- Bed and Breakfast from £20 per night

**14 St George's Road, Shanklin, Isle of Wight PO37 6BA • Tel: 01983 862821**

# Frenchman's Cove

◆◆◆

**ALUM BAY OLD ROAD, TOTLAND PO39 0HZ**

Our delightful family-run guesthouse is set amongst National Trust downland, not far from the Needles and safe sandy beaches. Ideal for ramblers, birdwatchers, cyclists and those who enjoy the countryside. We have almost an acre of grounds. Cots and high chairs are available. All rooms are en suite, with colour TV and tea/coffee making facilities. Guests can relax in the cosy bar or in the attractive lounge. Also available is the Coach House, a delightfully appointed apartment (ETC 3 Stars) for two adults and two children.

**Please contact Sue or Chris Boatfield for details.**

**Tel: 01983 752227 • www.frenchmanscove.co.uk**

# THE Bedford Lodge HOTEL

4 Chine Avenue, Shanklin Old Village,
Isle of Wight PO37 6AQ
Tel: 01983 862416 • Fax: 01983 868704
e-mail: mail@bedfordlodge.co.uk
www.bedfordlodge.co.uk

Privately owned and personally run, The Bedford Lodge Hotel is set in delightful gardens, in an elevated position giving easy access to both the Old Village and the beach. All bedrooms (some ground floor) are en suite with tea/coffee making facilities, central heating and TV. There is a licensed bar and non-smoking breakfast room. Private car park. Car ferry crossings can be arranged. *Please contact Richard & Ruth Carnall for full details.*

◆◆◆◆

*You can be assured of a warm welcome from Susan, Ginio and family at Ferrari's, in the heart of the Ribble Valley.*

# ferrari's

*Country House Hotel & Restaurant, Longridge*

The Country House offers 14 bedrooms, 5 of which are de luxe standard; some have jacuzzis and four-poster beds. As well as the main dining room which overlooks the beautifully laid out gardens, there are three further function rooms, a fully licensed bar and a residents' lounge. The proprietors pride themselves on satisfying the personal needs of their guests in a friendly and comfortable atmosphere. Whether for business or pleasure, Ferrari's will offer you the best in quality, service and value for money.

**Ferrari's Country House Hotel & Restaurant, Chipping Road, Thornley, Longridge, Preston, Lancashire PR3 2TB**

**Tel: 01772 783148 • info@ferrariscountryhouse.co.uk • www.ferrariscountryhouse.co.uk**

FHG DIPLOMA WINNER

# CASTLEMERE HOTEL

AA ◆◆◆

**13 Shaftesbury Avenue, North Shore, Blackpool FY2 9QQ • Tel: 01253 352430 • Fax: 01253 350116**
**e-mail: bookings@hotelcastlemere.co.uk or sue@hotelcastlemere.co.uk • web: www.hotelcastlemere.co.uk**

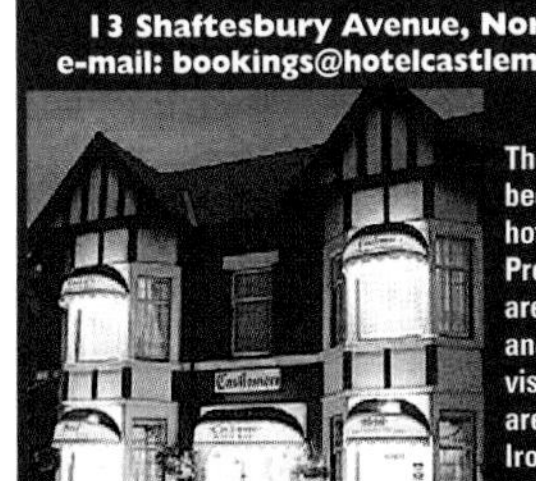

## Welcome Host & Welcome to Excellence Awards

The Castlemere is a licensed family run hotel. The resident proprietors Dave and Sue Hayward have been running the Castlemere for the past 11 years and have established an excellent clientele. The hotel is situated in the very pleasant North Shore area of Blackpool, adjacent to the delightful Queen's Promenade with its lovely views across the Irish Sea. The busy town centre, bus and train stations are convenient and a range of entertainment opportunities for all ages and tastes, including a Casino and Golf Course, are within an easy walk or a short tram ride. Blackpool is ideally situated for visiting the Dales, Lake District, "Bronte" Country and the Fylde Coast. Easy access to M55. All rooms are en suite with central heating, colour TV , alarm clock radios, tea-making facilities and hairdryers. Ironing facilities are also available. The Castlemere has a cosy bar, where evening snacks are available. Evening Dinner is optional. Open all year. Car Park. All major credit cards accepted.

**Terms from £22 per day per person, bed & breakfast.**

## NOTE

All the information in this guide is given in good faith in the belief that it is correct. However, the publishers cannot guarantee the facts given in these pages, neither are they responsible for changes in ownership or facilities that may take place after the date of going to press. Readers should always satisfy themselves that the facilities they require are available and that the terms, if quoted, still apply.

# *Beechwood Hotel*

Cromer Road, North Walsham,
Norfolk NR28 0HD
Tel: 01692 403231
www.beechwood-hotel.co.uk
info@beechwood-hotel.co.uk

*Winner of the 1999 Johansens Award for the Most Excellent Value for Money Hotel in the UK*

With two AA Red Stars and two Restaurant Rosettes, the Beechwood Hotel is one of the leading small hotels in the UK.
The combination of an elegant ivy-clad Georgian house dating back to 1800, surrounded by well-laid out gardens, with a lovely ambience generated by the proprietors' warm welcome and the attentive staff, has created a very special country house-style hotel in East Anglia.
The bedrooms are delightful, with big windows and antique furniture, and some have large Victorian-style bathrooms, featuring free-standing baths.
The atmosphere in the restaurant reflects the contentment of diners appreciating a menu that features fresh local produce and changes daily. It includes classic English dishes and Head Chef Steven Norgate's personal suggestions.

Gold
GOLD AWARD

*Winter and Spring Sundays with our compliments!*

*From 2 February-29 June and 2-30 November 2003 inclusive and on half-board Short Breaks of 2 nights, complimentary Sunday night accommodation and breakfast is available for a third night provided guests book a table in the restaurant for dinner.*

**Short Breaks**
**3/4 nights available all season from £58.**
**1st pet £5, 2nd pet free**

**A warm welcome for you and your pets. Inexpensive, 'live-as-you-please' self-catering holidays in beautiful Norfolk. Chalets, Bungalows, and Cottages near Great Yarmouth & Norfolk Broads.**

**Booking Hotline**
**Tel: 01493 732176**
**All calls personally answered**

**Debit/Credit cards accepted**

1-6 The Laurels: Close to beach

SUPERB VALUE FOR 2003 SEASON

**The Laurels** - Superb Bungalows close to beach. Private car park.
**The Jasmines** - Lovely cottages. 100 yards to golden sandy beach.
**Belle-Aire** - Family chalets, club-house. Free Electricity.
From £58 per short break

**Colour Brochure Tel: 01493 732176 7 days a week**
**Find us on the internet: www.carefree-holidays.co.uk**

## The Hope & Anchor • 44 Northumberland Street, Alnmouth, Northumberland NE66 2RA

Cosy coastal pub/hotel renowned for its friendly atmosphere and excellent freshly prepared home cooking. 8 en suite rooms. Beautiful beaches, golf, walking and cycling. Book the whole hotel - perfect for family get togethers or business conferences (special rates apply). Open all year.

**Tel: 01665 830363**
**www.hopeandanchorholidays.co.uk**
**e-mail: debbiephilipson@hopeandanchorholidays.fsnet.co.uk**

## Banbury Hill Farm

**Enstone Road, Charlbury, Oxfordshire OX7 3JH**

At Banbury Hill Farm we offer single, twin/double en suite and family rooms en suite. A number of en suite rooms are also available on the ground floor in the converted Old Piggery. All rooms have tea/coffee facilities and colour TV. In the morning all guests come to the main farmhouse for breakfast.

Also available are self-catering cottages, beautifully appointed with all modern facilities and extensive views of the Cotswold Hills.

**Freephone 0800 0853474 • Tel: 01608 810314 • Fax: 01608 811891**
**www.charlburyoxfordaccom.co.uk • bookings@gfwiddows.f9.co.uk**

## the Crown at Wells C. 1450 — Anton's Bistrot

A fifteenth century medieval coaching inn situated in the very heart of the historic City of Wells, within a minute's walk from the Cathedral and Bishop's Palace.
The Crown's central location makes it an excellent base from which to tour Wells City and the many surrounding attractions in this wonderful part of Somerset.
A range of comfortable, affordable en suite accommodation, including four-poster and family rooms. Private parking available.
A variety of mouth-watering dishes is served in Anton's Bistro, including delicious vegetarian options and tempting desserts. A buffet and tasty snacks are also available in the Penn Bar at lunchtimes and in the early evening. Prices from £30 pppn based on 2 people sharing. A warm welcome and friendly service in relaxed and comfortable surroundings.

The Market Place, Wells, Somerset BA5 2RP • Tel: 01749 673457 • Fax: 01749 679792
e-mail: reception@crownatwells.co.uk • www.crownatwells.co.uk

AA ★★

## Ralegh's Cross Inn

**Brendon Hill, Exmoor, Somerset TA23 0LN**

Perched high in the beautiful Brendon Hills, Exmoor National Park, Ralegh's Cross Inn offers comfortable and tastefully refurbished en suite rooms, some with four-poster beds, all non-smoking with colour TVs and hospitality trays.

A full and à la carte menu with freshly prepared starters, home-cooked main courses and home-made desserts is available daily. We're also famous locally for our tasty Farmer's Carvery.

A walker's, rider's and fisherman's paradise with many nearby places of interest for the tourist too.

Open all year, terms from £20 per night. Colour brochure available.

**Tel: 01984 640343**
**Fax: 01643 851227**
**E-mail: ruthattriscombe@aol.com**

# The Lion Hotel

The perfect headquarters for exploring the magic land of heather-clad moors, leafy lanes, nature trails, red deer and wild ponies of Exmoor, the attractive and comfortable Lion Hotel is set in the heart of the delightful little town of Dulverton, on Exmoor's southern fringe. Warm and friendly, the hotel takes great pride in the delicious home-cooked cuisine on offer in the charming restaurant. Alternatively, there is an extensive selection of meals available in the lounge bar. Full of character, guest rooms are fully en suite and have colour television, direct-dial telephone and beverage makers. Sporting activities available locally include riding, river and reservoir fishing, and golf. *AA* ★★

**Bank Square, Dulverton, Somerset TA22 9BU**

**Tel: 01398 323444**
**Fax: 01398 323980**

# CROFT HOLIDAY COTTAGES

**Anchor Street, Watchet, Somerset TA23 0BY**
**• Tel: 01984 631121 • Fax: 01984 631134**

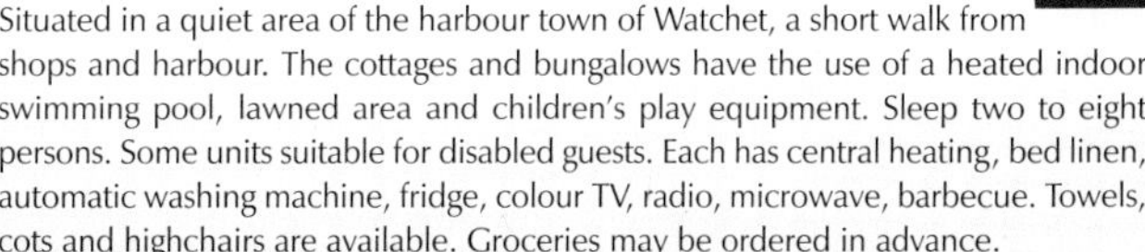

Situated in a quiet area of the harbour town of Watchet, a short walk from shops and harbour. The cottages and bungalows have the use of a heated indoor swimming pool, lawned area and children's play equipment. Sleep two to eight persons. Some units suitable for disabled guests. Each has central heating, bed linen, automatic washing machine, fridge, colour TV, radio, microwave, barbecue. Towels, cots and highchairs are available. Groceries may be ordered in advance.

**Watchet is an ideal centre for touring or walking the beautiful Exmoor, Brendon and Quantock Hills. Short Break details on request.**

**e-mail: croftcottages@talk21.com • Proprietors: A.M. & K.T. Musgrave**

# CHEDDAR – SUNGATE HOLIDAY APARTMENTS

***Church Street, Cheddar, Somerset BS27 3RA***

Delightful apartments in Cheddar village,
each fully equipped. Sleep 2/4. Laundry facilities.
Private parking.
Family, disabled, and pet friendly.

Contact: Mrs. M.M. Fieldhouse for brochure

**Tel: 01934 742264/842273**
**Fax: 01934 741411**

# THE *Old Malt House* HOTEL

Built in 1835 as a malt house for the local brewery, this family-run country hotel is situated in a small village surrounded by beautiful countryside just 6 miles from the historic city of Bath. You will be greeted with a warm, friendly welcome and it will be our pleasure to ensure your stay is enjoyable and relaxing. There are 11 tastefully decorated bedrooms, all with en suite bath/shower rooms, colour TV, tea and coffee making facilities and stunning views across the countryside. Our restaurant serves home-cooked food using fresh local produce. Before or after your meal you may wish to enjoy a relaxing drink by the log fire in the lounge bar, where a good selection of wines and beers is served. **AA** ★★

**Radford, Timsbury, Bath BA2 0QF • Tel: 01761 470106 • Fax: 01761 472726**
**e-mail: hotel@oldmalthouse.co.uk • website: www.oldmalthouse.co.uk**

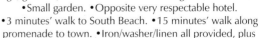

# LOWESTOFT

Newly decorated and furnished large, graceful, self-contained 2-bedroom ground floor flat.

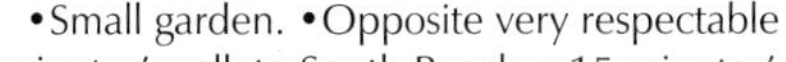

•Small garden. •Opposite very respectable hotel. •3 minutes' walk to South Beach. •15 minutes' walk along promenade to town. •Iron/washer/linen all provided, plus welcome grocery pack. •Outdoor drying facilities.

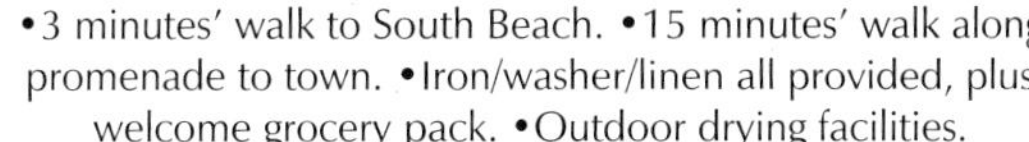

•Numerous events and attractions including Summer Carnival, French Market and Motorcycle Cavalcade.

**10 Banner Court, Kirkley Cliff Road, Lowestoft, Suffolk NR33 0DB**

**Tel: 01502 511876 • e-mail: aishakhalaf100@hotmail.com**

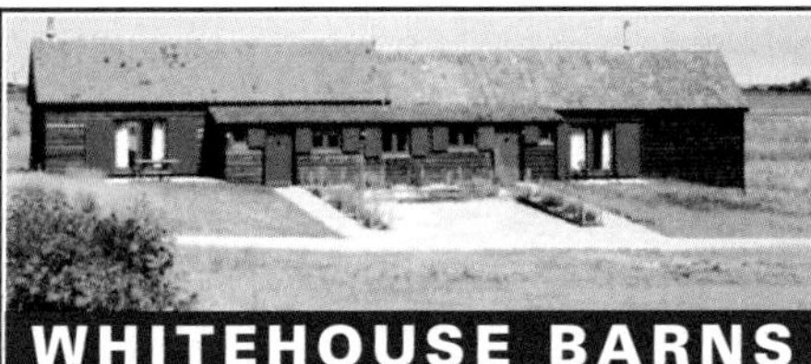

## WHITEHOUSE BARNS

**Blythburgh, near Southwold**
**Contact: Mrs P. Roskell-Griffiths**
**Tel/Fax: 0208 806 5969**
**www.whitehousebarns.co.uk**
**peneloperoskell@yahoo.co.uk**

Two beautiful well-appointed barn conversions in spectacular peaceful location overlooking the Blyth estuary. In two acres of land with stunning views all around, they are ideal for families, walkers and birdwatchers. Southwold and Walberswick sandy beaches 4 miles.

- Wood-burning stoves and full central heating.
- Sleep 5/6 and 8/9.
- Spacious playbarn and babysitting service available.
- Terms from £260 to £680.

AN AWARD WINNING HOTEL

*....with style, elegance, set in tranquil surroundings at affordable prices.*

## CHASE LODGE HOTEL

10 PARK ROAD, HAMPTON WICK,
KINGSTON-UPON-THAMES KT1 4AS

Quality en suite bedrooms • Full English breakfast
• A la carte menu • Licensed bar • Wedding receptions
• Honeymoon suite • 20 minutes from Heathrow Airport
London Tourist Board ★★★ • Easy access to Kingston town centre and all major transport links

*for business or pleasure... **Reservations 020 8943 1862 • Fax: 020 8943 9363***

AA/RAC ★★★ Les Routiers All major credit cards accepted.

## Dale Hill HOTEL & GOLF CLUB

Dale Hill

Situated in 350 acres of beautiful countryside, Dale Hill is an impressive modern hotel and is home to the Ian Woosnam designed golf course. Our guests can expect a warm and friendly welcome, excellent service, award-winning cuisine, the challenge of two golf courses and the latest fitness facilities, all in a quiet rural location.

From elegantly furnished public rooms and en suite bedrooms, to panoramic views over the Kentish Weald, the four-star Dale Hill Hotel is perfect for a relaxing and enjoyable break. Just an hour's drive from London and easily accessible from the M25.

**Ticehurst, Wadhurst, East Sussex TN5 7DQ • 01580 200112 • Fax: 01580 201249**
**e-mail: info@dalehill.co.uk • website: www.dalehill.co.uk**

## Bexhill-on-Sea • East Sussex

# MIRALEISURE

**Quietly exhilarating holidays in superior self-catering seafront accommodation**

infomira@waitrose.com
tel: 01424 730298 • fax: 01424 212500

## MAON HOTEL

**26 Upper Rock Gardens, Brighton BN2 1QE**

This is a completely non-smoking Grade II Listed building run by proprietors who are waiting with a warm and friendly welcome. No children. Established over 20 years. Our standard of food has been highly recommended by many guests who return year after year. Two minutes from the sea and within easy reach of conference and main town centres. All nine bedrooms are furnished to a high standard and have colour TV, radio alarm clock, hospitality tray and hairdryer and most are en suite. A lounge with colour TV is available for guests' convenience. Diningroom. Full central heating. Access to rooms at all times. Terms from £30. Brochure on request with SAE.

Tel: 01273 694400

## THE STAR INN, ALFRISTON

Prince Edward is among the guests who have visited this famous 14th century inn which was once a renowned meeting place for smugglers. Oak beams and open fires offer mellow reminders of the past and create an intimate atmosphere in the bar. Set in the South Downs, there are many fine walks. All rooms en suite, with tea/coffee making facilities, colour television and direct dial telephone.
Pets welcome with a charge.

Alfriston, near Polegate, East Sussex BN26 5TH
Tel: 0870 400 8102 • Fax: 0132 387 0922
E-Mail: HeritageHotels_Alfriston.Star_Inn@forte-hotels.com

FHG

## Visit the FHG website

www.holidayguides.com

**for details of the wide choice of accommodation featured in the full range of FHG titles**

ETC/AA ★★★★

## HONEYBRIDGE PARK

**Honeybridge Lane, Dial Post, Near Horsham
West Sussex RH13 8NX
Tel & Fax: 01403 710923**

Delightfully situated in 15 acres adjacent to woodlands, within an Area of Outstanding Natural Beauty. An ideal location for touring, convenient for the South Coast resorts and ferry ports, as well as Brighton and Chichester, yet only one hour from London by train; Horsham 10 miles. The park is maintained to the highest standards with generous-sized hard standing and grass pitches allowing comfort and privacy. Heated amenity block, storage, seasonal pitches; dogs welcome. Open all year.

**e-mail: enquiries@honeybridgepark.co.uk website: www.honeybridgepark.co.uk**

ETC/AA ◆◆◆◆

## ST ANDREWS LODGE

**Chichester Road, Selsey, West Sussex PO20 0LX
Tel: 01243 606899 • Fax: 01243 607826
e-mail: info@standrewslodge.co.uk
web: www.standrewslodge.co.uk**

Welcoming, family-run hotel with a reputation for an excellent hearty breakfast. Situated on the Manhood peninsula just south of Chichester, close to unspoilt beaches and countryside. Ten bedrooms, all en suite, with direct-dial telephones, TV, fridge and tea-making facilities; some on ground floor. Spacious lounges with log fire; friendly bar for residents only. Excellent Grade 1 (ETC Accessible Scheme) wheelchair access. Large secure car park. Evening meals by prior arrangement. Pets by arrangement. Apply for brochure and prices.

## White Rose Golf Breaks

**For your next golfing holiday visit Yorkshire's broad acres.**
**Wide range of courses and hotels across East, West and North Yorkshire.**

FOR OUR BROCHURE AND INFORMATION ON BOOKINGS CONTACT PETER GRAHAM TODAY

**tel: 01943 609888
e-mail: golf@wrgb.legend.yorks.com
www.whiterosegolfbreaks.co.uk**

## *The Fox & Hounds Inn*

Residential 16th Century Coaching Inn set amidst the beautiful North York Moors.
Freshly prepared dishes served every lunchtime and evening.
Superb en suite accommodation available, with all rooms having glorious views.
Open all year. Special Breaks available October to May.
Situated between Castleton and Danby on the Fryup Road.

ETC ◆◆◆◆ ***For bookings please***
***Tel: 01287 660218 or Fax: 01287 660030***
***Ainthorpe, Danby, Yorkshire YO21 2LD***

## THE BUCK INN

**Tel: 01677 422461 • Fax: 01677 422447**

**Thornton Watlass, Near Bedale, Ripon, North Yorkshire HG4 4AH**

- Friendly country inn overlooking the delightful cricket green in a peaceful village just five minutes away from the A1.
- Refurbished bedrooms, most with en suite facilities.
- Delicious freshly cooked meals served lunchtimes and evenings in the cosy bar and dining area. Hand-pulled cask beers.
- An ideal centre for exploring both the Yorkshire Dales and North York Moors.
- Children's playground in the secluded beer garden.
- Private fly fishing available on River Ure and six golf courses within 20 minutes' drive.

## New Close Farm

*A supa dupa cottage on New Close Farm in the heart of Craven Dales with panoramic views over the Aire Valley. Excellent area for walking, cycling, fishing, golf and touring.*

- Two double and one single bedrooms; bathroom.
- Colour TV and video.
- Full central heating and double glazing.
- Bed linen, towels and all amenities included in the price.
- Sorry, no young children, no pets.
- Non-smokers preferred.
- From £250-£300. Winter Short Breaks available.

*The weather can't be guaranteed but your comfort can*

**Kirkby Malham, Skipton BD23 4DP**
**Tel: 01729 830240 • Fax: 01729 830179**
**e-mail: brendajones@newclosefarmyorkshire.co.uk**
**website: www.newclosefarmyorkshire.co.uk**

## Castletown Golf Links Hotel

**Fort Island, Derbyhaven, Isle of Man**
**Tel: 01624 822201 • Fax: 01624 824633**
**e-mail: golflinks@manx.net • www.golfiom.com**

Whatever you might be looking for, from a holiday to remember and cherish to a great golfing experience, or a wonderful choice for a conference venue, a fabulous wedding destination with a honeymoon suite to dream about, we have it. In fact the Castletown Golf Links Hotel caters happily and easily for all our guests' needs and occasions. This character-filled hotel is situated on Fort Island with breathtaking views across the Irish Sea and panoramic views across the championship course. Only 5 minutes away from the airport, comfortable bedrooms, excellent restaurants, leisure facilities such as heated swimming pool, sauna and two snooker tables.

***So what are you waiting for? Get on the phone, fax or e-mail and find out what you have been missing!***

## NOTE

All the information in this guide is given in good faith in the belief that it is correct. However, the publishers cannot guarantee the facts given in these pages, neither are they responsible for changes in ownership or facilities that may take place after the date of going to press.

Readers should always satisfy themselves that the facilities they require are available and that the terms, if quoted, still apply.

# Other FHG Holiday and Accommodation Guides

## Recommended Country Hotels of Britain 2003

A quality selection of country hotels and country houses which offer the best of traditional hospitality and comfort.

This is a guide for those who appreciate good living with the high standards of food, wine, accommodation and service which that entails.

Mainly independent, with a resident proprietor. and often historic or with unique character, these hotels are ideal for quiet holidays in pampered surroundings.

Quick reference sections for Hotels with Leisure and Hotels with Conference Facilities

## Recommended Wayside & Country Inns of Britain 2003

This guide lists a large selection of inns, pubs and small hotels in every part of the country, all offering the same high-quality service, accommodation and, especially, cuisine as many of the bigger hotels, yet managing to retain that sense of history and the warm, friendly atmosphere for which the traditional inn is renowned. With separate supplements for Pet-Friendly and Family-Friendly Pubs to ensure that every member of the party receives a warm welcome when they stop for refreshment, the guide is an invaluable and informative source.

**Both guides available from most bookshops and larger newsagents**

**Only £5.99 each**

## THE PERFECT PLACE TO DISCOVER THE HIGHLANDS AND ISLANDS OF SCOTLAND.

ARDANAISEIG HOTEL, KILCHRENAN, BY TAYNUILT,
ARGYLL, SCOTLAND PA35 1HE • TEL: 01866 833333
FAX: 01866 833222 • WWW.ARDANAISEIG-HOTEL.COM
E-MAIL: ARDANAISEIG@CLARA.NET

IN A REMOTE PLACE OF QUIET TRANQUILLITY AND ALMOST SURREAL NATURAL BEAUTY, WHERE THE SLOPES OF BEN CRUACHAN FALL INTO THE CLEAR WATERS OF LOCH AWE, THERE IS A SMALL AND WILDLY ROMANTIC OLD COUNTRY HOUSE HOTEL. ARDANAISEIG SITS ALONE OVERLOOKING THE MYSTERIOUS ISLANDS AND CRANNOGS OF THE LOCH, IN WOODED GROUNDS TEEMING WITH WILDLIFE.

BUILT IN 1834, OVERLOOKING ITS OWN ISLAND, ARDANAISEIG, WITH ITS OWN LOG FIRES, FRESHLY PICKED FLOWERS, ANTIQUE FURNITURE AND FINE WORKS OF ART, HAS A SPECIAL STATELY AND TIMELESS ATMOSPHERE. IT IS IDEALLY SITUATED FOR VISITS TO ARGYLL'S MANY CASTLES AND SITES OF HISTORIC INTEREST.

THE RESTAURANT IS NOTED FOR ITS IMAGINATIVE USE OF FRESH PRODUCE, PARTICULARLY SEAFOOD. HERBS FROM THE WALLED GARDEN ENHANCE THE SUBTLE FLAVOURS CREATED BY THE YOUNG, AWARD-WINNING CHEF.

## Rockhill Waterside Country House

**Ardbrecknish, By Dalmally, Argyll PA33 1BH Tel: 01866 833218**

17th century guest house in spectacular waterside setting on Loch Awe with breathtaking views to Ben Cruachan, where comfort, peace and tranquillity reign supreme. Small private Highland estate breeding Hanoverian competition horses. 1200 metres free trout fishing. Five delightful rooms with all modern facilities. First-class highly acclaimed home cooking with much home-grown produce. Wonderful area for touring the Western Highlands, Glencoe, the Trossachs and Kintyre. Ideal for climbing, walking, bird and animal watching. Boat trips locally and from Oban (30 miles) to Mull, Iona, Fingal's Cave and other islands. Dogs' Paradise! Also Self-Catering Cottages.

## GIGHA HOTEL

Situated in the Inner Hebrides, the Community owned Isle of Gigha (God's Island) is surely one of Scotland's most beautiful and tranquil islands. Explore the white sandy bays and lochs. Easy walking, bike hire, birds, wildlife and wild flowers. Home to the famous Achamore Gardens with rhododendrons, azaleas and semi-tropical plants. Grass airstrip, 9 hole golf course and a regular ferry service (only 20 munutes from the mainland). We are dog friendly. Holiday cottages also available.

Gigha Hotel, Isle of Gigha, Argyll PA41 7AA
Tel: 01583 505254 Fax: 01583 505244
Website: www.isle-of-gigha.co.uk
STB ★★★ Small Hotel

## MELFORT PIER & HARBOUR

KILMELFORD, BY OBAN, ARGYLL PA34 4XD
Tel: 01852 200333 • Fax: 01852 200329
e-mail: melharbour@aol.com • website: scotland2000.com/melfort

Take a Relaxing and Romantic Short break in one of our Luxury Lochside Houses. Each with Sauna, Spa bath, Satellite TV, some with Sunbed, Logfire. Clean air, tranquil surroundings, superb views. Watersports, Riding, Golf, Fishing, Hillwalking, Castles. Bring your boat. Ideal base for touring.
Good restaurants, shopping and pubs nearby. Pets welcome.

CALL FOR SPECIAL PROMOTIONS. Start any day of the week. From £70.00 – £195.00 per house/night

# MILLARS HOTEL

**Market Square, Melrose TD6 9PQ**
**Tel: 01896 822645 Fax: 01896 823474**
**e-mail: Millars.Hotel@btinternet.com**

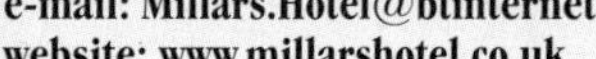

**website: www.millarshotel.co.uk**

Millars is an award-winning, traditional townhouse hotel situated at the foot of Eildon Hills making it an ideal location for walkers. For those who like fishing, there is the world famous River Tweed and for golfers there are 21 courses throughout the Borders; for everyone else there is plenty of opportunity for relaxation in Melrose, the Border's premier town. Quality accommodation, award-winning food and service makes Millars the perfect choice for a short break. All rooms are en suite and non-smoking with colour TV, telephone, complimentary tray, hairdryer, trouser press and radio/alarm. Dogs are accepted by arrangement. Credit/debit cards are accepted. Packages available throughout the year. Please call for details.

Scottish Tourist Board ★★★ Small Hotel · The Taste of Scotland

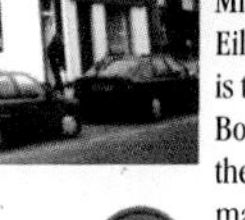


Green Tourism Bronze

---

# Creetown Caravan Park

**Silver Street, Creetown DG8 7HU**
**Tel/Fax: 01671 820377**
**e-mail: Beatrice.Mcneill@btinternet.com**
**website: www.creetown-caravans.co.uk**

Situated just off the A75, 6 miles east of Newton Stewart and 3 miles from the Galloway Forest Park, an ideal base for exploring this scenic area. Village shops and hotels only a two-minute walk.

SELECTION OF DE LUXE SIX-BERTH CARAVANS TO LET, ALL OF AN EXCELLENT STANDARD AND FULLY EQUIPPED.

Heated outdoor swimming pool (seasonal), children's play area, games room with video games and pool tables.
Creetown is part of the local designated cycle route.
*Facilities for touring caravans and tents.*

Scottish Tourist Board ★★★★ Holiday Park

---

# Mabie House Hotel

*Set in beautiful gardens, this 18th century Listed building is being carefully restored to its former glory.*

★ Bar Lounge ★ Log Fires
★ Dining Room ★ Fresh local food
★ Mahogany panelled entrance hall.
★ Eight fully refurbished en-suite rooms

**Mabie, Dumfries DG2 8HB**
**Tel: 01387 263188 • Fax: 01387 249696**
**e-mail: niki@mabiehouse.co.uk**
**website: www.mabiehouse.co.uk**

---

# Craigadam

Castle Douglas
Kirkcudbrightshire DG7 3HU

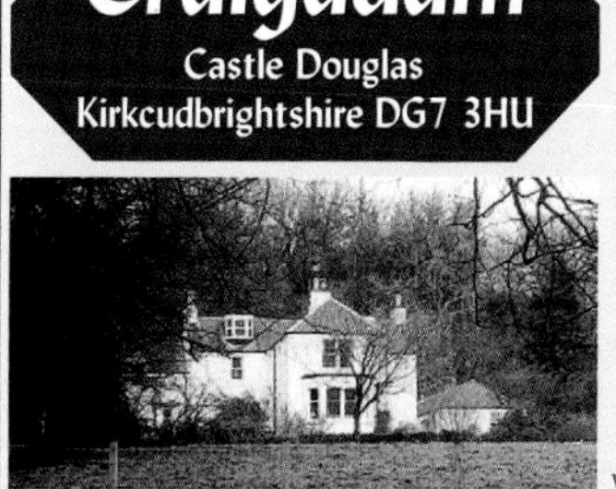

A family-run 18th century farmhouse situated in the hills looking across Galloway. All bedrooms are en suite and there is a lovely oak-panelled dining room which offers Cordon Bleu cooking using local produce such as venison, pheasant, salmon. Oak-panelled billiards room. Come home in the evening to comfort, warmth and good Scottish hospitality. Fish on our own trout loch. The area offers much to the traveller with its lovely beaches, hill and forest walks, sailing, fishing, bird watching, pony trekking, golfing, as well as many places of historic and local interest. Please telephone Richard or Celia for further details.

The Taste of Scotland
WINNER 2001

**website: www.craigadam.com**
**Tel & Fax: 01556 650233**
RAC ◆◆◆◆◆ Little Gem Award
AA ◆◆◆◆◆ Premier Collection

## Blenheim House Hotel

**14 Westgate, North Berwick, East Lothian EH39 4AF**
**Tel: 01620 892385 • Fax: 01620 894010**

The Blenheim offers an excellent base for discovering the surrounding beauty spots, of which there are many. The area is a 'golfers' paradise', with at least eighteen golf courses within half an hour's drive, including the famous Muirfield and four courses in nearby Gullane. The Blenheim itself is a few yards from the first tee of the North Berwick West Links Championship Golf Course. Children also have available a nine-hole course in North Berwick with competitions in the summer.

The Blenheim House Hotel is ideally situated in the main street of the picturesque seaside town of North Berwick with its own off-street parking. It is a family-run hotel open throughout the year. You can enjoy the uninterrupted panoramic views over the west bay, the Fife coast and beyond. We have eleven bedrooms, en suite, all with tea/coffee making facilities and colour television. We also have a private residents' lounge. We offer freshly-prepared home-cooked food using local produce, with a children's menu also available. Savour a glass of wine from our varied and interesting wine list whilst enjoying the splendid views to the sea, or take advantage of our sun patio and large garden with access to the putting greens and beach.

**e-mail: mail@blenheimhousehotel.com** **website: www.blenheimhousehotel.com**

## THE PEAT INN

**Cupar, Fife KY15 5LH**
**Tel: 01334 840206 • Fax: 01334 840530**
**e-mail: reception@thepeatinn.co.uk**

Situated just 6 miles from St Andrews in the village named after the Inn. 'The Residence', 8 luxurious suites, offer peace and comfort. The Restaurant has earned an international reputation over 28 years offering fresh Scottish produce, creativity and value.

AA
★★

**Tel: 01855 821236 • Fax: 01855 821550**
**e-mail: lochlevenhotel@lineone.net.**

The Loch Leven Hotel was originally built more than 300 years ago. It now combines the best of old and new. It is owned and run by Hilary and John who provide comfort in an informal setting. All 10 rooms are en suite and most have magnificent views.

Our Loch View Restaurant looks out to the loch and the magnificent mountains beyond. There is an extensive menu and a daily-changing set meal, all freshly prepared using the best Scottish produce. Most evenings you can also indulge in our own Oriental Menu. The comfortable Lounge Bar offers an impressive display of around 75 malts, and the Public Bar has a real fire and lots of atmosphere! There is a Family/Games Room for more relaxed dining.

**B&B from £25-£50pppn.** **Onich, By Fort William, Inverness-shire PH33 6SA**

## Nether Lochaber Hotel

**Onich, Fort William,**
**Inverness-shire PH33 6SE**
**Tel: 01855 821235**
**Fax: 01855 821545**

An ideal centre from which to explore Lochaber, the Ardnamurchan Peninsula and Glencoe. Traditional home cooking goes hand in hand with homely service, comfortable accommodation and private facilities.
The inn stands on the shores of beautiful Loch Linnhe at Corran Ferry.

# Bontddu Hall

## COUNTRY HOUSE HOTEL,

**Bontddu, Near Dolgellau, Gwynedd LL40 2UF**
**Tel: 01341 430661 • Fax: 01341 430284**

This historic Gothic mansion stands in 14 acres of landscaped gardens with breathtaking views of Cader Idris. First-class accommodation is offered in tastefully appointed bedrooms, each one with en suite facilities, colour television, clock radio, direct-dial telephone and tea and coffee-makers; there are also several luxury suites. The Restaurant is well noted for its gourmet specialities: regional and classical dishes are carefully prepared using the best of local produce. There is a wide variety of things to see and do in the vicinity and the historic castles of Caernarvon and Harlech are within easy reach. *WTB ★★★★ Hotel • AA ★★★ and Two Rosettes • RAC ★★★*

THE **GOLDEN PHEASANT** *Country* Hotel

Situated in the heart of the Ceiriog Valley, one of the most picturesque in North Wales. This 18th century hotel offers peace and tranquillity. All rooms en suite, some with whirlpool baths and four-poster beds. Excellent restaurant, old world charm bar with open fire, comfortable lounges, garden, patios and large car park. Pets welcome in all rooms except restaurants and lounge. 2 nights D,B&B from £100pp.

**Glyn Ceiriog, Near Llangollen LL20 7BB**
**Tel: 01691 718281 • Fax: 01691 718479**

AA ★★★

e-mail: goldenpheasant@micro-plus-web.net • website: www.goldenpheasanthotel.co.uk

# *The Lodge* Tal-y-Bont, Conwy, Gwynedd LL32 8YX

**e-mail: bbaldon@lodgehotel.co.uk • website: www.lodgehotel.co.uk**

Nestling in the lovely rolling hills of the beautiful Conwy Valley, our family-run, 14-bedroomed hotel has all the ingredients for a wonderful holiday. Enjoy peace and quiet, superb food, and attention from our friendly and efficient staff. Our lovely en suite bedrooms have that extra touch to make you feel at home. All major attractions are within easy reach, including Bodnant Gardens. Large private car park; extensive established grounds.

*Bed and Breakfast from £30 to £60 pppn; 2 nights Dinner, Bed and Breakfast from £88 to £100. Weekly terms on request.*

**Tel: 01492 660766 • Fax: 01492 660534 • Freephone: 0800 9176593**

Set in its own grounds overlooking the River Conwy and yet close to the town centre, Conwy Golf Club and the harbour, Castle Bank is the ideal centre for your visit to North Wales. All bedrooms have private toilet and shower and every room has tea/coffee facilities, TV and hairdryer. Before dining relax in our well stocked bar where our wine list offers a selection for all tastes. The Restaurant offers an imaginative and varied menu with great emphasis placed on quality. Ample parking. We are a non-smoking establishment.

***Two-day break: B&B from £35 single, £55 double***

**Castle Bank Hotel & Licensed Restaurant**
**Mount Pleasant, Conwy, North Wales LL32 8NY**
**Tel: 01492 593888 AA ★★**
e-mail: contact@castle-bank.co.uk
website: www.castle-bank.co.uk

## HEATHFIELD MANSION

**Letterston, Near Fishguard SA62 5EG**
**Tel & Fax: 01348 840263**

A Grade II Listed Georgian country house in 16 acres of pasture and woodland, Heathfield is the home of former Welsh rugby international, Clive Rees and his wife Angelica. This is an ideal location for the appreciation of Pembrokeshire's many natural attractions. There is excellent golf, riding and fishing in the vicinity and the coast is only a few minutes' drive away.

*The accommodation is very comfortable and two of the three bedrooms have en suite bathrooms. The cuisine and wines are well above average. This is a most refreshing venue for a tranquil and wholesome holiday.*

GWESTY ★★★ COUNTRY HOUSE

**Welcome Host Gold Award** **e-mail: angelica.rees@virgin.net**

WTB Self Catering ★★★★

## Gwarmacwydd

Gwarmacwydd is a country estate of over 450 acres, including two miles of riverbank. See a real farm in action, the hustle and bustle of harvest, newborn calves and lambs. Children are welcomed. On the estate are five character stone cottages, Tourist Board Grade Four. Each cottage has been lovingly converted from traditional farm buildings, parts of which are over 200 years old. Each cottage is fully furnished and equipped with all modern conveniences. All electricity and linen included. All cottages are heated for year-round use. Colour brochure available. Short break details on request.

**Tel: 01437 563260 Fax: 01437 563839**
**website: www.a-farm-holiday.org**
**e-mail: info@a-farm-holiday.org**

**Mrs Angela Colledge,**
**Llanfallteg, Whitland,**
**Pembrokeshire SA34 0XH**

## The Inn at the Elm Tree

**COUNTRY INN & RESTAURANT**

*A hidden retreat between two cities - Cardiff and Newport – just two miles from the M4 and a different world away.*

Originally an early 19th century barn, now transformed from a celebrated restaurant to an inn, the Elm Tree keeps the spirit of timeless hospitality alive, but with all the most modern appointments.

*Comfort epitomised, attention to detail paramount, relaxation assured.*

The Inn at the Elm Tree is the perfect retreat for a week or weekend, a special night stay, or simply a drink. The Restaurant has a long-standing reputation as one of the most distinguished in the area, using Wales' best natural produce. Bedrooms are all individually designed to the highest standards with lots of personal touches and luxuries.

St Brides, Wentlooge, Near Newport, South Wales NP10 8SQ
Tel: 01633 680225 • Fax: 01633 681035 • e-mail: inn@the-elm-tree.co.uk
website: www.the-elm-tree.co.uk WTB ★★★★★ Inn

## THE Rat Trap RESTAURANT & HOTEL

**Old Chepstow Road, Llangeview, Near Usk NP15 1EY**
**Tel: 01291 673288**

A family-run business, specialising in personal service. Situated in the heart of the Usk Vale, adjacent to the Wye Valley, centrally located for business or pleasure. Newport, Cwmbran, Pontypool and Cardiff all less than half an hour's drive. All rooms furnished and maintained to a high standard, with colour TV, direct-dial telephone, tea/coffee making and en suite facilities.

***Activities in the area include golf, gliding, grass skiing, horse riding, clay pigeon shooting, windsurfing, walking and cycling. Short Break details on request.***

GWESTY ★★★ HOTEL

**e-mail: info@rattraphotel.com • website: www.rattraphotel.com**

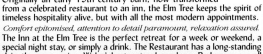

# Other FHG Holiday and Attractions Guides

100's of places to stay!

## SELF-CATERING HOLIDAYS in Britain

One of the best and perhaps the widest selection of self-catering accommodation, covering the whole of the UK. Established 30 years, and with over 1,000 entries it is firmly established as the market-leader for self-catering holiday choices throughout Britain.

From modern apartment complexes to hidden forest cabins, there is a holiday to suit every need. There is also a large selection of caravan holidays. The guide has proved popular with families and couples who enjoy the freedom of a direct-booked self catering holiday.

## CARAVAN & CAMPING HOLIDAYS

This handy sized guide is one of our most popular titles and has been a best-seller for over 20 years. This guide covers every type of caravan and camping facility with user-friendly symbols to show grading of standards and facilities. As a longtime best-seller our Guide to Caravan & Camping Holidays continues to offer advertisers low cost year-long exposure to the largest single category of holiday-maker throughout the UK.

## BRITAIN'S BEST HOLIDAYS

An extremely popular and inexpensive quick reference guide for all kinds of holiday opportunities throughout Britain. The extensive range of holidays is split into four main categories – Board (hotels, guest houses, farms, bed & breakfast, etc); Self-Catering (houses, cottages, flats, chalets); Caravans (solus sites, parks and camping sites); Activity holidays (camping, golfing, sporting holidays) This guide is very user-friendly with self-explanatory symbols to show services and amenities. It is most popular amongst families and those looking for the easiest route to making a direct booking.

FHG

Guides available from most bookshops and larger newsagents

FHG Publications Ltd. Abbey Mill Business Centre, Seedhill, Paisley PA1 1TJ

Prices: Caravan & Camping and Britains Best Holidays only £4.49

Self Catering Holidays only £5.99

# Ratings You Can Trust

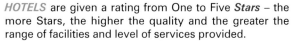

## ENGLAND

The ***English Tourism Council*** (formerly the English Tourist Board) has joined with the ***AA*** and ***RAC*** to create a new, easily understood quality rating for serviced accommodation, giving a clear guide of what to expect.

*HOTELS* are given a rating from One to Five ***Stars*** – the more Stars, the higher the quality and the greater the range of facilities and level of services provided.

*GUEST ACCOMMODATION*, which includes guest houses, bed and breakfasts, inns and farmhouses, is rated from One to Five ***Diamonds***. Progressively higher levels of quality and customer care must be provided for each one of the One to Five Diamond ratings.

*HOLIDAY PARKS, TOURING PARKS and CAMPING PARKS* are now also assessed using ***Stars***. Standards of quality range from a One Star (acceptable) to a Five Star (exceptional) park.

Look out also for the new *SELF-CATERING* Star ratings. The more ***Stars*** (from One to Five) awarded to an establishment, the higher the levels of quality you can expect. Establishments at higher rating levels also have to meet some additional requirements for facilities.

*NB Some self-catering properties had not been assessed at the time of going to press and in these cases the old-style **KEY** symbols will still be shown.*

## SCOTLAND

***Star Quality Grades*** will reflect the most important aspects of a visit, such as the warmth of welcome, efficiency and friendliness of service, the quality of the food and the cleanliness and condition of the furnishings, fittings and decor.

***THE MORE STARS, THE HIGHER THE STANDARDS.***

The description, such as Hotel, Guest House, Bed and Breakfast, Lodge, Holiday Park, Self-catering etc tells you the type of property and style of operation.

## WALES

Places which score highly will have an especially welcoming atmosphere and pleasing ambience, high levels of comfort and guest care, and attractive surroundings enhanced by thoughtful design and attention to detail

**STAR QUALITY GUIDE FOR**

**HOTELS, GUEST HOUSES AND FARMHOUSES**

**SELF-CATERING ACCOMMODATION**
**(Cottages, Apartments, Houses)**

**CARAVAN HOLIDAY HOME PARKS**
**(Holiday Parks, Touring Parks, Camping Parks)**

*Exceptional quality*
*Excellent quality*
*Very good quality*
*Good quality*
*Fair to good quality*

**In England, Scotland and Wales, all graded properties are inspected annually by Tourist Authority trained Assessors.**

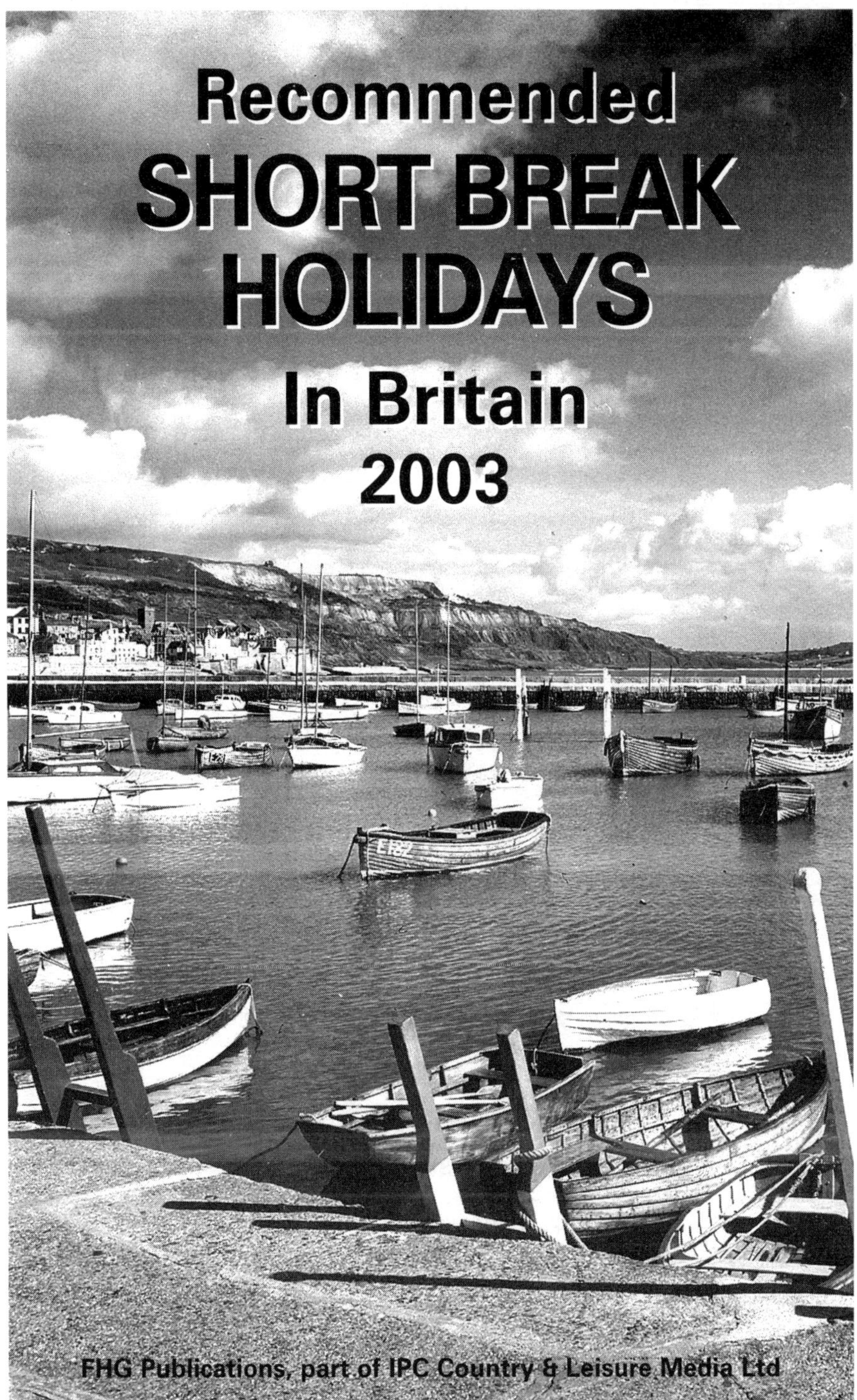
Recommended
SHORT BREAK
HOLIDAYS
In Britain
2003
FHG Publications, part of IPC Country & Leisure Media Ltd

**Other FHG Publications**

*Recommended Country Hotels of Britain*
*Recommended Wayside & Country Inns of Britain*
*Pets Welcome!*
*The Golf Guide: Where to Play/Where to Stay*
*Farm Holiday Guide to Coast & Country Holidays in England/Scotland/Wales/Ireland*
*Self-Catering Holidays in Britain*
*Britain's Best Holidays*
*Guide to Caravan and Camping Holidays*
*Bed and Breakfast Stops*
*Children Welcome! Family Holiday and Attractions Guide*

ISBN 185055 337 8


**Cover photographs**:
Towan Beach, supplied by Ivan J. Belcher; Loch Ard, supplied by V.K.Guy
**Cover design**: Focus Network


Cartography by GEO Projects, Reading
Maps are based on Ordnance Survey maps with the permission of Her Majesty's Stationery Office, crown copyright reserved.
Typeset by FHG Publications Ltd. Paisley.
Printed and bound in Great Britain by Polestar Wheatons Ltd, Exeter, Devon

Distribution. Book Trade: Plymbridge House, Estover Road, Plymouth PL6 7PY
Tel: 01752 202300; Fax: 01752 202333
News Trade: Market Force (UK) Ltd, 5th Floor Low Rise, King's Reach Tower, Stamford Street, London SE1 9LS
Tel: 0207 633 3450; Fax: 0207 633 3572

Published by FHG Publications Ltd., Abbey Mill Business Centre, Seedhill, Paisley PA1 ITJ (Tel: 0141-887 0428 Fax: 0141-889 7204).
e-mail: fhg@ipcmedia.com

*Recommended Short Breaks* is an FHG publication, published by IPC Country & Leisure Media Ltd, part of IPC Media Group of Companies.

## EXPLANATION OF SYMBOLS

| | |
|---|---|
| ★ | **Number of Stars (**English Tourism Council/AA/RAC) |
| ◆ | **Number of Diamonds** (English Tourism Council/AA/RAC) |
| (dog symbol) | **Pets Welcome** |
| (rocking horse symbol) | **Reductions for Children** |
| (tree symbol) | **Christmas Breaks** |
| ♿ | **Suitable for Disabled** |

The symbols are arranged in the same order throughout the book so that looking down each page will give a quick comparison.

# CONTENTS

# FHG Diploma Winners 2002

*Each year we award a small number of diplomas to holiday proprietors whose services have been specially commended by our readers. The following were our FHG Diploma Winners for 2002.*

## England

### DEVON

Woolacombe Bay Holiday Park,
Woolacombe, North Devon
EX34 7HW (01271 870343).

### LANCASHIRE

Mrs Holdsworth, Broadwater Hotel,
356 Marine Road, East Promenade
Morecambe, Lancashire LA4 5AQ
(01524 411333).

Peter & Susan Bicker,
Kelvin Private Hotel, Reads Avenue
Blackpool, Lancashire FY1 4JJ
(01253 620293).

### LINCOLNSHIRE

Sue and John Phillips,
Cawthorpe Farm, Cawthorpe
Bourne, Lincolnshire PE10 0AB
(01778 426697).

### OXFORDSHIRE

Liz Roach, The Old Bakery,
Skirmett, Nr Henley on Thames
Oxfordshire RG9 6TD
(01491 638309).

### SOMERSET

Pat & Sue Weir, Slipper Cottage,
41 Bishopston, Montacute,
Somerset TA15 6UX
(01935 823073)

## Scotland

### ARGYLL & BUTE

David Quibell,
Rosneath Castle Caravan Park
Near Helensburgh,
Argyll & Bute G84 0QS
(01436 831208)

### DUNDEE & ANGUS

Carlogie House Hotel,
Carlogie Road, Carnoustie,
Dundee DD7 6LD
(01241 853185)

### EDINBURGH & LOTHIANS

Geraldine Hamilton,
Crosswoodhill Farm, West Calder
Edinburgh & Lothians EH55 8LP
(01501 785205)

### FIFE

Mr Alastair Clark,
Old Manor Country House Hotel,
Lundin Links, Nr St Andrews
Fife KY8 6AJ
(01333 320368)

### HIGHLANDS

N & J McCallum, The Neuk
Corpach, Fort William PH33 7LE
(01397 772244)

**HELP IMPROVE BRITISH TOURISM STANDARDS**

## Recommended

# SHORT BREAK HOLIDAYS IN BRITAIN

For some people a short break holiday is a chance to have a complete rest while someone else takes care of the housework and cooking, while for others it is an ideal opportunity for exploring new places or perhaps trying out a different sport or pastime. There is plenty of choice for active or relaxing breaks in this 16th edition of RECOMMENDED SHORT BREAKS, and accommodation ranges from large hotels with full facilities, to B&Bs and self-catering properties at prices to suit every pocket.You will find that our proprietors and their staff do their best to ensure that you have an enjoyable visit.

To help you plan your holiday we have included some useful information on what to see and do within each area, and don't forget to use our Readers' Offer Vouchers (Pages 47 to 58) if you're near any of the attractions which are kindly participating.

Anne Cuthbertson, *Editor*

## The FHG Diploma

### HELP IMPROVE BRITISH TOURIST STANDARDS

You are choosing holiday accommodation from our very popular FHG Publications. Whether it be a hotel, guest house, farmhouse or self-catering accommodation, we think you will find it hospitable, comfortable and clean, and your host and hostess friendly and helpful.

Why not write and tell us about it?

As a recognition of the generally well-run and excellent holiday accommodation reviewed in our publications, we at FHG Publications Ltd. present a diploma to proprietors who receive the highest recommendation from their guests who are also readers of our Guides. If you care to write to us praising the holiday you have booked through FHG Publications Ltd. – whether this be board, self-catering accommodation, a sporting or a caravan holiday, what you say will be evaluated and the proprietors who reach our final list will be contacted.

The winning proprietor will receive an attractive framed diploma to display on his premises as recognition of a high standard of comfort, amenity and hospitality. FHG Publications Ltd. offer this diploma as a contribution towards the improvement of standards in tourist accommodation in Britain. Help your excellent host or hostess to win it!

---

We nominate ..........................................................................................................

..........................................................................................................................

Because

Your Name ............................................................................................................

Address ................................................................................................................

..............................................................................Telephone No............................................

# Ratings You Can Trust

## ENGLAND

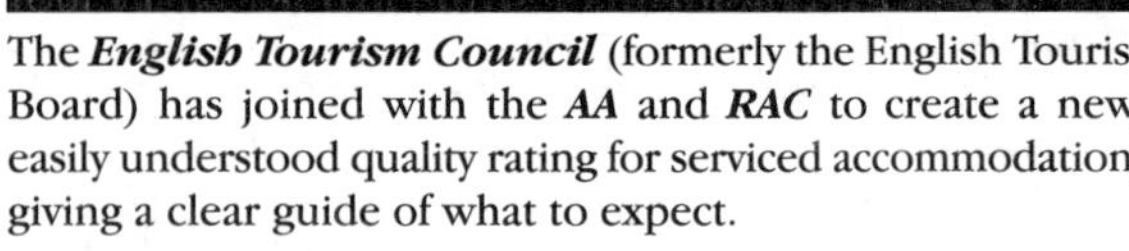

The ***English Tourism Council*** (formerly the English Tourist Board) has joined with the ***AA*** and ***RAC*** to create a new, easily understood quality rating for serviced accommodation, giving a clear guide of what to expect.

***HOTELS*** are given a rating from One to Five ***Stars*** – the more Stars, the higher the quality and the greater the range of facilities and level of services provided.

***GUEST ACCOMMODATION***, which includes guest houses, bed and breakfasts, inns and farmhouses, is rated from One to Five ***Diamonds***. Progressively higher levels of quality and customer care must be provided for each one of the One to Five Diamond ratings.

***HOLIDAY PARKS, TOURING PARKS and CAMPING PARKS*** are now also assessed using ***Stars***. Standards of quality range from a One Star (acceptable) to a Five Star (exceptional) park.

Look out also for the new ***SELF-CATERING*** Star ratings. The more ***Stars*** (from One to Five) awarded to an establishment, the higher the levels of quality you can expect. Establishments at higher rating levels also have to meet some additional requirements for facilities.

## SCOTLAND

***Star Quality Grades*** will reflect the most important aspects of a visit, such as the warmth of welcome, efficiency and friendliness of service, the quality of the food and the cleanliness and condition of the furnishings, fittings and decor.

***THE MORE STARS,***

***THE HIGHER THE STANDARDS.***

The description, such as Hotel, Guest House, Bed and Breakfast, Lodge, Holiday Park, Self-catering etc tells you the type of property and style of operation.

## WALES

Places which score highly will have an especially welcoming atmosphere and pleasing ambience, high levels of comfort and guest care, and attractive surroundings enhanced by thoughtful design and attention to detail

**STAR QUALITY GUIDE FOR**

**HOTELS, GUEST HOUSES AND FARMHOUSES**

**SELF-CATERING ACCOMMODATION**
**(Cottages, Apartments, Houses)**

**CARAVAN HOLIDAY HOME PARKS**
**(Holiday Parks, Touring Parks, Camping Parks)**

| | |
|---|---|
| ★★★★★ | *Exceptional quality* |
| ★★★★ | *Excellent quality* |
| ★★★ | *Very good quality* |
| ★★ | *Good quality* |
| ★ | *Fair to good quality* |

***In England, Scotland and Wales, all graded properties are inspected annually by Tourist Authority trained Assessors.***

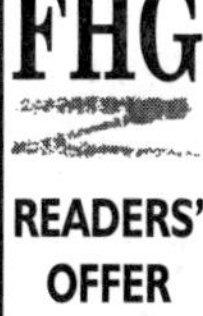


READERS' OFFER 2003

## Bekonscot Model Village

Warwick Road, Beaconsfield, Buckinghamshire HP9 2PL

Tel: 01494 672919 • e-mail: Bekonscot@dial.pipex.com
website: www.bekonscot.com

One child FREE when accompanied by full-paying adult

valid February to October 2003

NOT TO BE USED IN CONJUNCTION WITH ANY OTHER OFFER

READERS' OFFER 2003

## Tamar Valley Donkey Park

St Ann's Chapel, Gunnislake, Cornwall PL18 9HW

Tel: 01822 834072

e-mail: info@donkeypark.com • website: www.donkeypark.com

50p OFF per person, up to six persons

valid from Easter until the end of October 2003

NOT TO BE USED IN CONJUNCTION WITH ANY OTHER OFFER

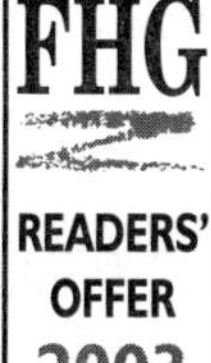


READERS' OFFER 2003

## Devonshire Collection of Period Costume

Totnes Costume Museum,
Bogan House, 43 High Street, Totnes TQ9 5NP

FREE child with a paying adult with voucher

valid from end of May to end of Sept 2003

NOT TO BE USED IN CONJUNCTION WITH ANY OTHER OFFER

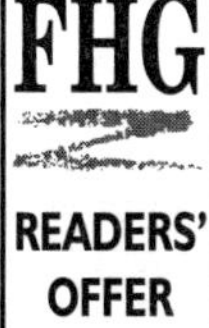


READERS' OFFER 2003

## Coldharbour Mill Visitor Centre & Museum

Coldharbour Mill, Uffculme, Cullompton, Devon EX15 3EE

Tel: 01884 840960 • e-mail: coldharbour@lineone.net
website: www.coldharbourmill.org.uk

TWO adult tickets for the price of ONE

valid during 2003

NOT TO BE USED IN CONJUNCTION WITH ANY OTHER OFFER

FHG

READERS' OFFER 2003

## Cider Museum & King Offa Distillery

21 Ryelands Street, Hereford HR4 0LW

Tel: 01432 354207 • Fax: 01432 371641

e-mail: info@cidermuseum.co.uk • website: www.cidermuseum.co.uk

50p reduction on entry fee

valid during 2003

NOT TO BE USED IN CONJUNCTION WITH ANY OTHER OFFER

*Be a giant in a magical miniature world of make-believe depicting rural England in the 1930's. "A little piece of history that is forever England."*

**Open:** 10am to 5pm daily 15th February to 26th October.

**Directions:** Junction 16 M25, Junction 2 M40.

**FHG PUBLICATIONS, ABBEY MILL BUSINESS CENTRE, PAISLEY PA1 1TJ**

---

*Cornwall's only Donkey Sanctuary set in 14 acres overlooking the beautiful Tamar Valley. Donkey rides, rabbit warren, goat hill, children's playgrounds, cafe and picnic area.*

**Open:** Easter to end of October and February half-term - daily from 10am to 5.30pm. November to March open weekends. Closed January.

**Directions:** Just off A390 between Callington and Gunnislake at St Ann's Chapel.

**FHG PUBLICATIONS, ABBEY MILL BUSINESS CENTRE, PAISLEY PA1 1TJ**

---

*Themed exhibition, changed annually, based in a Tudor house. Collection contains items of dress for women, men and children from 17th century to 1980s, from high fashion to everyday wear.*

**Open:** Open from May 27th to end of September. 11am to 5pm Monday to Friday.

**Directions:** Centre of town, opposite Market Square. Mini bus up High Street stops outside.

**FHG PUBLICATIONS, ABBEY MILL BUSINESS CENTRE, PAISLEY PA1 1TJ**

---

*A picturesque 200-year old woollen mill with machinery that spins yarn and weaves cloth. Mill machinery, restaurant, shop and gardens in a waterside setting and the largest stitched embroidery in the world.*

**Open:** March to December daily 10.30am to 5pm.

**Directions:** Two miles from Junction 27 M5; follow signs to Willand (B3181) then brown tourist signs to Museum

**FHG PUBLICATIONS, ABBEY MILL BUSINESS CENTRE, PAISLEY PA1 1TJ**

---

*Discover the fascinating history of cider making. There is a programme of temporary exhibitions and events plus free samples of Hereford cider brandy.*

**Open:** April to Oct 10am to 5.30pm (daily) Nov to Dec 11pm to 3pm (daily) Jan to Mar 11am to 3pm (Tues to Sun)

**Directions:** situated west of Hereford off the A438 Hereford to Brecon road.

**FHG PUBLICATIONS, ABBEY MILL BUSINESS CENTRE, PAISLEY PA1 1TJ**

FHG READERS' OFFER 2003

# Verulamium Museum

St Michael's, St Albans, Herts AL3 4SW

Tel: 01727 751810

e-mail: a.coles@stalbans.gov.uk • website: www.stalbansmuseums.org.uk

"Two for One"

valid from 1/8/03 until 31/12/03

NOT TO BE USED IN CONJUNCTION WITH ANY OTHER OFFER

FHG READERS' OFFER 2003

# DONINGTON GRAND PRIX COLLECTION

DONINGTON PARK

Castle Donington, Near Derby, Leics DE74 2RP

Tel: 01332 811027 • e-mail: enquiries@donington.co.uk

website: www.doningtoncollection.com

One child FREE with each full-paying adult

valid until 01/01/04

NOT TO BE USED IN CONJUNCTION WITH ANY OTHER OFFER

FHG READERS' OFFER 2003

# Snibston Discovery Park

Ashby Road, Coalville, Leicestershire LE67 3LN

Tel: 01530 278444 • Fax: 01530 813301

e-mail: snibston@leics.gov.uk • website: www.leics.gov.uk/museums

One FREE child with every full paying adult

valid until June 2003

NOT TO BE USED IN CONJUNCTION WITH ANY OTHER OFFER

FHG READERS' OFFER 2003

# Butterfly & Wildlife Park

Long Sutton, Spalding, Lincs PE12 9LE

Tel: 01406 363833

e-mail: butterflypark@hotmail.com • website: www.butterflyandwildlifepark.co.uk

One FREE child with one full-paying adult

valid April to October 2003 (Not Bank Holiday weekends)

NOT TO BE USED IN CONJUNCTION WITH ANY OTHER OFFER

FHG READERS' OFFER 2003

# PLEASURELAND

Marine Drive, Southport, Merseyside PR8 1RX

Tel: 08702 200204 • Fax: 01704 537936

e-mail: mail@pleasurelandltd.freeserve.co.uk • website: www.pleasureland.uk.com

3 for 2, if two all day wristbands purchased, third provided FREE
• offer not valid on Bank Holiday Weekends

valid from March to November 2003

NOT TO BE USED IN CONJUNCTION WITH ANY OTHER OFFER

*The museum of everyday life in Roman Britain. An award-winning museum with re-created Roman rooms, hands-on discovery areas, and some of the best mosaics outside the Mediterranean.*

**Open:** Monday to Saturday 10am-5.30pm Sunday 2pm-5.30pm.

**Directions:** St Albans.

FHG PUBLICATIONS, ABBEY MILL BUSINESS CENTRE, PAISLEY PA1 1TJ

*The world's largest collection of Grand Prix racing cars – over 130 exhibits within five halls, including McLaren Formula One cars.*

**Open:** Daily 10am to 5pm (last admission 4pm). Closed Christmas/New Year.

**Directions:** 2 miles from M1 (J23a/24) and M42/A42; to north-west via A50.

FHG PUBLICATIONS, ABBEY MILL BUSINESS CENTRE, PAISLEY PA1 1TJ

*Located in 100 acres of landscaped grounds, Snibston is a unique mixture, with historic mine buildings, outdoor science play areas, wildlife habitats and an exhibition hall housing five hands-on galleries. Cafe and gift shop.*

**Open:** Seven days a week 10am to 5pm.

**Directions:** Junction 22 from M1, Junction 13 from M42. Follow Brown Heritage signs.

FHG PUBLICATIONS, ABBEY MILL BUSINESS CENTRE, PAISLEY PA1 1TJ

*Large wildlife park with Reptile Land, Tropical House, Insectarium, Birds of Prey Centre, farm animals, wallaby enclosure, llamas; adventure playground, tea room and gift shop.*

**Open:** Daily from 10am April to 28th October 2003

**Directions:** Off A17 at Long Sutton.

FHG PUBLICATIONS, ABBEY MILL BUSINESS CENTRE, PAISLEY PA1 1TJ

*Over 100 rides and attractions, including the Traumatizer - the UK's tallest, fastest suspended looping coaster and the new Lucozade Space Shot.*

**Open:** March to November, times vary.

FHG PUBLICATIONS, ABBEY MILL BUSINESS CENTRE, PAISLEY PA1 1TJ

FHG READERS' OFFER 2003

## The New Metroland

39 Garden Walk, Metrocentre, Gateshead NE11 9XY

Tel: 0191 4932048 • Fax: 0191 4932904

e-mail: enquiries@metroland.uk.com • website: www.metroland.uk.com

TWO all day unlimited ride passes for the price of ONE

valid until 31/12/03 except Bank Holiday Weekends

NOT TO BE USED IN CONJUNCTION WITH ANY OTHER OFFER

FHG READERS' OFFER 2003

## Chesters Walled Garden

Chollerford, Hexham NE46 4BQ

Tel: 01434 681483

website: www.chesterswalledgarden.co.uk

One FREE adult with one paying adult

valid Easter to end of August 2003

NOT TO BE USED IN CONJUNCTION WITH ANY OTHER OFFER

FHG READERS' OFFER 2003

## Galleries of Justice

Shire Hall, High Pavement, Lace Market, Nottingham NG1 1HN

Tel: 0115 9520555 • Fax: 0115 9939828

e-mail: info@galleriesofjustice.org.uk • website: www.galleriesof justice.org.uk

TWO for ONE with full paying adult (one free visit per voucher)

Valid from Jan to Dec 2003, not Bank Holidays

NOT TO BE USED IN CONJUNCTION WITH ANY OTHER OFFER

FHG READERS' OFFER 2003

## The White Post Modern Farm Centre

Farnsfield, Nottingham NG22 8HL

Tel: 01623 882977 • e-mail: tim@whitepostfarmcentre.co.uk

Fax: 01623 883499 • website: www.whitepostfarmcentre.co.uk

10% off entry to the farm with voucher

valid during 2003

NOT TO BE USED IN CONJUNCTION WITH ANY OTHER OFFER

FHG READERS' OFFER 2003

## Cogges Manor Farm Museum

Church Lane, Witney, Oxfordshire OX28 3LA

Tel: 01993 772602

Two for the price of one

Valid April to end of November 2003

NOT TO BE USED IN CONJUNCTION WITH ANY OTHER OFFER

*Europe's largest indoor family funfair, with exciting rides like the new rollercoaster, disco dodgems and swashbuckling pirate ship. There's something for everyone whatever the weather!*

**Open:** Open daily except Christmas Day. 10am to 8pm Monday to Saturday, 11am to 6pm Sunday. (Open from 12 noon Monday to Friday during term time).
**Directions:** Signposted from the A1

**FHG PUBLICATIONS, ABBEY MILL BUSINESS CENTRE, PAISLEY PA1 1TJ**

*Beautiful walled garden with famous collections of herbs and herbaceous plants, including Roman Garden, National Thyme and Marjoram Collections. There is also a woodland walk. Gift shop.*

**Open:** From Easter to the end of October 10am to 5pm daily.

**Directions:** Six miles north of Hexham off B6318 next to Chesters Roman Fort.

**FHG PUBLICATIONS, ABBEY MILL BUSINESS CENTRE,PAISLEY PA1 1TJ**

*Journey with us through 300 years of Crime and Punishment on this unique atmospheric site. Witness a real trial in the authentic Victorian courtroom. Prisoners and gaolers act as guides as you becomepart of history.*

**Open:** Tuesday to Sunday 10am to 5pm peak season 10am to 4pm off-peak.

**Directions:** from Nottingham city centre follow the brown tourist signs.

**FHG PUBLICATIONS, ABBEY MILL BUSINESS CENTRE, PAISLEY PA1 1TJ**

*A modern working farm with displays indoors and outdoors designed to help visitors listen, feel and learn whilst having fun. Daily baby animal holding sessions plus a large indoor play barn.*

**Open:** Daily 10am to 5pm.

**Directions:** 12 miles from Nottingham on A614 or follow Robin Hood signs from J27 of M1.

**FHG PUBLICATIONS, ABBEY MILL BUSINESS CENTRE, PAISLEY PA1 1TJ**

*Historic manor house and farm with traditional animals. Baking in the Victorian kitchen every afternoon.*

**Open:** April to December: Tuesday to Friday 10.30am to 5.30pm. Saturday and Sunday 12-5.30pm.

**Directions:** Just off A40 Oxford to Cheltenham road at Witney.

**FHG PUBLICATIONS, ABBEY MILL BUSINESS CENTRE, PAISLEY PA1 1TJ**

FHG

READERS' OFFER 2003

## Wookey Hole Caves & Papermill

Wookey Hole, Wells, Somerset BA5 1BB

Tel: 01749 672243

e-mail: witch@wookey.co.uk • website: www.wookey.co.uk

£1 per person OFF full admission price (up to max. 5 persons)

valid during 2003

NOT TO BE USED IN CONJUNCTION WITH ANY OTHER OFFER

FHG

READERS' OFFER 2003

## Royal Doulton Visitor Centre

Nile Street, Burslem, Stoke-on-Trent, Staffs ST6 2AJ

Tel: 01782 292434 • Fax: 01782 292424

e-mail: visitor@royal-doulton.com • website: www.royal-doulton.com

Two admissions for the price of one – does not apply to factory tours

valid during 2003

NOT TO BE USED IN CONJUNCTION WITH ANY OTHER OFFER

FHG

READERS' OFFER 2003

## New Pleasurewood Hills

Leisure Way, Corton, Lowestoft, Suffolk NR32 5DZ

Tel: 01502 508200 • Fax: 01502 567393

e-mail: info@pleasurewoodhills.com • website: www.pleasurewoodhills.com

'3 for 2' One FREE adult/child with two full paying adults

valid during 2003, except special events and at Christmas

NOT TO BE USED IN CONJUNCTION WITH ANY OTHER OFFER

FHG

READERS' OFFER 2003

## PARADISE PARK & GARDENS

Avis Road, Newhaven, East Sussex BN9 0DH

Tel: 01273 512123 • Fax: 01273 616000

e-mail: enquiries@paradisepark.co.uk • website: www.paradisepark.co.uk

Admit one FREE adult or child with one adult paying full entrance price

valid during 2003

NOT TO BE USED IN CONJUNCTION WITH ANY OTHER OFFER

FHG

READERS' OFFER 2003

## Wildfowl & Wetlands Trust

District 15, Washington, Tyne & Wear NE38 8LE

Tel: 0191 416 5454

e-mail: wetlands@euphony.net • website: www.wwt.org.uk

One FREE admission with full-paying adult

valid from 1st Jan 2003 to 30th Sep 2003

NOT TO BE USED IN CONJUNCTION WITH ANY OTHER OFFER

** Britain's most spectacular caves*
** Traditional paper-making*
** Penny Arcade*
** Magical Mirror Maze **

**Open:** Summer 10am to 5pm last tour; Winter 10.30am to 4.30pm last tour. Closed 17-25 Dec.
**Directions:** From M5 J22 follow brown-and-white signs via A38 and A371. Two miles from Wells.

FHG PUBLICATIONS, ABBEY MILL BUSINESS CENTRE, PAISLEY PA1 1TJ

*Extensive displays of Royal Doulton products both past and present including figures, giftware, tableware and crystal. Live demonstrations, museum area, restaurant and shop. Factory Tours by prior booking weekdays only.*

**Open:** Monday to Saturday 9.30am to 5pm; Sundays 10.30am to 4.30pm Closed Christmas/New Year period.

**Directions:** From M6 Junction 15/16; follow A500 to exit for A527. Follow signs for about one mile.

FHG PUBLICATIONS, ABBEY MILL BUSINESS CENTRE, PAISLEY PA1 1TJ

*With over forty rides, shows and attractions set in fifty acres of parkland - you'll have everything you need for a brilliant day out. The mixture of old favourites and exciting new introductions are an unbeatable combination.*

**Open:** From 10am. Closing time varies depending on season.

**Directions:** Off A12 between Great Yarmouth and Lowestoft.

FHG PUBLICATIONS, ABBEY MILL BUSINESS CENTRE, PAISLEY PA1 1TJ

*A plant lover's paradise with outstanding themed gardens and extensive Museum of Natural History. Conservatory gardens contain a large and varied collection of the world's flora. Sussex History Trail. Dinosaur Museum. Rides and amusements.*

**Open:** Open daily, except Christmas Day and Boxing Day.

**Directions:** Signposted off A26 and A259.

FHG PUBLICATIONS, ABBEY MILL BUSINESS CENTRE, PAISLEY PA1 1TJ

*100 acres of parkland, home to hundreds of duck, geese, swans and flamingos. Discovery centre, cafe, gift shop; play area.*

**Open:** Every day except Christmas Day

**Directions:** Signposted from A19, A195, A1231 and A182.

FHG PUBLICATIONS, ABBEY MILL BUSINESS CENTRE, PAISLEY PA1 1TJ

FHG READERS' OFFER 2003

## The Grassic Gibbon Centre

Arbuthnott, Laurencekirk, Aberdeenshire AB30 1PB
Tel: 01561 361668 • e-mail: lgginfo@grassicgibbon.com
website: www.grassicgibbon.com

TWO for the price of ONE entry to exhibition (based on full adult rate only)

Valid during 2003 (not groups)

NOT TO BE USED IN CONJUNCTION WITH ANY OTHER OFFER

FHG READERS' OFFER 2003

## Scottish Maritime Museum

Harbourside, Irvine KA12 8QE
Tel: 01294 278283 • e-mail: smm@tildesley.fsbusiness.co.uk
website: www.scottishmaritimemuseum.org • Fax: 01294 313211

TWO for the price of ONE

Valid from January to December 2003

NOT TO BE USED IN CONJUNCTION WITH ANY OTHER OFFER

FHG READERS' OFFER 2003

## CREETOWN GEM ROCK MUSEUM

Chain Road, Creetown, Near Newton Stewart, Kirkcudbrightshire DG8 7HJ
Tel: 01671 820357 • e-mail: gem.rock@btinternet.com
website: www.gemrock.net

10% off admission prices

valid during 2003

NOT TO BE USED IN CONJUNCTION WITH ANY OTHER OFFER

FHG READERS' OFFER 2003

## Edinburgh Crystal Visitor Centre

Eastfield, Penicuik, Midlothian EH26 8HB
Tel: 01968 675128 • Fax: 01968 674847
e-mail: VisitorCentre@edinburgh-crystal.co.uk • website: www.edinburgh-crystal.com

TWO adults for the price of ONE

valid during 2003

NOT TO BE USED IN CONJUNCTION WITH ANY OTHER OFFER

FHG READERS' OFFER 2003

## Deep Sea World

North Queensferry, Fife KY11 1JR
Tel: 01383 411880 / 0906 941 0077 (24hr info line, calls cost 10p per minute)
info@deepseaworld.com • www.deepdseaworld.com

One child FREE with a full-paying adult

valid until end 2003

NOT TO BE USED IN CONJUNCTION WITH ANY OTHER OFFER

*Visitor centre dedicated to the much-loved Scottish writer Lewis Grassic Gibbon. Exhibition, cafe, gift shop. Outdoor children's play area. Disabled access throughout.*

**Open:** Daily April to October 10am to 4.30pm. Groups by appointment including evenings.

**Directions:** On the B967, accessible and signposted from both A90 and A92.



*Scotland's seafaring heritage is among the world's richest and you can relive the heyday of Scottish shipping at the Maritime Museum.*

**Open:** all year except Christmas and New Year Holidays.
10am - 5pm

**Directions:** Situated on Irvine harbourside and only a 10 minute walk from Irvine train station.

FHG PUBLICATIONS, ABBEY MILL BUSINESS CENTRE, PAISLEY PA1 1TJ

*Worldwide collection of gems, minerals, crystals and fossils*
*•Erupting Volcano•Audio Visual•*
*•Crystal Cave•Unique Giftshop•*
*•Relax in our themed tea room•*
*•Internet Cafe*

**Open:** Open daily Easter to 30th November; December to February – weekends only.

**Directions:** 7 miles from Newton Stewart, 11 miles from Gatehouse of Fleet; just off A75 Carlisle to Stranraer road.

FHG PUBLICATIONS, ABBEY MILL BUSINESS CENTRE, PAISLEY PA1 1TJ

*Watch the craftsmen, feel the passion and discover the history of the UK's favourite crystal on tours of the glasshouse. Plus great shopping.*

**Open:** Monday to Saturday 10am to 5pm, Sundays 11am to 5pm. Tour not available during Christmas and New Year fortnight

**Directions:** 30 minutes south of Edinburgh city centre. From city bypass, take A701 to Peebles, following the signs for Penicuik.

FHG PUBLICATIONS, ABBEY MILL BUSINESS CENTRE, PAISLEY PA1 1TJ

*Scotland's award-winning aquarium where you can enjoy a spectacular diver's eye view of our marine environment through the world's longest underwater safari. New 'Amazing Amphibians' display, (Cayman crocodile), behind the scenes tours. Aquamazing entertainment for all the family*

**Open:** Daily except Christmas Day.

**Directions:** From Edinburgh follow signs for Forth Road Bridge, then signs through North Queensferry. From North, follow signs through Inverkeithing and North Queensferry.

FHG PUBLICATIONS, ABBEY MILL BUSINESS CENTRE, PAISLEY PA1 1TJ

FHG READERS' OFFER 2003

## Highland Folk Museum

Aultlarie Crofthouse, Newtonmore, Inverness-shire PH20 1AY

Tel: 01540 661307 • Fax: 01540 661631

e-mail: highland.folk@highland.gov.uk • website: www.highlandfolk.com

One child FREE with each adult paying full admission price

valid from May to October 2003

NOT TO BE USED IN CONJUNCTION WITH ANY OTHER OFFER

FHG READERS' OFFER 2003

## Speyside Heather Garden & Visitor Centre

Speyside Heather Centre, Dulnain Bridge, Inverness-shire PH26 3PA

Tel: 01479 851359 • Fax: 01479 851396

e-mail: enquiries@heathercentre.com • website: www.heathercentre.com

FREE entry to 'Heather Story' exhibition

valid during 2003

NOT TO BE USED IN CONJUNCTION WITH ANY OTHER OFFER

FHG READERS' OFFER 2003

## New Lanark World Heritage Site

New Lanark Mills, New Lanark, Lanarkshire ML11 9DB

Tel: 01555 661345• Fax: 01555 665738

e-mail: development@newlanark.org • website: www.newlanark.org

One FREE child with every full price adult

valid until 31st October 2003

NOT TO BE USED IN CONJUNCTION WITH ANY OTHER OFFER

FHG READERS' OFFER 2003

## Alice in Wonderland Centre

3/4 Trinity Square, Llandudno, Conwy, North Wales LL30 2PY

Tel: 01492 860082 • e-mail: alice@wonderland.co.uk

website: www.wonderland.co.uk

One child FREE with two paying adults. Guide Dogs welcome

valid during 2003

NOT TO BE USED IN CONJUNCTION WITH ANY OTHER OFFER

FHG READERS' OFFER 2003

## Rhondda Heritage Park

Lewis Merthyr Colliery, Coed Cae Road, Trehafod, Near Pontypridd CF37 7NP

Tel: 01443 682036 • e-mail: info@rhonddaheritagepark.com

website: www.rhonddaheritagepark.com

Two adults or children for the price of one

Valid until end 2003 for full tours only. Not valid on special event days.

NOT TO BE USED IN CONJUNCTION WITH ANY OTHER OFFER

| | |
|---|---|
| *300 years of history has been recreated in a thriving township from the 1700s, a working Highland farm with old breed horses, cattle, ducks, farm machinery and an old tin school where the teacher rules!* | **Open:** Mid-April to October. Check for opening times.<br><br>**Directions:** Follow signs from A9 to Newtonmore. North end of Newtonmore on A86. |

**FHG PUBLICATIONS, ABBEY MILL BUSINESS CENTRE, PAISLEY PA1 1TJ**

| | |
|---|---|
| *Award-winning attraction with unique 'Heather Story' exhibition, extensive giftshop. Large garden centre selling 300 different heathers, antique shop, children's play area and famous Clootie Dumpling restaurant.* | **Open:** All year except Christmas Day.<br><br>**Directions:** Just off A95 between Aviemore and Grantown-on-Spey. |

**FHG PUBLICATIONS, ABBEY MILL BUSINESS CENTRE, PAISLEY PA1 1TJ**

| | |
|---|---|
| *A beautifully restored cotton mill village close to the Falls of Clyde. Explore the fascinating history of the village, try the 'New Millennium Experience', a magical chair ride which takes you back in time to discover what life used to be like.* | **Open:** 11am to 5pm daily. Closed Christmas and New Year. |

**FHG PUBLICATIONS, ABBEY MILL BUSINESS CENTRE, PAISLEY PA1 1TJ**

| | |
|---|---|
| *Walk through the Rabbit Hole to the colourful scenes of Lewis Carroll's classic story set in beautiful life-size displays. Recorded commentaries and transcripts available in several languages.* | **Open:** 10am to 5pm daily (closed Sundays Easter to November); closed Christmas/Boxing/New Year's Days.<br><br>**Directions:** situated just off the main street, 250 yards from coach and rail stations. |

**FHG PUBLICATIONS, ABBEY MILL BUSINESS CENTRE, PAISLEY PA1 1TJ**

| | |
|---|---|
| *Make a pit stop whatever the weather! Join an ex-miner on a tour of discovery, ride the cage to pit bottom and take a thrilling ride back to the surface. Multi-media presentations, period village street, children's adventure play area, restaurant and gift shop. Full disabled access.* | **Open:** Open daily 10am to 6pm (last tour 4.30pm). Closed Mondays October to Easter, also Christmas/Boxing days.<br><br>**Directions:** Exit Junction 32 M4, signposted from A470 Pontypridd. Trehafod is located between Pontypridd and Porth. |

**FHG PUBLICATIONS, ABBEY MILL BUSINESS CENTRE, PAISLEY PA1 1TJ**

# London & The South East

*The Great Gatehouse of Hampton Court Palace*

WITH A POPULATION of almost seven million, London is by far the largest city in Europe, sprawling over an area of 620 square miles. For first-time visitors a city sight-seeing tour by double-decker bus or by boat along the River Thames is a 'must'. Even for those already familiar with the main attractions, there's always something new in London. Buckingham Palace is now open to the public and proving a very popular attraction. Visitors are welcome from August until October and will see 18 out of the 660 rooms in the Palace, including the Throne Room and most of the other State apartments.

The Crown Jewels are on display in their splendid new home in the Tower of London – the Jewel House. It cost £10 million, but it's three times as large as the old place, with state-of-the-art lighting and security control.

If you haven't visited London recently, consider calling in at The Celebration Story, located inside Tower Bridge. Animatronic characters, a simulated bridge lift, video, light and sound bring to life the story of the construction of Tower Bridge. A visit to London is not complete without seeing the new Docklands – an 8½ square mile area with a fantastic range of old and new architecture (including Britain's tallest building), pubs and restaurants, shops, visitor attractions and parks – all just a short journey from the City Centre. With its orchards, hopfields, bluebell woods and vineyards it's not surprising that Kent is known as 'The Garden of England'. Historic Kent towns like Canterbury, Rochester and Broadstairs are a contrast with Dover, still the busiest passenger seaport in Europe and gateway to the Channel Tunnel.

In Dover, the White Cliffs Experience

tells the story of the town and its strategic importance in both World Wars. The South East has many and varied resorts. Several have royal connections such as Bognor – patronised by George V when the suffix 'Regis' was added. The most famous 'royal' resort in Sussex is Brighton, with its two piers, prom, graceful Georgian houses, antique shops, and the famous Royal Pavilion, built at the request of the Prince of Wales, later Prince Regent and George IV. Eastbourne is another fine family resort, while in the quieter nearby town of Bexhill, low tides reveal the remains of a forest – part of the land bridge by which Britain was joined to Europe 10,000 years ago.

Seaside towns also cluster along the Hampshire coast around the port of Southampton, itself a picturesque town. And in the extreme east of the county is Portsmouth, a town irrevocably tied to its seafaring heritage. There are naval museums and ships to see, including Nelson's famous flagship from Trafalgar, *The Victory.*

# Great Days Out – Visits and Attractions

**London Aquarium**
*South Bank, London SE1 • 020 7967 8000*
Hundreds of varieties of fish and sea life from all over the world, displayed around two huge tanks representing the Atlantic and Pacific oceans.

**Tate Modern**
*London • 020 7887 8734*
International modern art from 1900 to the present day, in a massive exhibition space. Cafe with outstanding views of the river.

**National Portrait Gallery**
*St Martin's Place, London WC2 • 0870 0660597*
The largest collection of portraiture in the world, with over 10, 000 images of Men and women who have shaped the history and culture of the nation. Varied programme of special exhibitions throughout the year.

**West Wycombe Caves**
*Near High Wycombe, Bucks • 01494 533739.*
A fun experience for the whole family. Follow the winding passage through the caves until you find yourself 300ft down. Cafe.

**Marwell**
*Near Winchester, Hants • 07626 943163*
*website: www.marwell.org.uk*
World famous for its dedication to the conservation of endangered species. Nearly 1000 animals in acres of beautiful parkland.

**Eagle Heights**
*Near Dartford, Kent • 01322 866466*
*website: www.eagleheights.co.uk*
Birds of prey housed undercover – eagles, hawks, falcons, owls and vultures. Flying demonstrations daily; snake handling and reptile room; play areas.

**Brooklands Museum**
*Weybridge, Surrey • 01932 857381*
*website: www.motor-software.co.uk*
Set on 30 acres of the original motor racing circuit. Racing cars, motorcycles and bikes, and the new 'Fastest on Earth' exhibition.

**Royal Pavilion**
*Brighton, East Sussex • 01273 290900*
*website: www.royalpavilion.brighton.co.uk*
Decorated in Chinese taste with an Indian exterior, this Regency Palace was built for George IV and features superb craftsmanship and extravagant decoration. Guided tours, tearooms and shop.

**Arundel Castle**
*Arundel, West Sussex • 01903 883136*
*website: www.arundelcastle.org*
The family home of the Dukes of Norfolk for over 850 years. Superb collection of paintings, furniture and armour; restored Victorian kitchen; grounds with chapel.

**Weald & Downland Open Air Musem**
*Chichester, West Sussex • 01243 811348*
*website: www.wealddown.co.uk*
Over 40 historic buildings carefully re-constructed, including medieval farmstead, working flour mill, Victorian rural school, and 16th century market place. Visitors can see working horses and demonstrations of building crafts and countryside skills.

**Isle of Wight Waxworks**
*Brading, Isle of Wight • 01983 487286*
See the Rectory Mansion, The Chamber of Horrors, The World of Nature, Professor Copperthwaite's Exhibition of Oddities, and demonstrations of the fascinating art of candle carving.

# The South West

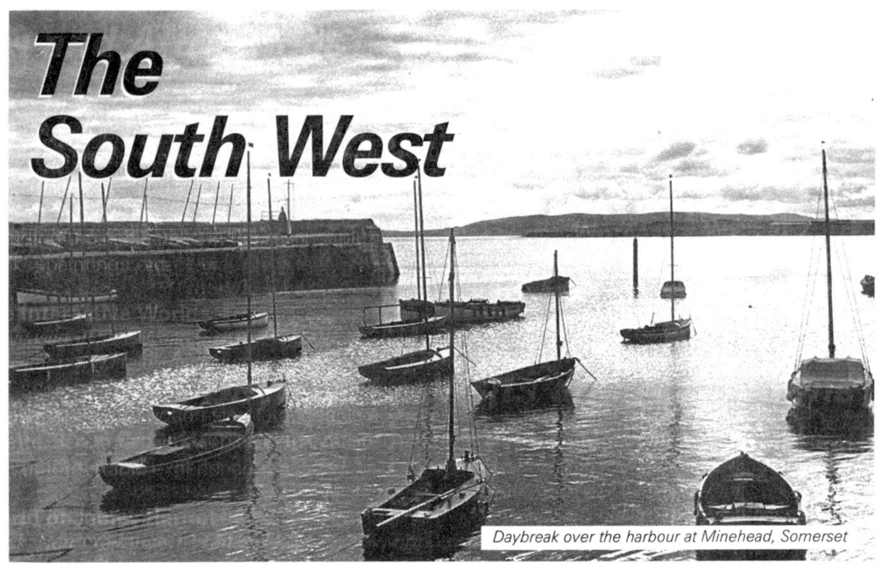

Daybreak over the harbour at Minehead, Somerset

WHATEVER SORT of holiday destination you're looking for, you'll find it in South-West England. As well as the elegant shops and Georgian crescents of Bath, other south-west towns have the very latest in big shopping centres, speciality shops and nightlife. There are stretches of wild moorland, chalk hills, limestone gorges and thatched-house villages and there are miles of golden sand washed by Atlantic breakers. Stop at a Dorset village to enjoy a glass of real Dorset ale in a thatch-roofed pub and you'll understand why almost the whole of Dorset has been designated as an Area of Outstanding Natural Beauty.

Devon has both coast and countryside. Plymouth on the south coast has been a naval base of the greatest importance to the defence of the realm since the days of Sir Francis Drake The city was hastily rebuilt after destruction in the Second World War, but nothing can spoil the glorious vista of the Sound viewed from Plymouth Hoe where Drake finished his game of bowls.

Cornwall reaches into the Atlantic Ocean for almost 100 miles.Take a walk along any part of this strikingly beautiful coast, enjoy a cream tea in one of the charming villages sheltering in a cove and you will understand why Cornwall has been the inspiration for so many artists, novelists and poets. Often free from frost in winter, the soft spring climate favours Cornwall as an ideal destination for holiday breaks.

Say Somerset and most people would automatically think of cider, Cheddar cheese and county cricket matches. But there's a lot more to Somerset – there's Exmoor which is Lorna Doone territory and home to the wild Exmoor ponies and herds of red deer. The National Park of Exmoor has a coastline with some marvellous clifftop walks. Further along this coast are Somerset's main seaside resorts, Minehead and Burnham-on-Sea.

## WEST COUNTRY TOURIST BOARD

*• Bath • Bristol • Cornwall • Devon • Western Dorset • Somerset • Wiltshire • Isles of Scilly*

**60 St. David's Hill, Exeter EX4 4SY**
**Tel: 0870 442 0880**
**Fax: 0870 442 0881**
**www.westcountrynow.com**

## SOUTHERN TOURIST BOARD

*• East Dorset and North Dorset*

**40 Chamberlayne Road, Eastleigh, Hampshire S050 5JH**
**Tel: 023 8062 5400**
**Fax: 023 8062 0010**
**www.visitsouthernengland.com**

# *Great Days Out – Visits and Attractions*

**The Eden Project**
*Near St Austell, Cornwall • 01726 811911*
*website: www.edenproject.com*
A gateway into the fascinating interaction of plants and people. Two gigantic geodesic conservatories - the Humid Tropics Biome and the Warm Temperate Biome - set amidst landscaped outdoor terraces.

**Goonhilly Earth Station**
*Helston, Cornwall • 01326 221333*
*website: www.goonhilly.bt.com*
Explore the wonders of pioneering technology at one of the most important communication stations in the world. Scan the skies by operating an IV dish aerial yourself.

**Quince Honey Farm**
*South Molton, Devon • 01769 572401*
The world's largest living honey bee exhibition, where the hives can be viewed in complete safety. Ideal for all ages, with fascinating videos and well-stocked shop.

**Tuckers Maltings**
*Newton Abbot, Devon • 01626 334734*
England's only working malthouse open to the public. See how barley is turned into malt for brewing beer and sample Devonshire Real Ale. Speciality shop.

**Sherborne Castle**
*Sherborne, Dorset • 01935 813182*
*website: www.sherbornecastle.com*
Built by Sir Walter Raleigh in 1594 and home to the Digby family since the early 17th century. Splendid collection of art, furniture and porcelain.

**Abbotsbury Swannery**
*Near Bridport, Dorset • 01305 871858*
Up to 600 free-flying swans – help feed them twice daily. Baby swans hatch May/June. AV show, coffee shop and gift shop.

**Wookey Hole Caves**
*Wells, Somerset • 01749 672243*
*website: www.wookey.co.uk*
Spectacular showcaves with ancient history and legends. Victorian papermill with traditional papermaking, magical mirror maze, old penny arcade, caves museum

**West Somerset Railway**
*Bishops Lydeard (near Taunton) to Minehead • 01643 704996*
Enjoy 20 miles of glorious Somerset countryside as the steam train gently rolls back the years. Break your journey at any one of ten restored stations along the route. For 24hr talking timetable call 01643 707650..

**Dunster Water Mill**
*Dunster, Somerset • 01643 821759*
The West Country's finest working water mill, set alongside the River Avill. See how flour is produced, then visit the Mill Shop where stoneground floor, home-made muesli and other products are available.

**Bowood House & Gardens**
*Calne, Wiltshire • 01249 812102*
*website: www.bowood.org*
Set in parkland, the magnificent home of the Marquis and Marchioness of Lansdowne, with adventure playground and rhododendron walks (April to mid-June).

# East of England

The village of Cavendish in Suffolk

EAST ANGLIA, once a Saxon kingdom cut off from the rest of England by marshland and forest, remains to this day a relatively unexplored part of Britain. It is an area of low, chalky hills, pleasant market towns, working windmills adding charm to the fields, wide sweeping views over the flattest land and glorious sunsets. Along East Anglia's North Sea coast, the visitor can choose between bustling seaside resorts or long stretches of deserted sandy beaches. Boating enthusiasts come from all over the world for holidays afloat on the Norfolk Broads, an ancient man-made network of shallow tree-fringed lakes, rivers and canals. East Anglia's inland towns are full of history and proud to tell their stories at visitor centres and museums. Specialist museums abound. The Imperial War Museum at Duxford Airfield has the largest collection of military and civil aircraft in Britain. Duxford was a Battle of Britain station and the flatness of East Anglia gave it the wartime distinction of having the largest number of airfields in the country. Steam, vintage and miniature railway museums, classic car collections, bicycle museums: East Anglia has them all, as well as the famous Lace Museum (with magnifying glasses provided) in Norfolk and a Working Silk Museum at the restored silk mills in Braintree and a National Motorboat Museum tracing the history of motor boats, racing hydroplanes and leisure boats. At Lowestoft harbour you can step aboard the last survivor of more than 3000 drifters that came every autumn to Yarmouth and Lowestoft, following the plentiful shoals of herring. Visual displays portray the hardships of the herring workers, male and female, who brought prosperity to the two ports for more than a century but only poverty to themselves.

It was a different way of life – above stairs at least – for the inhabitants of the great mansion houses of East Anglia in their hey-day. The Queen's favourite country seat in England, Sandringham House, is open to the public except when members of the Royal Family are in residence, for two weeks in late July or early August.

**EAST OF ENGLAND TOURIST BOARD**

*• Bedfordshire • Cambridgeshire • Essex • Hertfordshire • Lincolnshire • Norfolk • Suffolk*

**Toppesfield Hall, Hadleigh, Suffolk IP7 5DN**
**Tel: 0870 225 4800**
**Fax: 0870 225 4890**
**www.eastofenglandtouristboard.com**

## Great Days Out – Visits and Attractions

**The Shuttleworth Collection**
*Biggleswade, Bedfordshire • 01767 626227*
*website: www.shuttleworth.org*
A world-famous collection of 40 aircraft, plus veteran and vintage cars, motorcycles and horse-drawn vehicles. All are kept in working condition; flying displays monthly.

**Fitzwilliam Museum**
*Cambridge, Cambridgeshire • 01223 332904*
*website: www.fitzmuseum.cam.ac.uk*
One of the UK's finest collections of armour, antiquities, sculpture, furniture, pottery, paintings, prints, coins and much more.

**Colchester Zoo**
*Colchester, Essex • 01206 331292*
*website: www.colchester-zoo.co.uk*
Set in 60 acres of grounds, over 150 species in award-winning enclosures. Over 15 unique daily displays from elephant bathtime to penguin parades .

**Knebworth House**
*Near Stevenage, Herts • 01438 812661*
*website: www.knebworthhouse.com*
Home of the Lytton family since 1490, with fine collections of manuscripts, portraits and furniture. Set in 250 acre country park with formal gardens and large adventure playground. Gift shop and cafeteria.

**Natureland Seal Sanctuary**
*Skegness, Lincolnshire • 01754 764345*
Famous for its work with abandoned baby seal pups, this conservation centre has aquaria, butterflies, pets' comer. A highlight is feeding time for the seals and penguins.

**Norfolk Shire Horse Centre**
*Near Cromer, Norfolk • 01263 837339*
*website: www.norfolk-shirehorse-centre.co.uk*
Entertaining - Educational - Nostalgic. Wet or fine, a perfect visit for all the family, with cart rides for children. Daily demonstrations; ponies and farm animals, displays.

**Pensthorpe Waterfowl Trust**
*Fakenham, Norfolk • 01328 851465*
Over 120 species of waterfowl from all over the world make this Europe's finest collection of endangered and exotic waterbirds, with over 200 acres of lakes, woodland and meadows to explore.

**Pettitts Animal Adventure Park**
*Near Great Yarmouth, Norfolk • 01493 701403*
Three parks in one - fun for all the family. Rides, play area, adventure golf course, animals galore. Children's entertainment daily.

**National Horse Racing Museum**
*Newmarket, Suffolk • 01638 667333*
*website: www.nhrm.co.uk*
Five permanent galleries tell the story of the development of the "sport of kings" over 400 years. Guided tours by arrangement to the studs, racing yards and training facilities.

**Suffolk Wildlife Park**
*Kessingland, Suffolk • 01502 740291*
*website: www.suffolkwildlifepark.co.uk*
Take a walk in the wilds of Africa and create your own safari adventure amidst an abundance of wildlife from the African continent. Roadtrain, daily feeding talks and displays, indoor and adventure play areas.

# The Midlands

The old stone bridge at Eastleach Martin in Gloucestershire

FOLLOWING THE Romantic Road is not what immediately comes to mind when the English Midlands are being considered as a holiday destination. Nevertheless, the Romantic Road is a very suitable title for a guide to the picture-postcard villages of the Cotswolds which is available from Cheltenham Tourism. The gentle hills and honey-coloured houses of the Cotswolds are deservedly popular with tourists in summer. Quieter, but just as beautiful in their way, are other scenic areas of the Midlands: the Wye Valley, the Vale of Evesham, Sherwood Forest, once the haunt of the legendary Robin Hood and, near the Welsh border, the wooded valleys known as the Marches around the towns of Hereford and Shrewsbury

In a secluded valley in this area a discovery was made that changed the face of the world when Abraham Darby perfected his revolutionary techniques for the mass production of cast iron. Today there are no fewer than seven museums in the Gorge, which has been designated a World Heritage Site.

To keep the children happy there is also a Teddy Bear Museum and the Ironbridge Toy Museum. Children are welcome at the Heritage Motor Centre at Gaydon, the largest collection of British cars in the world; quad biking over rough terrain track is available for children.

Staffordshire is the home of the Potteries and some of the best china and porcelain in the world is made there. Visit Stoke-on-Trent for the complete China Experience, factory tours, ceramic museums and, to take home as a souvenir of the Midlands, world famous names like Wedgwood, Royal Doulton and Spode china at amazing discounts.

The so-called 'industrial' Midlands has also been the birthplace of writers and composers – the Stratford-upon-Avon of Shakespeare, the Lichfield of Dr Samuel Johnson, the Gloucestershire villages of Laurie Lee's "Cider With Rosie" fame, and the Malvern Hills of Elgar's inspiration.

*Local tourist offices offer free advice and guidance on all aspects of your holiday, from mapping out a touring route, local travel and excursions, to ideas on what to do and places to visit throughout the year. Don't hesitate to ask. . . !*

**HEART OF ENGLAND TOURIST BOARD**

• *Gloucestershire* • *Herefordshire* • *Shropshire* • *Staffordshire* • *Warwickshire* • *Worcestershire* • *West Midlands* • *Cherwell* • *West Oxfordshire* • *Derbyshire* • *Leicestershire* • *Northamptonshire* • *Rutland* • *Nottinghamshire*

**Woodside, Larkhill Road, Worcester WR5 2EZ**
**Tel: 01905 761100**
**www.visitheartofengland.com**

## *Great Days Out – Visits and Attractions*

**Royal Crown Derby Visitor Centre**
*Derby, Derbyshire • 01332 712800*
*website: www.royal-crown-derby.co.uk*
Guided tours of the working factory and demonstrations of key skills. Factory shop, restaurant and museum

**Conkers – National Forest Centre**
*Moira, Leicestershire • 01283 216633*
*website: www.visitconkers.com*
Discover how the National Forest is transforming the Heart of England. Walk amongst the treetops, explore the woodland trails, relax by the lakeside. Woodland garden, adventure playground, restaurant and shop.

**The Galleries of Justice**
*Nottingham, Notts • 0115 952 0555*
*website: www.galleriesofjustice.org.uk*
Step back in time and take an unrivalled tour through 2½ centuries of crime, punishment and law. Interactive exhibits and a cast of costumed characters make this an experience to remember.

**Acton Scott Historic Working Farm**
*Church Stretton, Shropshire • 01694 781306*
A fascinating working farm using heavy horses and 19th century techniques, designed to show agricultural life from years past. Daily demonstrations of farming, butter making and traditional crafts.

**Tamworth Castle**
*Tamworth, Staffs • 01827 709629*
*website: www.tamworth.gov.uk*
This dramatic Norman castle is reputedly haunted by lady ghosts. Lots of hands-on activities for children.

**Heritage Motor Centre**
*Gaydon, Warwickshire • 01926 641188*
*website: www.heritage.org.uk*
The largest collection of British cars in the world. 4-wheel drive demonstration circuit, children's roadway, cafe and gift shop.

**Hatton Country World**
*Hatton, Warwickshire • 01926 843411*
*website: www.hattonworld.com*
Rural crafts, farm park and shopping village. Craft gifts and antiques, plus factory outlets and speciality foods. Children can enjoy the soft play centre; displays of traditional farming methods and lots of animals.

**Museum of British Road Transport**
*Coventry, West Midlands • 024 7683 2425*
*website: www.mbrt.co.uk*
The largest display in the world of British-made road transport, from buses to bikes. Tiatsa Model Collection, Coventry Blitz Experience and lots more.

**Cadbury World**
*Bournville, West Midlands • 0121 451 4180*
*website: www.cadburyworld.co.uk*
The chocoholic's paradise. Chocolate-making demonstrations (with free samples!). Something for everyone, from the magic of Cadbury Land to irrestible liquid chocolate.

**Avoncroft Museum**
*Near Bromsgrove, Worcs • 01527 831363*
*website: www.avoncroft.org.uk*
Historic buildings saved from destruction, including a working windmill, furnished houses and the National Telephone Kiosk Collection.

# The North

*Friars Crag on the shores of Derwentwater, Cumbria*

THERE ARE SOME PEOPLE who prefer a holiday where every day is packed with action and every evening filled with fun. Others see a holiday as the exact opposite, a chance to get some peace and quiet in the wide open spaces. Whatever sort of holidaymaker you are, the North of England has plenty to offer you. What's more, touring the North of England can be a great learning experience – and if that sounds boring, it isn't! The North has some of the best living museums and 'hands-on' visitor centres in Britain, where the latest presentation techniques are equally fascinating to adults and children. How does the world look to a fish, a dog, a bee? Find out – and learn to make rainbows too – at the Colour Museum in the once-grimy city of Bradford. Also in Bradford is the National Museum of Photography, Film and Television which has Britain's biggest cinema screen, a thousand times bigger than your TV screen at home – and not content with that, it also has the world's only Cinerama cinema, the world's biggest lens, smallest camera and first-ever photographic likeness! Just as interesting are the smaller heritage museums to be found in practically every town and village in the North. Britain's National Railway Museum is in York, the birthplace of the steam railway. If a day trip behind a steam engine is more your style, ask for the Yorkshire Tourist Board's leaflet 'Steaming Along' with details of seven steam railways and the dates of the kiddies' specials – the Thomas the Tank Engine week-ends.

The seaside resorts of the North have provided happiness for children and relaxation for Mums and Dads for generations. In Lancashire, on the west coast, Southport, St Annes,

Blackpool, Morecambe – often it's the same resort families choose year after satisfied year. The twin resorts of Whitley Bay and Tynemouth are on the North Tyneside coast. Whitley Bay has the noise and thrills of the famous Spanish City fun park, Tynemouth has the attractive Long Sands. From bright lights to walking on the fells, from heritage visits to Sunday shopping, you'll find them all in the North of England!

*Local tourist offices offer free advice and guidance on all aspects of your holiday, from mapping out a touring route, local travel and excursions, to ideas on what to do and places to visit throughout the year. Don't hesitate to ask. . . !*

**CUMBRIA TOURIST BOARD**

*• Cumbria*

**Ashleigh, Holly Road,**
**Windermere, Cumbria LA23 2AQ**
**Tel: 015394 44444**
**Fax: 015394 44041**
**www.golakes.co.uk**

**NORTHUMBRIA TOURIST BOARD**

*• Durham • Northumberland • Tees Valley • Tyne & Wear*

**Aykley Heads,**
**Durham DH1 5UX**
**Tel. 0191 375 3010**
**Fax: 0191 386 0899**
**www.visitnorthumbria.com**

**YORKSHIRE TOURIST BOARD**

*•Yorkshire • Northern Lincolnshire*

**312 Tadcaster Road,**
**York YO24 1GS**
**Tel: 01904 707961**
**Brochure Line: 01904 707070**
**www.yorkshirevisitor.com**

**N.W. TOURIST BOARD**

*• Cheshire • Greater Manchester • Lancashire • Merseyside • High Peak of Derbyshire*

**Swan House,**
**Swan Meadow Road,Wigan Pier,**
**Wigan WN3 5BB**
**Tel: 01942 821222**
**Fax: 01942 820002**
**website: www.visitnorthwest.com**

PLEASE MENTION THIS GUIDE WHEN YOU WRITE OR PHONE TO ENQUIRE ABOUT ACCOMMODATION

IF YOU ARE WRITING, A STAMPED, ADDRESSED ENVELOPE IS ALWAYS APPRECIATED

# Great Days Out – Visits and Attractions

**Rheged Discovery Centre**
*Off M6 Junction 40, A66 • 01768 868000*
*website: www.rheged.com*
The Lake District's most spectacular attraction, and Britain's largest grass-covered building. Six-storey high cinema screen takes you on a journey through 2000 years of Cumbria's history, myths and legends.

**Cumberland Pencil Museum**
*Keswick, Cumbria • 017687 73626*
*website: www.pencils.co.uk*
The fascintating history of the humble pencil, from the discovery of Borrowdale graphite to present day manufacture. See the world's largest colouring pencil, Shop.

**Killhope Lead Mining Centre**
*Near Alston, Co Durham • 01388 537505*
Get a glimpse of a vanished way of life with a trip to Park Level Mine, and a re-creation of the appalling working and living conditions of the late 19th century. A real 'hands on' adventure which brings the past vividly to life.

**National Football Museum**
*Preston, Lancashire• 01772 908442*
*www.nationalfootballmuseum.com*
The story of the world's greatest game. In two distinctive halves, it can be enjoyed by supprters of all ages. Shop and restaurant.

**Hat Works**
*Stockport • 0161-355 7770*
*website: www.hatworks.org.uk*
Uncover the fascinating world of hats. Fully restored working machinery, with workshops and demonstrations; displays of historical and contemporary headgear. Cafe and shop.

**Grace Darling Museum**
*Bamburgh, Northumberland • 01668 214465*
Commemorates the rescue by Grace and her father of the nine survivors of the wreck of the Forfarshire. Many original relics, including the cable used in the rescue, plus books, paintings etc.

**Life Interactive World**
*Newcastle, Tyne & Wear • 0191-243 8210*
*website: www.lifeinteractiveworld.co.uk*
The secret of life – how it works, what it means. A thrilling motion-simulator ride, live theatre, 3D interactive exhibits, virtual reality – an unforgettable experience.

**World of James Herriot**
*Thirsk, North Yorkshire • 01845 524234*
*website: www.worldofjamesherriot.org*
Combines history, humour, nostalgia, science and education in a unique tribute to the creator of the famous "vet' novels. Set in the original 'Skeldale House'.

**Magna**
*Rotherham, South Yorkshire • 01709 720002*
*website: www.magnatrust.org.uk*
The UK's first Science Adventure Centre explores the four elements of Fire, Earth, Air and Water. Experience sound and light shows, fire giant water cannons, and lots more!

**Thackray Medical Museum**
*Leeds, West Yorkshire • 0113 244 4343*
*website: www.thackraymuseum.org*
This interactive museum shows how medicine has changed our lives. Walk through the slums of 1840 Leeds, experience surgery without anaesthetics, see live leeches, and in Bodyworks enter the giant gut.

# Elstead Hotel

Set in a quiet, tree-lined avenue in central Bournemouth, the Elstead is a very special hotel with an elegance and warmth which creates its own character and ambience.

• You are assured of a warm welcome at the Elstead. Fifty comfortable en suite bedrooms blend with delightful lounges and bars and a superb restaurant to ensure a memorable stay in a Hotel which is renowned for its personal service, fine cuisine and the warmth of its welcome.

• Close to the heart of Bournemouth and a short stroll from the beach, yet conveniently placed for all major road and rail links, and with ample car parking, the Elstead Hotel is the perfect base for both business and pleasure.

• You can be sure of a very comfortable and enjoyable stay. All of our bedrooms are equipped to the standard you would expect of a very good, quality Hotel.

• The Elstead Hotel is proud of its reputation for good home cooked food and can cater for special diets with advance notice. Whether you choose to eat in the elegant restaurant or in the more casual surroundings of the bar or terrace you can be sure of good service and excellent food. Our restaurant is non-smoking and there is also a non-smoking lounge. We also offer both smoking and non-smoking bedrooms.

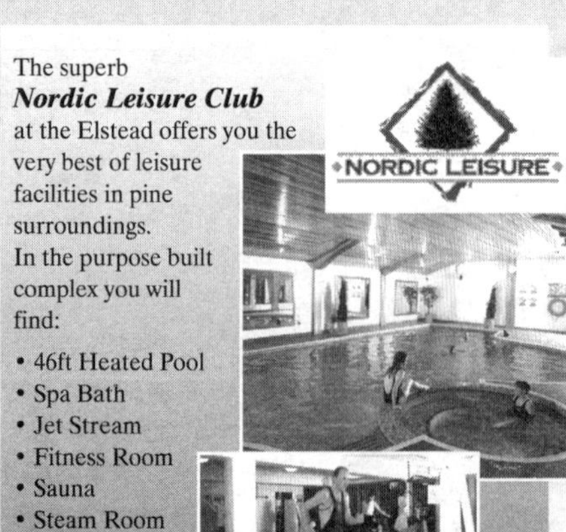

# Greater London

## FALCON HOTEL

ETC ★★

See also Colour Advertisement on page 3

**11 Norfolk Square, Hyde Park North, London W2**
**Tel: 020 7723 8603 • Fax: 020 7402 7009**
**e-mail: info@aafalcon.co.uk • website: www.aafalcon.co.uk**

Central London B&B Hotel. Family-friendly and very clean and comfortable. Established 30 years. In a tranquil position in a garden square, two minutes from Paddington Station. Airlines check-ins 15 minutes to Heathrow on Express Link. Close to tourist attractions and shops. En suite facilities; triple and family rooms. Full freshly cooked English breakfasts. Our guests first and always.

£ **Affordable prices from £35 single, £55 double. Please call for latest seasonal prices.**

## ELIZABETH HOTEL

See also Colour Advertisement on page 3

**37 Eccleston Square, Victoria, London SW1V 1PB**
**Tel: 020 7828 6812 • Fax: 020 7828 6814**
**e-mail: info@elizabethhotel.com • website: www.elizabethhotel.com**

Quiet, convenient town house overlooking the magnificent gardens of Eccleston Square. Only a short walk from Buckingham Palace and other tourist attractions. Easy access to Knightsbridge, Oxford Street and Regent Street. Extremely reasonable rates in a fantastic location. Visa, Mastercard, Switch, Delta and JCB are all accepted.

£ **Details on request.**

## DALMACIA HOTEL

**71 Shepherds Bush Road, Hammersmith, London W6 7LS**
**Tel: 020 7603 2887 • Fax: 020 7602 9226**
**website: www.dalmacia-hotel.co.uk**

Conveniently located for visiting all of London's attractions, offering comfortable, value-for-money accommodation. Single and double/twin rooms are available, all en suite with remote-control satellite TV and direct-dial telephones. All major credit cards accepted. Les Routiers and London Tourist Board Listed. Brochure available.

£ **Terms on request.**

## ADRIA HOTEL

**44 Glenthorne Road, Hammersmith, London W6 0LS**
**Tel: 020 7603 2887**
**website: www.dalmacia-hotel.co.uk**

This newly refurbished hotel is conveniently situated just 100 metres from the Underground, making it ideal for exploring all the historic, cultural, leisure and entertainment amenities of the capital. Accommodation is available in 15 comfortable bedrooms, all en suite, and offering superb value for money. Major credit cards accepted. Parking available.

£ **Single room from £35; double room from £55.**

---

## QUEENS HOTEL

ETC ◆◆

**33 Anson Road, Tufnell Park, London N7**
**Tel: 020 7607 4725 • Fax: 020 7697 9725**
**e-mail: queens@stavrouhotels.co.uk • website: http://www.stavrouhotels.co.uk**

See also Colour Advertisement on page 4

The Queens Hotel is a large double-fronted Victorian building standing in its own grounds five minutes' walk from Tufnell Park Station. Quietly situated with ample car parking spaces; 15 minutes to West End and close to London Zoo, Hampstead and Highgate. Two miles from King's Cross and St Pancras Stations. Many rooms en suite.

£ **All prices include full English breakfast and VAT. Children half price; discounts on longer stays. Singles from £23-£34; doubles/ twins from £30-£48; triples and family rooms from £16pp.**

---

## GOWER HOTEL

ETC ◆◆

**129 Sussex Gardens, Hyde Park, London W2 2RX**
**Tel: 020 7262 2262 • Fax: 020 7262 2006**
**e-mail: gower@stavrouhotels.co.uk • website: http://www.stavrouhotels.co.uk**

See also Colour Advertisement on page 4

The Gower Hotel is a small family-run Hotel, centrally located, within two minutes of Paddington Station and the Heathrow Express. Excellent for sightseeing London's famous sights and shops. Hyde Park, Madame Tussaud's, Oxford Street, Marble Arch, Buckingham Palace and many more close by. All rooms have private shower, WC, radio, TV (includes satellite and video channels), direct dial telephone and tea and coffee facilities. All recently refurbished and fully centrally heated.

£ **All prices inclusive of full English breakfast and VAT. Credit cards welcome. Single rooms £30-£54; double/twin room £26-£36; triple/family rooms from £20-£30 – all prices are per person.**

---

## ATHENA HOTEL

ETC ◆◆◆

**110-114 Sussex Gardens, Hyde Park, London W2 1UA**
**Tel: 020 7706 3866 • Fax: 020 7262 6143**
**e-mail: athena@stavrouhotels.co.uk • website: http://www.stavrouhotels.co.uk**

Family-run hotel in restored Victorian building. Professionally designed, including a lift to all floors and exquisitely decorated, we offer the ambience and hospitality necessary for a relaxing and enjoyable stay. Extremely well-positioned for sightseeing London's famous sights and shops; Hyde Park, Madame Tussaud's, Oxford Street, Marble Arch, Knightsbridge, Buckingham Palace and many more all within walking distance. Tastefully decorated bedrooms with en suite, TV, telephone and tea/coffee facilities. Ample car parking. Travel connections to all over London only minutes away. See also Advertisement on Inside Back Cover.

£ **Single Rooms from £50-£65, Double/Twin Rooms from £60-£89, Triple and Family Rooms from £25 per person.**

See also Colour Advertisement on page 5

## BLAIR VICTORIA HOTEL

LTB ◆◆

**78-84 Warwick Way, Victoria, London SW1V 1RZ**
**Tel: 020 7828 8603**
**e-mail: sales@blairvictoria.com • website: www.blairvictoria.com**

An impressively furnished and friendly London town house, in an excellent location for all tourist attractions. Within easy walking distance of Buckingham Palace, St James's Park, Westminster Abbey, the Embankment and The Apollo and Palace Theatres.

£ **Single room from £35, double room from £55.**

See also Colour Advertisement on page 4

## HAVEN HOTEL

**6-8 Sussex Gardens, Paddington, London W2 1UL**
**Tel: 020 7723 5481/2195 • Fax: 020 7706 4568**

Very centrally situated Bed and Breakfast. First hotel in Sussex Gardens from Edgware Road. Parking available. Reasonable rates. Major shops and attractions nearby. Nearest Underground stations Edgware Road, Paddington, Marble Arch, Lancaster Gate.

£ **Short break details on request.**

See also Colour Advertisement on page 4

## EUROPA HOUSE HOTEL

ETC ◆◆

**151 Sussex Gardens, Hyde Park, London W2 2RY**
**Tel: 020 7723 7343 • Fax: 020 7224 9331 • e-mail: europahouse@enterprise.net**
**web: www.europahousehotel.org.uk/www.europahousehotel.com/www.europahousehotel.net**

Europa House is a small privately-owned hotel which aims to give personal service of the highest standard. Full central heating, all rooms en suite. Within easy reach of the West End. Situated close to Paddington Station. Double and twins. Singles. Family rooms available. Special rates for children under 10 years. Full English breakfast.

£ **Terms available on request.**

## HAZELWOOD HOUSE

**865 Finchley Road, Golders Green, London NW11 8LX**
**Tel: 020 8458 8884**

Enjoy luxury in a friendly atmosphere at our SRAC listed establishment. Whether on holiday or business, this hotel is famous for its "home from home" atmosphere in London's exclusive district of Golders Green. Private forecourt parking for 5/6 cars. Children over 10 years, animals accepted.

£ **Single room with breakfast from £28.00 per night, double room with breakfast from £38 per night.**

See also Colour Advertisement on page 3

## THE ELYSEE HOTEL

ETC ★★

**25/26 Craven Terrace, London W2 3EL**
**Tel: 020 7402 7633 • Fax: 0207 402 4193**
**e-mail: information@elyseehotel-london.co.uk • web: www.elyseehotel-london.co.uk**

Unbeatable value in the heart of London facing Hyde Park. Near London's famous tourist and shopping areas. Rooms with attached bath/shower and toilets. Lifts to all floors. Tea/coffee making facilities, hairdryers, cable TV, security safes. Rates include Continental breakfast. Three minutes from Lancaster Gate Underground and six minutes from Paddington Railway Station for Heathrow Express.

£ **Single £50.00; Twin/Double £55.00 (for room); Family £75.00 (up to 3 persons); Family £95.00 (up to 5 persons).**

## RASOOL COURT HOTEL

ETC ◆◆

**19-21 Penywern Road, Earls Court, London SW5 9TT**
**Tel: 020 7373 8900 • Fax: 020 7244 6835**
**e-mail: rasool@rasool.demon.co.uk • website: www.rasoolcourthotel.com**

The Rasool Court is a family-run hotel with 58 bedrooms. We are 2 Diamonds rated by the London Tourist Board. All bedrooms have colour TV with satellite channels, and direct-dial telephones. The hotel is located in fashionable Kensington and close to the heart of the city.

£ **Single from £33.00; Double/Twin from £48.00; Triple from £75.00.**

## EXPLANATION OF SYMBOLS

|  |  |
|---|---|
| ★ | Number of Stars (English Tourism Council/AA/RAC) |
| ◆ | Number of Diamonds (English Tourism Council/AA/RAC) |
| | Pets Welcome |
| | Reductions for Children |
| | Christmas Breaks |
| | Suitable for Disabled |

The symbols are arranged in the same order throughout the book so that looking down each page will give a quick comparison.

## PUBLISHER'S NOTE

While every effort is made to ensure accuracy, we regret that FHG Publications cannot accept responsibility for errors, misrepresentations or omissions in our entries or any consequences thereof. Prices in particular should be checked because we go to press early. We will follow up complaints but cannot act as arbiters or agents for either party.

# Buckinghamshire

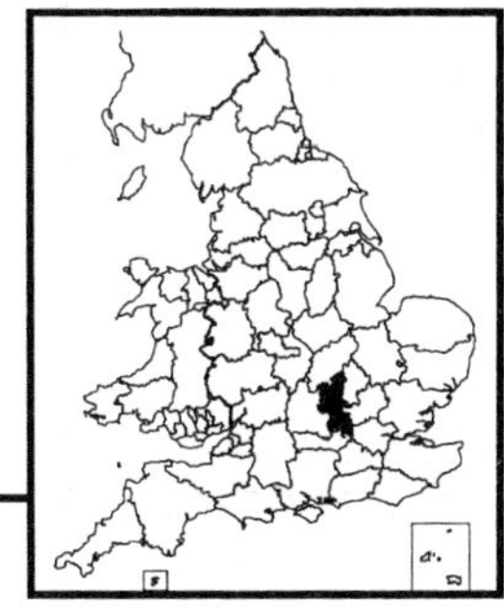

See also Colour Advertisement on page 5

## EXPRESS BY HOLIDAY INN

**Eastlake Park, Tongwell Street, Milton Keynes MK15 0YA**

**Tel: 01908 681000 • Fax: 01908 609429**

**e-mail: exhimiltonkeynes@aol.com • website: www.eastlakehospitality.com**

Award-winning Express by Holiday Inn, Milton Keynes, is the perfect venue for short breaks. Milton Keynes is the UK's best action-packed destination with real-snow skiing, water sports, shopping and dining. The local area offers a taste of Britain's heritage as well as fun with Woburn Abbey and Safari Park, Silverstone Racing circuit and Gulliver's Land theme park all nearby. Our quality rooms all have en suite shower, satellite TV, in-house movies, tea and coffee making facilities and direct dial telephone.

**£ Family rooms for two parents and two children up to 19 years old from £50 pn (Fri-Sat) including continental buffet breakfast for all. Special rates for families at weekends. Please quote ref SBMK when booking.**

# Cambridgeshire

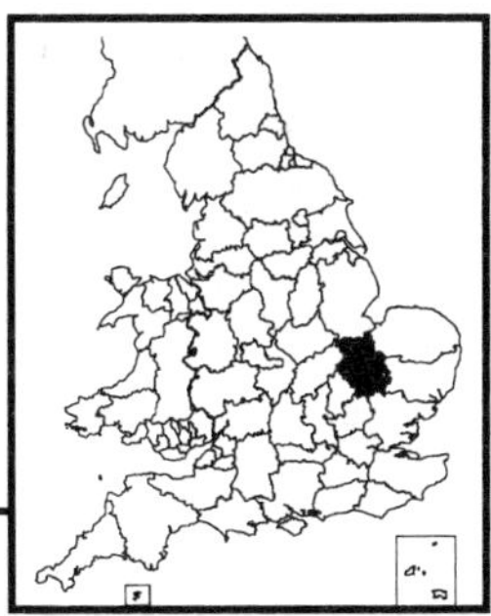

## CATHEDRAL HOUSE

**ETC ◆◆◆◆**

**17 St Mary's Street, Ely CB7 4ER**

**Tel & Fax: 01353 662124**

**e-mail: farndale@cathedralhouse.co.uk • website: www.cathedralhouse.co.uk**

Cathedral House is situated in the centre of Ely and within the shadow of its famous cathedral. A Grade II Listed house, it retains many original features and has a delightful walled garden. There is one twin, one double and one family bedrooms. All overlook the garden and are comfortably furnished with tea/coffee facilities, TV, central heating and en suite bathrooms. An ideal base for touring East Anglia, within easy reach of Cambridge, Welney and Wicken Fen Wildlife Reserves, Newmarket, Bury St. Edmunds and several National Trust properties. Open all year. Parking. No smoking. Newly available, quaint coachhouse for self-catering. ETC Silver Award 99.

**£ Based on 2 persons sharing twin/double: 2 nights midweek £110; 3 nights midweek £160. One week from £385. Offers not applicable Bank Holidays or High Season. Self-catering tariff on application.**

# Cheshire

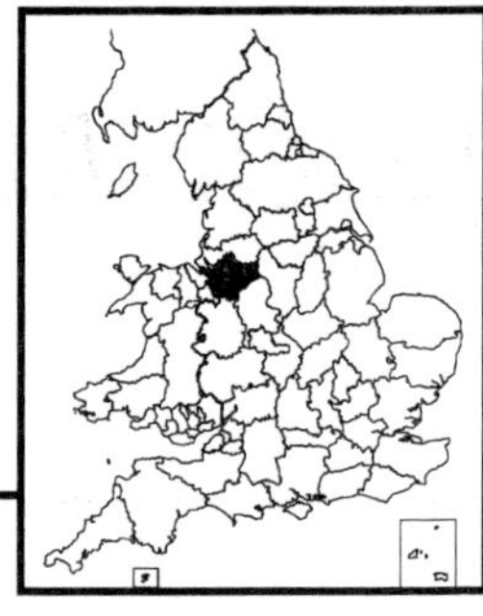

**GEORGE & DRAGON HOTEL**
**Liverpool Road, Chester CH2 1AA**
**Tel: 01244 380714 • Fax: 01244 380782**

Situated just two minutes' walk from the famous City Walls, with its own car park, the George & Dragon is a traditional hostelry where you can be assured of a warm welcome and a pleasant stay, and will be ideally situated for discovering historic Chester. It has 14 new en suite bedrooms, double, twin and single, all with colour TV and tea/coffee making facilities. The hotel boasts the largest selection of real ales in Chester and there is a separate dining area serving freshly prepared lunches, evening meals and bar snacks daily.

£ **Details of special breaks and business packages on request.**

## • • *Some Useful Guidance for Guests and Hosts* • •

Every year literally thousands of holidays, short breaks and ovemight stops are arranged through our guides, the vast majority without any problems at all. In a handful of cases, however, difficulties do arise about bookings, which often could have been prevented from the outset.

*It is important to remember that when accommodation has been booked, both parties – guests and hosts – have entered into a form of contract. We hope that the following points will provide helpful guidance.*

**GUESTS:**

- When enquiring about accommodation, be as precise as possible. Give exact dates, numbers in your party and the ages of any children.
- State the number and type of rooms wanted and also what catering you require – bed and breakfast, full board etc. Make sure that the position about evening meals is clear – and about pets, reductions for children or any other special points.
- Read our reviews carefully to ensure that the proprietors you are going to contact can supply what you want. Ask for a letter confirming all arrangements, if possible.
- If you have to cancel, do so as soon as possible. Proprietors do have the right to retain deposits and under certain circumstances to charge for cancelled holidays if adequate notice is not given and they cannot re-let the accommodation.

**HOSTS:**

- Give details about your facilities and about any special conditions. Explain your deposit system clearly and arrangements for cancellations, charges etc. and whether or not your terms include VAT.
- If for any reason you are unable to fulfil an agreed booking without adequate notice, you may be under an obligation to arrange suitable alternative accommodation or to make some form of compensation.

*While every effort is made to ensure accuracy, we regret that FHG Publications cannot accept responsibility for errors, omissions or misrepresentations in our entries or any consequences thereof. Prices in particular should be checked because we go to press early. We will follow up complaints but cannot act as arbiters or agents for either party.*

# Cornwall

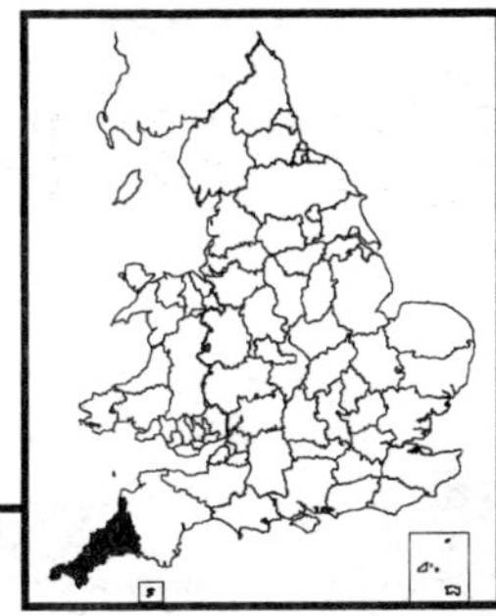

See also Colour Advertisement on page 6

## DUCHY HOLIDAYS

**St Georges Hill, Perranporth TR6 0DZ**
**Tel & Fax: 01872 572971**
**e-mail: duchy.holidays@virgin.net • website: www.duchyholidays.co.uk**

A selection of seaside and countryside holiday homes located throughout Cornwall. A luxury bungalow with a private swimming pool, farmhouse with lake fishing, beachside cottages, lodges and villas with swimming pools and entertainment. All properties are inspected and personally supervised.

£ **Short Breaks and long weekends available from £85 (excluding school holidays).**

## PENROSE BURDEN HOLIDAY COTTAGES

**St Breward, Bodmin PL30 4LZ**
**Tel: 01208 850277/850617 • Fax: 01208 850915**

Situated within easy reach of both coasts and Bodmin Moor on a large farm overlooking a wooded valley with own salmon and trout fishing. Close to Eden Project. These stone cottages with exposed beams and quarry tiled floors have been featured on TV and are award winners. Home-made meals can be delivered daily. All are suitable for wheelchair users and dogs are welcomed. Our cottages sleep from two to seven and are open all year. Please write or telephone Nancy or Rodney Hall for a colour brochure.

£ **Short break details on request.**

See also Colour Advertisement on page 6

## HIGHBRE CREST

**ETC ◆◆◆◆**

**Whitstone, Holsworthy, Near Bude EX22 6UF**
**Tel: 01288 341002**

Stunning views to coasts and moors make this very spacious house a special destination for your holiday. With the added bonus of peace, tranquillity and delicious home-made country cooking, how can you resist paying us a visit? We are well situated for the coast and moors in Devon and Cornwall, including the Eden Project. Two double and one twin room, all en suite. Games room with full-size snooker table, dining room, and comfortable large conservatory with spectacular coastal views. Garden for guests' use; car parking. Non-smoking establishment. Children over 12 years welcome.

£ **B&B from £20, optional Evening Meal from £10. Open February to November.**

## BOWOOD PARK HOTEL & GOLF COURSE

ETC/AA ★★★

**Lanteglos, Camelford PL32 9RF**
**Tel: 01840 213017 • Fax: 01840 212622**
**e-mail: golf@bowoodpark.com • website: www.bowoodpark.com**

Set in 230 acres of rolling hills and woodlands, Bowood Park Estate once formed part of the 13th century deer park owned by the Black Prince. Conveniently situated less than one hour by car from Exeter, the idyllic countryside of North Cornwall is on your doorstep, with the spectacular coastline of rugged cliffs and beautiful sandy beaches, the Camel Estuary and busy harbours. Accommodation is available in 31 en suite bedrooms, most overlooking the golf course. Enjoy fine dining in our new 2,000 sq. ft. restaurant with panoramic views over the course. Bowood Park is now home to the John Phillips Golf Academy – teaching breaks available. Golf World Gold Award, S. B. Golf Monthly Gold Award.

£ **From £40 in low season to £59.50 in high season (£69.50 weekends). Superior and terrace rooms are available at an extra charge.**

## PENMORVAH MANOR HOTEL

ETC/AA ★★★

**Budock Water, Near Falmouth TR11 5ED**
**Tel: 01326 250277 • Fax: 01326 250509**
**e-mail: reception@penmorvah.co.uk • website: www.penmorvah.co.uk**

A three-star Country House Hotel and self-catering courtyard cottages situated in six acres of mature grounds and woodland, close to Falmouth and coastal paths. This secluded hotel serves quality cuisine in a friendly, relaxed atmosphere. It is ideally situated for visiting Cornwall's superb gardens. Well behaved dogs welcome. Ground floor bedrooms available. Ample car parking. The 3 self-catering cottages are in a converted barn complex and offer privacy and flexibility, with the added benefit of the hotel facilities.

£ **Short break details on request.**

## TRELAWNE HOTEL

AA/ETC ★★★

**Mawnan Smith, Falmouth TR11 5HS**
**Tel: 01326 250226 • Fax 01326 250909**

See also Colour Advertisement on page 7

Nestling on the coastline between the Helford and Fal rivers in a beautiful and tranquil corner of Cornwall, this fine country house hotel enjoys a magnificent outlook across Falmouth Bay to the Roseland Peninsula. The tastefully furnished and centrally heated bedrooms have en suite facilities, as well as colour television, radio, telephone and tea and coffee makers. There is a charming cocktail bar and an indoor pool and games room. The cuisine comes high on the list of attractions at this well-run hotel and is backed by an extensive wine list. AA 2 Rosettes. ETC Silver Award.

£ **"Slipaway" Autumn and Winter Breaks: 2 nights minimum stay from £43 pppn Dinner, Bed and Breakfast. October-December, February and March.**

## TREVAYLOR

ETC ◆◆◆◆

**8 Pennance Road, Falmouth TR11 4EA**
**Tel: 01326 313041 • Fax: 01326 316899**
**e-mail: stay@trevaylor.co.uk**

You are assured of a warm welcome in pleasant surroundings. Small detached hotel situated between town and beach. En suite rooms with TV, tea/coffee making facilities and full central heating. Full English Breakfast or vegetarian alternative. Walking, sailing, tennis, golf and fishing nearby. Non-smoking establishment. Children welcome. Pets by arrangement.

£ **Bed and Breakfast from £21, special weekly and winter rates. Open all year.**

## THE COTTAGES AT TREFANNY HILL

Trefanny Hill, Duloe, Liskeard PL14 4QF
Tel: 01503 220622
e-mail: enq@trefanny.co.uk • website: www.trefanny.co.uk

COTTAGES FOR ROMANITICS. A Country Lover's Paradise ~ with an abundance of country walks from your garden gate and coastal walks only 4 miles away. Old world charm, log fires, antiques ~ beautifully furnished with the comforts of home. Private gardens, spectacular views ~ peace for families, friends and couples to enjoy. Nestling on a south facing hillside, near coast ~ heated pool, tennis, badminton, lake, shire horses, etc. Enchanting 70 acre estate with bluebell wood, walking and wildlife. Delicious fare also available by candlelight 'at home' or in our tiny inn.

£ **Short Break details on request**

## MARAZION HOTEL

The Square, Marazion TR17 0AP
Tel: 01736 710334 • Fax: 01736 719180

The Marazion Hotel is 50 yards from the beach, sailing club and causeway to St Michael's Mount. It is fully licensed and open throughout the year. Bedrooms are comfortably furnished with colour TV, tea and coffee making facilities, private shower or bathroom en suite: many have sea views. The restaurant, open to non-residents, offers a wide choice of dishes using fresh local produce. There is ample free car parking, and the hotel is ideally situated for touring Land's End and Lizard peninsula.

£ **B&B: one night Low Season from £25pp; DB&B: one night Low Season from £40pp.**

## WHITE LODGE HOTEL

Mawgan Porth Bay, Near Newquay TR8 4BN
Tel: 01637 860512
e-mail: adogfriendly@aol.com • website: www.white-lodge-hotel.co.uk

Family-run hotel overlooking Mawgan Porth Bay, with fantastic sea views from most rooms. All rooms have colour TV, tea/coffee maker, radio and heater, and most are en suite. Well stocked residents' lounge bar, dining room and sun patio. Dogs most welcome. Direct access to sandy beach and coastal path. NOW OPEN ALL YEAR ROUND – Winter Break packages

£ **Dinner, B&B from £35 per night. Details of Christmas and New Year Breaks on request.**

## THE PHILADELPHIA

19 Eliot Gardens, Newquay TR7 2QE
Tel: 01637 877747 • e-mail: stay@thephiladelphia.co.uk
website: www.thephiladelphia.co.uk or www.thephiladelphia.org.uk

See also Colour Advertisement on page 5

Newquay's premier smoke-free guest house, recommended by Which? as one of their Top 20 Guest Houses. Quiet tree-lined avenue, award-winning gardens, car park, private patio and hot tub. Bright and spacious quality accommodation in tastefully themed rooms, all with superb en suite facilities, colour TV and complimentary beverages. Extensive choice for breakfast. Short walk to beaches, town and Trenance Gardens. Short drive to the famous Eden Project and Heligan Gardens. Special breaks in quality surroundings, relaxed and friendly atmosphere, comfort, good food and great hospitality – you'll be made very welcome at The Philadelphia.

£ **B&B from £25.00pppn; four-night Eden Break £99.00.**

See also Colour Advertisement on page 5

## HOTEL VICTORIA

ETC ★★★

**East Street, Newquay TR7 1DB**
**Tel: 01637 872255 • Fax: 01637 859295**
**website: www.hotel-victoria.co.uk**

113 en suite rooms; 7 new luxury suites. Unique lift through cliff to beach. Victoria Health Club with indoor pool, spa bath, sauna and sunbeds. Ideal for a golfing holiday - Newquay, Perranporth, Treloy, Lanhydrock and St Mellion courses nearby. Please see website for further details.

£ **Inclusive golf packages available: 5 nights, 4 rounds of golf from £265pp; 3 nights, 2 rounds of golf from £150pp.**

## RAINTREE HOUSE HOLIDAYS

**Padstow**
**Tel: 01841 520228 • Fax: 01841 520130**

A range of well equipped houses and bungalows near Trevose Golf Club, sandy beaches, scenic walks. Details from Mrs Watts, "Whistlers", Treyarnon Bay, Padstow PL28 8JR

£ **Short Break details on request.**

## PENALVA PRIVATE HOTEL

**Alexandra Road, Penzance TR18 4LZ**
**Tel: 01736 369060**

The hotel is TOTALLY NON-SMOKING, offering full central heating, fresh immaculate interior, en suite facilities, excellent food and a real welcome with courteous service. Penalva is a well positioned imposing late Victorian hotel set in a wide tree-lined boulevard with ample parking, close to promenade and shops. Perfect centre for enjoying the wealth of beautiful sandy coves, historical remains and magnificent walks. Large guest lounge and separate dining room. Colour TV and tea/coffee making facilities in bedrooms. Open all year. Special diets by prior arrangement. Sorry, no pets. Highly recommended. SAE, please, for brochure.

£ **Bed and Breakfast from £16 to £21. Weekly reductions. Children 6 to 12 half-price if sharing family rooms.**

See also Colour Advertisement on page 6

## PENVENTON PARK HOTEL

AA ★★★

**Redruth TR15 1TE**
**Tel: 01209 203000 • Fax: 01209 203001**
**e-mail: penventon@bigfoot.com • website: www.penventon.com**

A beautiful 18th century country mansion house set in acres of parkland, ideally situated for touring Cornwall and the Eden Project. A health and leisure spa offers indoor swimming, sauna, spa bath, gym, beautician and masseur. The famous Dining Galleries Restaurant serves a large choice of locally caught fish, meat and home-produced vegetables. Extensive à la carte menus – many food awards. Resident pianists nightly. All bedrooms are en suite, with colour TV and tea/coffee making facilities. A Cornish welcome awaits you.

£ **Weekend rates from £44 DBB. Would you like a FREE ROOM? – phone for details**

## PENKERRIS

ETC/AA/RAC ◆◆

**Penwinnick Road, St Agnes TR5 0PA**
**Tel & Fax: 01872 552262**
**e-mail: info@penkerris.co.uk • website: www.penkerris.co.uk**

A creeper-clad Edwardian residence with lawned garden in unspoilt Cornish village. A home-from-home offering real food. Comfortable bedrooms with facilities (TV, radio, kettle, washbasin). Dining room serving breakfast; dinner available by arrangement. Bright cosy lounge with a log fire in winter, colour TV, video and piano. Licensed. Ample parking. Dramatic cliff walks and beaches with good surfing nearby. Easy to find on B3277 road from big roundabout on A30 and just by village sign.

£ **Bed and Breakfast from £17.50 to £25.00 per night; Dinner from £12.50**

## TRENCREEK FARM HOLIDAY PARK

AA ✓✓✓

**Hewaswater, St Austell PL26 7JG**
**Tel: 01726 882540**
**website: www.trencreek.co.uk**

See also Colour Advertisement on page 7

Are you visiting the Eden Project in Cornwall? Then we may be able to help you with your accommodation. We have available self-catering and camping facilities and can provide two and three bedroom units to sleep up to eight. Heated outdoor swimming pool, tennis court and fishing lakes. Children and pets welcome.

£ **Self-catering accommodation available from £50 for 2 nights.**

## RIVENDELL

RAC ◆◆◆◆

**7 Porthminster Terrace, St Ives TR26 2DQ**
**Tel & Fax: 01736 794923**
**e-mail: rivendellstives@aol.com • website: www.rivendell-stives.co.uk**

Our family-run guest house is in a superb location, with a reputation for excellent meals prepared by resident chef. Homely atmosphere. Close to town, beaches and all amenities. Full central heating, en suite rooms available. Colour TV and beverage facilities in all rooms. Television and video in lounge. Fire certificate. Parking available. Open all year (including Christmas and New Year). RAC Sparkling Diamond Award for excellent standards of cleanliness; Dining Award. Phone or send SAE to Angela Walker for brochure.

£ **Short break terms on request. Reduced rates for children and off-peak discounts for over 60s and Countdown cardholders.**

## WILLAPARK MANOR HOTEL

ETC ★★

**Bossiney, Tintagel PL34 0BA**
**Tel: 01840 770782**
**website: www.willapark.co.uk**

See also Colour Advertisement on page 6

Willapark Manor is a lovely character house in a beautiful setting amidst 14 acre grounds, overlooking Bossiney Bay. Surrounded by woodland, it is secluded and has direct access to the coastal path and beach. It is a family-run hotel with a friendly and informal atmosphere, excellent cuisine and a well stocked cocktail bar. Beautifully appointed bedrooms, all en suite and with colour TV and tea/coffee making facilities. Some four-posters. A warm welcome and a memorable holiday assured.

ONE OF THE MOST BEAUTIFULLY SITUATED HOTELS IN ENGLAND.

£ **Dinner, bed and breakfast from £275 weekly, from £46 daily (incl. VAT). Bed and breakfast from £28.50 daily.**

## LANDS VUE

**Three Burrows, Truro TR4 8JA**
**Tel: 01872 560242**

You will find a warm welcome at our peaceful Country House, set in two acres of garden where you may spend time relaxing. There are three lovely bedrooms, all en suite, with tea-making facilities. There is a cosy lounge with open fire and large dining room with superb views over the Cornish countryside where we serve a delicious farmhouse breakfast. Being very central for all Cornwall's famous gardens and coastline, Lands Vue is an ideal base highly recommended by many of our guests who return year after year. Write or phone Mandy Gill for further information.

£ **B&B from £25. Closed Christmas and New Year.**

## GUNVENNA TOURING CARAVAN & CAMPING PARK

**St Minver, Wadebridge PL27 6QN**
**Tel: 01208 862405**

The Park is a well drained site of level grassland on 10 acres commanding uninterrupted views of the countryside within five minutes' drive of safe golden sandy beaches. Local activities include golf, fishing, tennis, surfing and swimming. Site facilities include two modern toilet and shower blocks, launderette and ironing room, children's play area, children's games room (9am to 10pm), barbecue area, dog exercise area, shop, telephone, etc. We also have an indoor heated swimming pool.

£ **Please send for brochure and prices.**

## CORNISH COTTAGE

**Bodieve, Wadebridge**

300 year old farmhouse, with sunny gardens and ample parking. Only three miles from the sandy beaches at Rock and Daymer Bay, and close to the ancient fishing harbour of Padstow. Ideal for surfing, safe bathing, walking, fishing, sailing, golf, cycling. Lounge with colour TV; large cosy, well equipped kitchen/diner; laundry room; three bedrooms - large master bedroom, one twin bedroom and a bedroom with bunk beds. Linen and towels at extra charge. Bathroom, shower, toilet. Night storage heaters. Pets by arrangement. Available all year. Apply: Mrs Holder, Cross Wood House, Roseley, Wadebridge PL27 6EG.

£ **For prices, please enquire on telephone no. 01208 813024**

PLEASE MENTION THIS GUIDE WHEN YOU WRITE

OR PHONE TO ENQUIRE ABOUT ACCOMMODATION

IF YOU ARE WRITING, A STAMPED, ADDRESSED

ENVELOPE IS ALWAYS APPRECIATED

# Cumbria

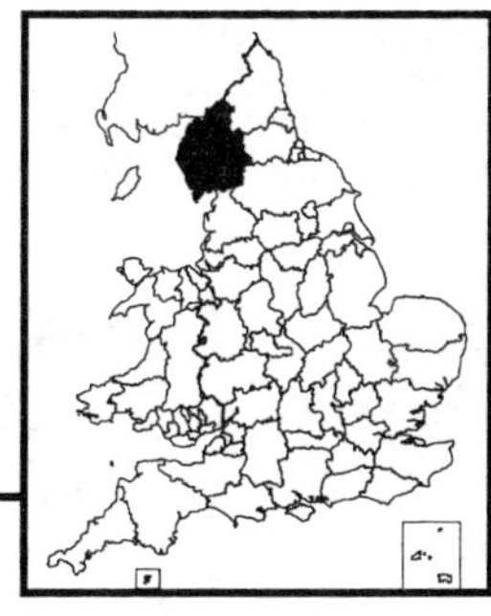

## GREENHOWE CARAVAN PARK

**Great Langdale, Ambleside, English Lakeland LA22 9JU**
**Tel: 015394 37231 • Fax: 015394 37464 • Freephone 0800 0717231**

Greenhowe is a permanent caravan park with self-contained holiday accommodation. Subject to availability, holiday homes may be rented for short or long periods from 1st March to mid-November. The park is situated in the heart of the Lake District, some half a mile from Dungeon Ghyll at the foot of the Langdale Pikes. It is an ideal centre for climbing, fell walking, riding, swimming, water ski-ing or just a lazy holiday. Please ask about short breaks and free colour brochure. Rose Award Park, David Bellamy Award.

£ **Short break details on request.**

## FERNDALE HOTEL

**ETC ◆◆◆**

See also Colour Advertisement on page 8

**Lake Road, Ambleside LA22 0DB**
**Tel: 015394 32207**
**e-mail: ferndalehotel@btconnect.com • website: www.ferndalehotel.com**

The Ferndale Hotel is a small, family-run hotel where you will find a warm, friendly welcome and personal attention at all times. Excellent accommodation with good home-cooked English or vegetarian breakfast. The 10 attractive bedrooms have all been individually decorated and furnished, each with full en suite facilities, colour TV, and tea/coffee making tray. Full central heating; several rooms have views of the fells; some ground floor bedrooms. The Ferndale is open all year round with a car park, is licensed, offers packed lunches, hairdryer, clothes/boot drying and ironing facilities. A wide choice of places to dine within minutes' walking distance, ranging from excellent pub food to superb restaurants, will complete your day.

£ **Bed and Breakfast from £22-£26; weekly from £145-£165.**

## ROTHAY HOUSE

**Rothay Road, Ambleside LA22 0EE**
**Tel & Fax: 015394 32434**
**e-mail: e-mail@rothay-house.com • website: www.rothay-house.com**

Rothay House is an attractive modern detached guest house set in pleasant gardens with views of the surrounding fells. All bedrooms are comfortable and well furnished with en suite facilities, colour TV, tea and coffee trays. Robin and Margaret combine 20 years quality hotel experience with a friendly atmosphere in clean, attractive surroundings. The house is within easy walking distance of the village centre. Ambleside has a variety of interesting shops and restaurants and makes an ideal base for walking, touring or enjoying sailing, watersports and angling on Lake Windermere. Car not essential, but ample parking. Open all year. Children welcome; sorry, no pets.

£ **B&B from £25 to £30; Winter Weekend Breaks available.**

## ROTHAY MANOR HOTEL

**Ambleside LA22 0EH**
**Tel: 015394 33605 • Fax: 015394 33607**
**e-mail: hotel@rothaymanor.co.uk • website: www.rothaymanor.co.uk**

ETC★★★

An elegant Regency country house situated in the heart of the Lake District, ¼ mile from the head of Lake Windermere and a short walk from the centre of Ambleside. Personally managed by the Nixon family it retains the comfortable relaxed atmosphere of a private house. Renowned for its cuisine, Rothay Manor is an excellent base for a short break - whether it be walking or sightseeing. The hotel has 15 bedrooms and 3 suites situated in the grounds of the hotel. The dining room and one of the lounges are non-smoking. Families and disabled guests welcome. Residents have free use of a nearby leisure club. Specialised holidays available October to May. All major credit cards accepted.

£ **Special breaks available – details on request.**

See also Colour Advertisement on page 7

## THE SAWREY HOTEL

**Far Sawrey, Near Ambleside LA22 0LQ**
**Tel & Fax: 015394 43425**

ETC/RAC ★★

This fully licensed 18th century free house stands within easy reach of all parts of Lakeland, just one mile from Windermere car ferry and 2½ miles from Hawkshead. It is an ideal centre for touring, walking, pony trekking, sailing and water ski-ing, and all the other activities that this beautiful area is renowned for. There are 18 bedrooms, all with colour TV, tea/coffee facilities, telephone and private bathrooms. Excellent cuisine is available in the restaurant, and the Claife Crier Bar serves an extensive range of hot and cold snacks. Under the personal management of the proprietors.

£ **2 day breaks (with private bathroom) £76 DB&B. 4 day breaks (midweek between Sun. night and Fri. morning) £120. Available November 2002 to April 2003 excluding Christmas and New Year.**

## THE EYRIE

**Lake Road, Ambleside**
**Tel: 01844 208208**

A really delightful, characterful flat nestling under the eaves of a converted school with lovely views of the fells, high above the village. Large airy living/diningroom with colour TV. Comfortably furnished as the owners' second home. Well equipped kitchen with spacious airing cupboard; three bedrooms sleeping six; attractive bathroom (bath/WC/ shower) carpets, gas central heating, use of separate laundry room. Terrace garden with fine views. Children welcome. Sorry, but no pets. Available all year. Sleeps 6. Free parking permit provided for one car. Many recommendations. Brochure available. Telephone Mrs Clark for details.

£ **Weekly rates £200 to £370. Short breaks available.**

## GREY FRIAR LODGE COUNTRY HOUSE HOTEL

**Clappersgate, Ambleside LA22 9NE**
**Tel & Fax: 015394 33158**
**e-mail: greyfriar@veen.freeserve.co.uk • website: www.cumbria-hotels.co.uk**

ETC/AA ◆◆◆◆◆

Overlooking the lovely Brathay River Valley, this most comfortable house offers excellent accommodation as well as warm hospitality backed by professional expertise. Bedrooms are individually designed and all have private facilities as well as such amenities as colour television, radio clock alarm, tea/coffee making facilities, central heating plus several thoughtful extras. The cuisine is a revelation from the four-course breakfast to dinners which feature English cooking at its very best. The house is set in sheltered gardens just a mile from Lake Windermere. ETC Silver Award.

£ **Details on request.**

## BARBON INN

**Barbon, Via Carnforth LA6 2LJ**
**Tel & Fax: 015242 76233**

If you are torn between the scenic delights of the Lake District and the Yorkshire Dales, then you can have the best of both worlds by making your base this friendly 17th century coaching inn nestling in the pretty village of Barbon. Individually furnished bedrooms provide cosy accommodation, and for that extra touch of luxury enquire about the elegant mini-suite with its oak four-poster bed. Fresh local produce is featured on the good value menus presented in the bar and restaurant, and the Sunday roast lunch with all the trimmings attracts patrons from near and far. A wide range of country pursuits can be enjoyed in the immediate area, and the helpful staff will be happy to give information.

£ **Terms on request.**

## GLEN GARTH HOTEL

**359 Abbey Road, Barrow-in-Furness LA13 9JY**
**Tel: 01229 825374 • Fax: 01229 811744**

See also Colour Advertisement on page 8

The hotel is close to historic Furness Abbey but is only a short step away from the town centre and all its amenities as well as the train station. The area's top tourist attraction, South Lakeland Wild Animal Park, is only three quarters of a mile away. There is a leisure centre close by with sports, swimming and gym facilities as well as an 18 hole golf course within one mile. Barrow-in-Furness is an ideal location for tourists, surrounded by beautiful beaches and within easy reach of everything the Lake District National Park has to offer. Accommodation is available in 15 comfortable en suite bedrooms (executive single and double/twin), all with TV and radio; there is a four poster room for that special occasion. The Hotel is licensed with a popular restaurant and can provide the perfect venue for wedding receptions and celebration dinners. Children are welcome, and cots and high chairs can be provided.

£ **B&B from £28.00 to £35.00pp**

## THE LEATHES HEAD HOTEL & RESTAURANT

**Borrowdale CA12 5UY**
**Tel: 017687 77247 • Fax: 017687 77363**
**website: www.leatheshead.co.uk**

See also Colour Advertisement on page 9

The Leathes Head is an 11-bedroom hotel located in the spectacular Borrowdale Valley, in three acres of secluded formal lawns and woodland, with wonderful views of the surrounding fells and Derwentwater. There are three lounges, a fully licensed bar and an award-winning restaurant. The menus, changed daily, put the emphasis on fresh local produce prepared by our acclaimed local chef. Health Club, croquet and boules, terrace seating, ample parking.

£ **Short break details on request.**

## NEW HOUSE FARM

AA ◆◆◆◆◆

**Lorton, Buttermere CA13 9UU**
**Tel: 01900 85404**
**e-mail: hazel@newhouse-farm.co.uk • website: www.newhouse-farm.co.uk**

See also Colour Advertisement on page 8

Situated in the quietest and most beautiful part of the Lakes, New House Farm has 15 acres of open fields, ponds, streams and woods, which guests may wander around at leisure and there is easy access to nearby lakes and fells. All bedrooms are en suite. There is a cosy dining room and two comfortable sitting rooms with open log fires. The food served is fine traditional fare. Which? Hotel Guide Hotel of the Year Award Winner (Cumbria). "The Lorton Vale – A Place for All Seaons".

£ **Bed and Breakfast from £42; Dinner, Bed and Breakfast from £60.**

## NEW PALLYARDS

ETC ◆◆◆◆

**Hethersgill, Carlisle CA6 6HZ**
**Tel: 01228 577308).**
**e-mail: info@newpallyards.freeserve.co.uk • website: www.newpallyards.freeserve.co.uk**

Farmhouse filmed for BBC TV. Relax and see beautiful North Cumbria and the Borders. A warm welcome awaits you in our country farmhouse tucked away in the Cumbrian countryside, yet easily accessible from M6 Junction 44. In addition to the surrounding attractions there is plenty to enjoy, including hill walking, peaceful forests and sea trout/salmon fishing or just nestle down and relax with nature. Two double en suite rooms and one twin/single bedroom, all with tea/coffee making equipment. Self-catering is also available. We are proud to have won a National Salon Culinaire Award for the "Best Breakfast in Britain". ETC Gold Award.

£ **Short Break terms on request. B&B from £22pp, DB&B from £160 to £170 weekly.**

## LIGHTWOOD COUNTRY GUEST HOUSE

ETC ◆◆◆◆

**Cartmel Fell LA11 6NP**
**Tel & Fax: 015395 31454**
**e-mail: enquiries@lightwoodguesthouse.com • website: www.lightwoodguesthouse.com**

Lightwood is a charming 17th century farmhouse retaining original oak beams and staircase. It stands in two acres of lovely gardens with unspoilt views of the countryside. Excellent fell walking area. 2½ miles from Lake Windermere; many stately homes within easy reach. All rooms are en suite, tastefully decorated and furnished, with central heating, tea/coffee making facilities; some with colour TV. Cosy lounge with log fire and TV. We serve a high standard of home cooking with seasonal home-grown produce. Restricted smoking. No pets. Children welcome. "Which?" Guide recommended.

£ **Bed and Breakast from £28; Dinner, Bed and Breakfast from £44.50. Short Breaks available all year. Closed Christmas.**

See also Colour Advertisement on page 9

## MANOR HOUSE GUEST HOUSE

**Oughterside, Aspatria, Cumbria CA7 2PT.**
**Tel & Fax: 016973 22420**
**e-mail: richardandjudy@themanorhouse.net • website: www.themanorhouse.net**

We will make you very welcome at our lovely old manor farmhouse. The rooms are spacious with kingsize beds, large en suite bathrooms, tea and coffee making facilities, TVs and lots of extras. The seven acres of grounds are home to many birds, including barn owls, as well as horses, donkeys, a mule and even sheep! Although there is easy access to the nearby Western Lakes and Solway Coast, guests enjoy the peace of our rural setting. Inside bike storage, drying facilities. Local inspection. Silver Environmental Award.

£ **Bed & Breakfast from £21 to £30. Dinner from £7. Special prices for longer stays.**

See also Colour Advertisement on page 9

## THE COPPERMINES & CONISTON COTTAGES

ETC ★★/★★★★★

**Tel: 015394 41765 (24hrs) • Mobile: 07721 584488**
**website: www.coppermines.co.uk**

Fifty unique lakeland cottages for two to thirty, of quality and character in stunning mountain scenery. Log fires, exposed beams. Weekends and short breaks available. Pets very welcome.

£ **Short break details on request.**

See also Colour Advertisement on page 8

## CLARENCE HOUSE COUNTRY HOTEL

**Skelgate, Dalton-in-Furness LA15 8BQ**
**Tel: 01229 462508 • Fax: 01229 467177**
**e-mail: clarencehsehotel@aol.com • website: www.clarencehousehotel.com**

A beautiful mid-Victorian mansion set in over 3 acres of landscaped gardens overlooking St Thomas' Valley. With an enviable reputation as being one of the best hotels in the area offering excellent accommodation, fine dining and a warm and friendly atmosphere. Situated on the Furness peninsula and surrounded by beaches and open countryside. All of the 17 bedrooms have private facilities, colour television, telephone, radio, trouser press, hairdryer and hospitality tray. Our residents keep coming back time after time to enjoy our warm hospitality and speciality dining. At Clarence House we realise the importance of simply getting away from it all.

£ **Tariff from £75 to £105 per person. Special weekend breaks from £95 per person per weekend.**

## LAKEVIEW COUNTRY HOUSE

ETC ◆◆◆◆

**Lake View Drive, Grasmere, Ambleside LA22 9TD**
**Tel: 015394 35384**
**e-mail: sbh@lakeview-grasmere.com • website: www.lakeview-grasmere.com**

Lakeview Country House is set in magnificent surroundings overlooking Grasmere Lake amidst substantial gardens with private lakeshore access (fishing can be arranged). Guests are assured of a warm welcome and delicious English bereakfasts. This is a non-smoking establishment. Ground floor accommodation is available and pets are welcome. Three flats, each sleeping two to five persons, also provide self-catering accommodation. Please contact Stephen and Michelle King for full details. Which 'Good Bed & Breakfast Guide'.

£ **Terms available on request.**

## CRAGG FARM

ETC ◆◆◆

**New Hutton, Near Kendal LA8 0BA**
**Tel & Fax: 01539 721760**
**e-mail: knowles.cragg@ukgateway.net • website: www.craggfarm.com**

A delightful 17th century oak beamed farmhouse which retains its character yet has all the modern comforts. This 280 acre working dairy/sheep farm is set in peaceful countryside and ideally positioned for exploring the Lake District and Yorkshire Dales, and makes an ideal stopover between England and Scotland. We have one double, one family and one single bedrooms, all with tea/coffee making facilities; bathroom with shower and toilet; lounge/dining room with colour TV. Full central heating. Full English Breakfast served. Families are welcome. Open March to November. Self-catering caravan also available. Welcome Host.

£ **Short break terms on request. B&B from £18 to £20 per person.**

## LAKESIDE STUDIOS

**Derwentwater Marina, Portinscale, Keswick CA12 5RF**
**Tel: 017687 72912 • Fax: 017687 72924**
**website: www.derwentwatermarina.co.uk**

Three self-catering apartments, all with stunning views of the Lake and fells, are fully equipped for two or a couple and small child. They have en suite bath or shower, TV and stereo radio/CD, and make an extremely comfortable base for a family holiday, whether you are a sailing enthusiast, a fell walker or just want a relaxing time away from it all. Children are especially welcome, and a cot and high chair are available. The Marina is an ideal location for water or mountain-based activities, and facilities include changing rooms with showers, and a well-stocked chandlery. RYA registered sailing and windsurfing centre; tuition available. Please contact Chris Bowns for details.

£ **Terms on request.**

See also Colour Advertisement on page 7

## HILTON KESWICK LODORE

ETC ★★★★

**Keswick CA12 5UX**
**Tel: 017687 77285 • Central Reservations: 08705 909090**

Overlooking Derwentwater, this elegant hotel is set in stunning Lake District scenery, yet less than half an hour from the M6. Facilities include 71 bedrooms, including suites and Lake view rooms, a health club with swimming pools, solarium, sauna and fitness suite, massage and beauty salon, games room, and children's play area. The Lodore Restaurant offers a delicious choice of table d'hôte and à la carte menus. Situated in 40 acres of beautiful countryside, this hotel offers a delightful base from which to explore fells and woodland trails.

£ **Short break details on request**

## SECLUDED COTTAGES with Private Fishing

ETC ★★★

**Crossfield Cottages, Kirkoswald, Penrith CA10 1EU**
**Tel & Fax: 01768 898711 (6-10pm bookings, 24hr brochure line)**
**e-mail: info@crossfieldcottages.co.uk • website: www.crossfieldcottages.co.uk**

Total peace and tranquillity. Quality cottages overlooking two fishing lakes amid Lakeland's beautiful Eden Valley countryside. Central for Ullswater, North Pennines, Hadrian's Wall and Scottish Borders. Beds freshly made for you, freedom to roam. Residents' exclusive coarse and fly fishing on doorstep. Cottages sleep 2-6. Guaranteed clean, well maintained and equipped. Laundry area. Pets Welcome. Golf courses nearby. Exceptional wildlife and walking area. Relax and escape to your home in the country. Telephone or SAE for details and availability.

£ **Open all year. Inclusive flexible terms for breaks.**

## GREENAH CRAG

**Troutbeck, Penrith CA11 0SQ**
**Tel: 017684 83233**

Enjoy a relaxing break at Greenah Crag, a 17th century former farmhouse peacefully located in the Lake District National Park, just 10 miles from Keswick and only eight miles from the M6 motorway. Ideal for exploring Northern Lakes, Eden Valley, Carlisle, Hadrian's Wall and the Western Pennines. Accommodation is in two double bedrooms with bathroom en suite, and one twin-bedded room with washbasin, all with tea/coffee making facilities. The guests' sittingroom with TV and woodburning stove is a cosy place on the coldest days! A full breakfast is served in the oak-beamed diningroom. Excellent choice of pubs/restaurants within 3 miles, nearest three quarters of a mile. Regret no pets or smoking in the house. Please telephone for brochure.

£ **Bed and Breakfast from £17.50 per person.**

## SUN INN

**Pooley Bridge, Penrith CA10 2NN**
**Tel: 017684 86205 • Fax: 017684 86913**
**e-mail: michaeljane66@btopenworld.com**

Dating from the mid 1700's, the inn has nine bedrooms, all en suite, comprising five doubles, one twin, two singles and a family room. There is a no smoking policy in the bedrooms and also in the 30-seater dining room, the lobby and lounge bar. The Public bars attract the colourful local people, walkers, fishermen and sportsmen who enjoy rugby and football on our big screen. The inn enjoys a certain atmosphere, especially in busy times during the season. Visitors are encouraged to enjoy the inn and the area in the winter when we offer special rates. Dogs are most welcome.

£ **Short Break terms on request.**

## PRIMROSE COTTAGE B&B or SELF-CATERING

ETC/RAC ◆◆◆◆

**Orton Road, Tebay CA10 3TL**
**Tel: 015396 24791**
**e-mail: primrosecottebay@aol.com • website: www.primrosecottage.co.uk**

Excellent rural location for North Lakes and Yorkshire Dales. Superb facilities include jacuzzi bath and four-poster bed. Self-contained ground floor flat available and (new for 2002) beautiful detached bungalow set in one-acre garden with private drive; easy parking for loading and security. Accommodation comprises two bedrooms, one en suite and one with bathroom designed for use by disabled guests. Fire alarms and many extras. Proprietor available at all times, very friendly. Pets most welcome. Views of fells from all windows. Close to M6 at Junction 38, but quiet location. Nearby pub for meals. Telephone Helen Jones for details.

£ **Bungalow, suitable for disabled, £250 to £450 per week, daily rates available; Flat £180 to £220 per week; B&B £20 to £25pppn.**

---

## GLENTHORNE GUESTHOUSE

**Princes Road, Windermere LA23 2DD**
**Tel: 015394 47558**
**website: www.glenthorne-guesthouse.co.uk**

A cosy family-run guesthouse in an ideal location to explore the Lake District. Situated midway between Windermere village and Bowness. Within easy walking distance of shops, cafes, pubs and restaurants, railway and bus station. All rooms tastefully decorated with colour TV, tea, coffee, hairdryer and radio. A hearty breakfast is served to start your day, with vegetarian options. Books and maps are available to help plan your holiday.

£ **Rates from £19 per person per night. 3 night special from £50 per person. Four-poster 3 nights £60 per person.**

---

## GILPIN LODGE

ETC/AA/RAC ★★★

See also Colour Advertisement on page 9

**Crook Road, Near Windermere LA23 3NE**
**Tel: 015394 88818 • Fax: 015394 88058**
**e-mail: hotel@gilpin-lodge.co.uk • website: www.gilpin-lodge.co.uk**

A friendly, luxurious hotel with an atmosphere redolent of an elegant private house. Set in 20 acres of woodland, moors and country gardens, only 2 miles from Lake Windermere and 12 miles from the M6. All the charming bedrooms have en suite facilities; some have jacuzzis and some have four-poster beds, French windows and private patios. Dinner is the highlight of the day, with an interesting yet unpretentious style of cooking which has won many awards. Near Windermere Golf Club, and guests have free use of a nearby leisure club.

£ **Terms available on request.**

---

## "THE BEAUMONT"

ETC/AA/RAC ◆◆◆◆◆

**Holly Road, Windermere LA23 2AF**
**Tel & Fax: 015394 47075**
**e-mail: thebeaumonthotel@btinternet.com • website: www.lakesbeaumont.co.uk**

Should you wish to have a relaxing break in luxurious accommodation offering superb food, sincere hospitality and tranquillity, yet only two minutes' walk to the centre of Windermere, look no further – The Beaumont is for you! Private car park. Non-smoking. Children over 12 years. ETC Silver Award. RAC Sparkling Diamond and Warm Welcome. Ashley Courtenay Recommended. Which? Hotel Guide. Frommers Highly Recommended.

£ **Prices from £30.**

# Derbyshire

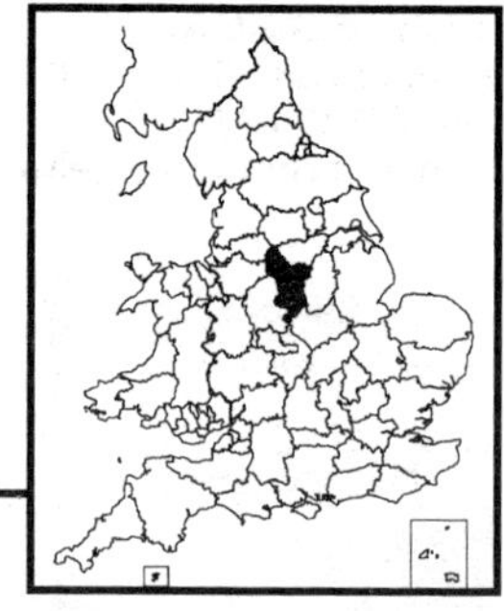

## THE DOG AND PARTRIDGE COUNTRY INN

ETC ★★

**Swinscoe, Ashbourne DE6 2HS**
**Tel: 01335 343183 • Fax: 01335 342742**
**e-mail: info@dogandpartridge.co.uk • website: www.dogandpartridge.co.uk**

Mary and Martin Stelfox welcome you to a family-run 17th century inn and motel set in five acres, 5 miles from Alton Towers and close to Dovedale and Ashbourne. We specialise in family breaks, and special diets and vegetarians are catered for. All rooms have private bathrooms, colour TV, direct-dial telephone, tea-making facilities and baby-listening service. Ideal for touring Stoke Potteries, Derbyshire Dales and Staffordshire moorlands. Restaurant open all day, non-residents welcome. Open Christmas and New Year.

£ **Any 2 nights Dinner, B&B midweek £95, weekend £105 per person.**

## DOVE COTTAGE

ETC ★★★

**Church Lane, Mayfield, Ashbourne**
**Tel: 01335 324443 or 324279**

See also Colour Advertisement on page10

This modernised 200-year-old cottage in Mayfield village is ideally situated for shops, pubs, busy market towns, sporting facilities, lovely Dove Valley, Alton Towers, Peaks and Staffordshire Moorlands and many other places of interest. The cottage is comfortably furnished and well-equipped with TV, fridge, automatic washing machine, gas central heating. The fenced garden overlooks farmland. Sleeps seven. Garage and parking. Children welcome. Pets by arrangement. Available for long and short lets, also mid-week bookings. Further details from: Arthur Tatlow, Ashview, Ashfield Farm, Calwich, Ashbourne DE6 2EB

£ **Price and brochure on request.**

## NEW HOUSE ORGANIC FARM

**Kniveton, Ashbourne DE6 1JL**
**Tel: 01335 342429**

Organic family farm in the Derbyshire Dales, near Matlock, Bakewell, Dove Dale; one mile from Carsington Watersports Centre. We serve organic, free-range and fair-traded foods; vegetarian and other diets welcome. Children's teas, babysitting and play area available; pets, horses, bicycles and children welcome. B&B in annexe which is suitable for asthma/allergy sufferers; also self-catering in six berth mobile home, gypsy caravan sleeping two/four, two small caravans sleeping two/four; space for tourers and camping. Free working holidays can be arranged. Members ECEAT and affiliated to Environmental Tourism Association.

£ **Bed and Breakfast from £10; self-catering from £80 per week.**

## THE OLD BARN

**Middle Lane, Brassington DE4 4HL**
**Tel: 01629 540317**
**e-mail: tyler.family@lineone.net**

Brassington is an unspoilt village on the edge of the Peak National Park, two miles from Carsington Water. The Old Barn is in a truly quiet rural setting on the edge of the village, which has two pubs and a post office/shop within easy walking distance. There is plenty of walking, cycling, horse riding and water sports close by. Chatsworth House, Haddon Hall, Sudbury Hall and the pretty market towns of Ashbourne and Bakewell are all within a 20 minute drive. The National Tramway Museum, Peak Steam Railway, The Heights of Abraham and Alton Towers are less than 30 minutes away.

£ **Short break details available on request. B&B from £23 pp.**

## THE CHARLES COTTON HOTEL

**Hartington, Near Buxton SK17 0AL**
**Tel: 01298 84229 • Fax: 01298 84301**
**e-mail: dogpart@fsbdial.co.uk • website: www.charlescotton.co.uk**

The Charles Cotton is a small, comfortable hotel which lies in the heart of the Derbyshire Dales, pleasantly situated in the village square of Hartington, with nearby shops catering for all needs. It is renowned throughout the area for its hospitality and good home cooking. Pets and children are welcome; special diets catered for. The Charles Cotton makes the perfect centre to relax and explore the area, whether walking, cycling, brass rubbing, pony trekking or even hang-gliding. Open Christmas and New Year.

£ **3 nights Dinner, B&B £135, one week £295.**

## BIGGIN HALL

ETC ★★

**Biggin-by-Hartington, Buxton SK17 0DH**
**Tel: 01298 84451 • Fax: 01298 84681**
**website: www.bigginhall.co.uk**

Tranquilly set 1,000 ft up in the White Peak District National Park, 17th century Grade II* Listed Biggin Hall – now one of the 'World's Best Loved Hotels' where guests experience the full benefits of the legendary Biggin Air – has been sympathetically restored, keeping its character while giving house room to contemporary comforts. Rooms are centrally heated with bathrooms en suite, colour TV, tea-making facilities, silent fridge and telephone. Those in the main house have stone arched mullioned windows, others are in converted 18th century outbuildings. Centrally situated for stately homes and for exploring the natural beauty of the area. Return at the end of the day to enjoy your freshly cooked dinner alongside log fires and personally selected wines.

£ **Call for brochure or details of special breaks.**

## YE OLDE CHESHIRE CHEESE

ETC ◆◆◆◆

**How Lane, Castleton S33 8WJ**
**Tel: 01433 620330 • Fax: 01433 621847**
**e-mail: kslack@btconnect.com • website: www.peakland.com/cheshirecheese**

This delightful 17th century free house is situated in the heart of the Peak District and is an ideal base for walkers and climbers; other local attractions include cycling, golf, swimming, gliding, horse riding and fishing. All bedrooms are en suite with colour TV and tea/coffee making facilities. A "Village Fayre" menu is available all day, all dishes home cooked in the traditional manner; there is also a selection of daily specials. Full Fire Certificate. Large car park.

£ **B&B from £25.00pp.**

# Devon

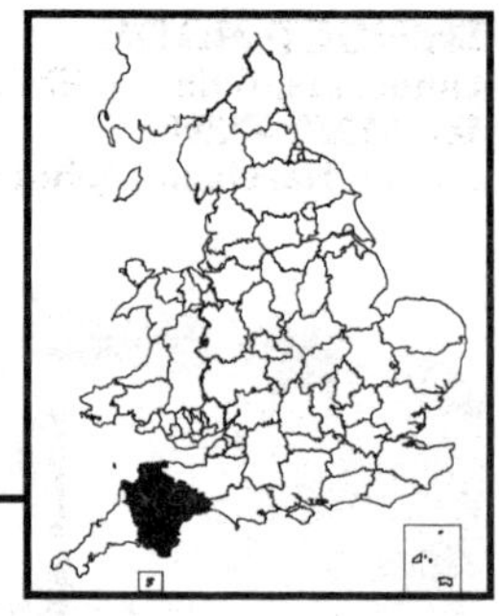

## BRADDON COTTAGES

**Ashwater, Beaworthy EX21 5EP**
**Tel & Fax: 01409 211350**
**e-mail: holidays@braddoncottages.co.uk • website: www.braddoncottages.co.uk**

**ETC ★★★**

Six secluded cottages in quiet countryside of meadow and woodland, on 500 acre site. Four barn conversions and two purpose-built houses surrounded by gardens and lawns, with views over lake to Dartmoor. All-weather tennis court; adults' snooker room and children's games room. Licensed shop. Very comfortable, with gas central heating, wood fires, dishwashers, washing machines, clothes dryers, microwaves and payphones. Bed linen and towels supplied. Pleasant walks; large summer house with barbecue; free fishing. Resident owners George and Anne Ridge. Open all year. Credit cards accepted.

£ **From £60 for two persons for two nights, £90 for two persons for one week. September to May, except public holidays.**

See also Colour Advertisement on page 11

## ANCHORAGE HOTEL

**Babbacombe, Torquay**
**Tel: 01803 326175**
**e-mail: anchorage@aol.com • website: www.anchoragehotel.co.uk**

**AA/RAC ★★**

Set in quiet Cary Park adjacent to the bowling green. All 56 bedrooms are en suite with tea making facilities, colour TV and all non-smoking. Outdoor heated pool. Fully licensed. Regular entertainment, car parking and lift to most rooms.

£ **Short break details available on request.**

## LEE HOUSE

**Marwood, Barnstaple EX31 4DZ**
**Tel: 01271 374345**

Stone-built Elizabethan Manor House dating back to 1256, standing in its own secluded gardens and grounds with magnificent views over rolling Devon countryside. James II ceilings, an Adam fireplace, antiques and the work of resident artist add interest. Easy access to coast and moor. Family-run, friendly and relaxing atmosphere. Walking distance to local pub with excellent food. Marwood Gardens one mile. Open April to October. One double, one twin room and one four-poster room, all en suite with colour TV and tea/coffee making facilities. Children over 12 years welcome. No smoking.

£ **Bed and Breakfast: one night from £22pppn, two nights or more from £20pppn.**

## SUNSET HOTEL

ETC/AA ◆◆◆

**Landcross, Bideford EX39 5JA**
**Tel: 01237 472962**
**e-mail: HazelLamb@hotmail.com**

SOMEWHERE SPECIAL in North Devon. Small Country Hotel in quiet, peaceful location, overlooking spectacular scenery in an area of outstanding natural beauty, one and a half miles from Bideford town. Beautifully decorated and spotlessly clean. Highly recommended quality accommodation. All en suite with colour TV, tea/coffee facilities. Superb cooking, everything home-made with all fresh produce. Vegetarians and special needs catered for. Excellent reputation. Book with confidence in a NON-SMOKING ESTABLISHMENT. Licensed. Private parking. Visa, Mastercard. Adult only.

£ **B&B £30-£32.50. BB&EM £43-£46. BB&EM per week £290-£305.**

## THE EDGEMOOR

ETC/AA/RAC ★★★

**Lowerdown Cross, Bovey Tracey TQ13 9LE**
**Tel: 01626 832466 • Fax: 01626 834760**
**e-mail: edgemoor@btinternet.com • website: www.edgemoor.co.uk**

Charming country house hotel in peaceful wooded setting adjacent Dartmoor National Park, yet only two miles from A38 trunk road. Ideal for walking, touring and relaxing, with golf, riding, fishing and shooting all nearby. Beautiful gardens, friendly atmosphere, award-winning food. Nine NT properties within 35 miles. Beautiful bedrooms including some four-posters. RAC Dining Award, Johansens, "Which?" Hotel Guide. See colour pictures on our Web Page.

£ **2 nights Dinner, Bed and Breakfast from £110 to £130 per person dependent on season.**

## DEVONCOURT HOLIDAY FLATS

**Berryhead Road, Brixham TQ5 9AB**
**Tel: 01803 853748 • Fax: 01803 855775**
**e-mail: devoncourt@devoncoast.com**

The Devoncourt Holiday Flats are a modern, purpose built block of 24 flats, containing all modern conveniences. The flats offer accommodation for up to six persons, with private bathrooms and colour television. They have their own private balconies overlooking Brixham Marina and Torbay. Linen on hire if required. Boating and open air swimming pool only 200 yards away. Beautiful beach opposite. Fishing available. Car parking. Open all year.

£ **£35 per night per flat. October to May.**

## HOOPS INN

RAC ★★

**Horns Cross, Near Clovelly, Bideford EX39 5DL**
**Tel: 01237 451222 • Fax: 01237 451247**
**e-mail: sales@hoopsinn.co.uk • website: www.hoopsinn.co.uk**

This lovingly cared for, picturebook thatched country inn blends 13th century charm with 21st century luxury and extends a warm welcome to its guests. Relax by one of the open log fires to soak up the olde worlde atmosphere while enjoying a real ale or wine before dining on the best of local fish, game or meat. All bedrooms are en suite, individually furnished and well appointed. Special golfing breaks available. The Hoops is a splendid base for a combined sea, country or touring holiday, with historic gardens, houses, and the world-famous fishing village of Clovelly on the doorstep, and Dartmoor and Exmoor within easy reach. RAC Three Dining Ribbons, Which?, CAMRA, AA Pick of Pubs.

£ **Terms available on request.**

See also Colour Advertisement on page 14

See also Colour Advertisement on page 12

## THE NEW INN

ETC/AA ★★

High Street, Clovelly, Near Bideford EX39 5TQ
Tel: 01237 431303 • Fax: 01237 431636
website: www.clovelly.co.uk

This unspoilt heritage village is filled with colourful flower-covered cottages that seem to tumble over one another down the steep and narrow cobbled street which descends towards the tiny harbour. To stay at the New Inn in the heart of the village is to wake up to the sights and sounds of a seafaring way of life that has changed little over the last hundred years. Each of the hotel bedrooms is beautifully decorated. The magic touch of a talented interior designer is to be seen everywhere. The restaurant serves local and regional specialities. This really is a short break paradise. AA ★★ 73%.

£ **Dinner, Bed and Breakfast from £38.25pppn (low season, seven-night stay) to £65.00pppn (high season, one-night stay).**

See also Colour Advertisement on page 10

## PRINCE HALL HOTEL

ETC/AA ★★

Two Bridges, Dartmoor PL20 6SA
Tel: 01822 890403 • Fax: 01822 890676
e-mail: bookings@princehall.co.uk • website: www.princehall.co.uk

The Prince Hall Hotel is a small, friendly and relaxed country house hotel, in a peaceful and secluded setting, commanding glorious views over open moorland. Nine en suite bedrooms, two with four posters, all rooms have colour TV, direct-dial telephone, refreshment tray. The hotel offers peaceful surroundings, a warm welcome, log fires, good books, gourmet cooking by the owner/chef and an excellent wine list. Marvellous walks from the hotel; fishing, riding and golf nearby. AA Two Rosettes for Food, Good Hotel Guide, 'Which?' Hotel Guide Best Loved Hotels. Voted "Best West Country Hotel Restaurant" in 2000. Supreme Accolade 2003 - voted one of the AA Top 200 hotels in Britain and Ireland.

£ **3-day break from £240pp for four course dinner, bed and breakfast.**

See also Colour Advertisement on page 14

## CHERRYBROOK HOTEL

ETC/AA ◆◆◆◆

Two Bridges, Yelverton, Devon PL20 6SP
Tel: 01822 880260
e-mail: info@cherrybrook-hotel.co.uk • website: www.cherrybrook-hotel.co.uk

Get away from it all! There will always be times when you wish there was somewhere you could go to get away from it all, relax in beautiful surroundings, and sample delicious food. The Cherrybrook Hotel is the ideal choice and you will find the warmest of welcomes. Set in the heart of Dartmoor National Park, Cherrybrook is an excellent base for walking, touring or simply enjoying the breathtaking scenery. To find out more, telephone or fax Margaret or Andy Duncan.

£ **Terms available on request.**

## THE ROYAL OAK INN

Dunsford, Near Exeter EX6 7DA
Tel: 01647 252256

Enjoy a friendly welcome in our traditional Country Pub in the picturesque thatched village of Dunsford. Quiet en suite bedrooms are available in the tastefully converted cob barn. An ideal base for touring Dartmoor, Exeter and the coast, and the beautiful Teign Valley, six miles from Exeter and four miles from Moretonhampstead. Real ale and home-made meals are served. Well behaved children and dogs are welcome. The accommodation is suitable for disabled guests and non-smokers. CAMRA, Good Pub Guide.

£ **Please ring Mark or Judy Harrison for further details.**

See also Colour Advertisement on page 15

## THE LORD HALDON COUNTRY HOUSE HOTEL

ETC/AA ★★★

**Dunchideock, Near Exeter EX6 7YF**
**Tel: 01392 832483 • Fax: 01392 833765**
**e-mail: enquiries@lordhaldonhotel.co.uk • website: www.lordhaldonhotel.co.uk**

The Lord Haldon Country House Hotel is the perfect venue for a quiet get-away break. The hotel stands in its own grounds, four miles south west of Exeter, set 400 feet above sea level. It is family run by the Preece family, owners for over 21 years. The hotel has two Red Rosettes for its restaurant, which is open seven days a week, and there is also an intimate Lounge Bar which serves bar food.The Lord Haldon is the only hotel in Devon that is a member of Relais du Silence, an independent hotel consortium dedicated to fine food, service, peace and quiet. For further information, please telephone for a free hotel brochure.

£ **Short break details on request.**

See also Colour Advertisement on page 15

## GLEBE HOUSE COTTAGES

ETC ★★★★

**Bridgerule, Holsworthy EX22 7EW**
**Tel: 01288 381272**
**e-mail: fhg@glebehousecottages.co.uk • website: www.glebehousecottages.co.uk**

Grade II Listed Georgian Estate with original Coach House, Stables and Barns beautifully converted into seven spacious, warm and comfortable cottages sleeping from two to twelve. Exposed beams, some four-poster beds, double-sized spa baths and en suite facilities. Set in five acres of beautiful, tranquil countryside, but only 10 minutes' drive from sandy beaches. Games room, children's play area, cellar bar and à la carte restaurant with log fire. Superb home cooked food.

£ **Short Break terms on request.**

See also Colour Advertisement on page 13

## THE AVONCOURT HOTEL

**Torrs Walk Avenue, Ilfracombe**
**Tel: 01271 862543**

Chris and Tony welcome you to their friendly family-run hotel. The hotel is situated in a quiet private road adjacent to National Trust land. It faces south with panoramic views of town and countryside. All bedrooms are on first or ground floor and the excellent food and relaxed atmosphere will make your holiday a memorable one. The heated rooms are en suite with tea/coffee making facilities and colour TV. There is also a cosy licensed bar and a TV lounge. Ample parking.

£ **Short break details available on request.**

See also Colour Advertisement on page 11

## VARLEY HOUSE

ETC/AA ◆◆◆◆

**Chambercombe Park, Ilfracombe EX34 9QW**
**Tel: 01271 863927 • Fax: 01271 879299**
**e-mail: info@varleyhouse.co.uk • website: www.varleyhouse.co.uk**

Varley generates a feeling of warmth and relaxation, combined with an enviable position overlooking Hillsborough Nature Reserve. Winding paths lead to the Harbour and several secluded coves. Our attractive, spacious, fully en suite, non-smoking bedrooms all have colour TV, central heating, generous beverage tray, hairdryer, clock-radio-alarm and lots of thoughtful extras. Superb food, beautiful surroundings and that special friendly atmosphere so essential to a relaxing holiday. Cosy separate bar. Car park. Children over 5 years of age. Dogs by arrangement. We want you to want to return.

£ **Bed and Breakfast from £26pppn. Weekly from £170 per person. Dinner available £15.**

## MOUNTS FARM TOURING PARK

**The Mounts, Kingsbridge TQ9 7QJ**
**Tel: 01548 521591**

Mounts Farm is a family-run site in the heart of south Devon. On site facilities include FREE hot showers, flush toilets, FREE hot water in washing-up room, razor points, laundry and information room, electric hook-ups and site shop. We welcome tents, touring caravans and motor caravans. Large pitches in level, sheltered fields. No charges for awnings. Children and pets welcome. Situated three miles north of Kingsbridge, Mounts Farm is an ideal base for exploring Dartmouth, Salcombe, Totnes, Dartmoor and the many safe, sandy beaches nearby. Please telephone or write for a free brochure.Self-catering cottage also available.

£ **Short Break details available on request.**

See also Colour Advertisement on page 13

## THE CROWN (Hospitality since 1760)

**Market Street, Lynton, North Devon EX35 6AG**
**Tel: 01598 752253 • Fax: 01598 75331**
**website: www.thecrown-lynton.co.uk**

Nestling in the heart of Exmoor National Park Conservation Area, this Old Village Inn is privately owned, family-managed and continually striving to maintain the reputation it has achieved during its present ownership. The ambience of The Crown is enhanced by the high standard of hospitality, comfortable lounge bar, bustling bar/restaurant and covered terrace. Non-smoking areas include the hotel dining room and library. We offer an extensive menu using fresh local produce, when available, prepared by a team of young but experienced chefs, complemented by genuinely friendly and efficient front of house staff. Open all year.

£ **Winter-3 nights DB&B from £130pp. Summer-3 nights DB&B from £180pp. Concessions for group bookings.**

## MOORLANDS

**Woody Bay, Parracombe, Near Lynton EX31 4RA**
**Tel: 01598 763224**

Moorlands (formerly the Station Hotel) is a family-run establishment in a most beautiful part of North Devon, surrounded by Exmoor countryside and within two miles of the spectacular coastline. Very comfortable and quiet double or family suite accommodation suitable for two persons or a family of four, all en suite with shower, colour TV, and tea/coffee making facilities. Moorlands has a licensed restaurant and residents' lounge, and private outdoor swimming pool, all set in six acres of gardens. Open all year except Christmas, a perfect retreat for the country lover. Some ground floor rooms. Details from Christine and Ian Corderoy.

£ **Dinner, Bed and Breakfast from £33-£35. 3 nights DB&B £99pp, B&B £22.50pp – reductions for family of four.**

See also Colour Advertisement on page 13

## LAMBSCOMBE FARM

ETC ★★★★

**North Molton, Devon EX36 3JT**
**Tel: 01598 740558**
**e-mail: richardboulter@supanet.com • website: www.lambscombefarm.co.uk**

Medieval farmhouse and luxury barn conversions around cobbled courtyard overlooking wooded valley full of wildlife. Set in 6 secluded acres with stream, large children's play/picnic area, games room. Every home comfort including log fires and some en suite bathrooms. All inclusive rates. Open all year. Two night breaks available. Sleep 2 to 14.

£ **Short break details available on request.**

See also Colour Advertisement on page 15

## NEWBARN FARM COTTAGES

ETC ★★★★

**Totnes Road, Paignton TQ4 7PT**
**Tel: 01803 553602 • Fax: 01803 553637**
**e-mail: info@newbarnfarm.com • website: www.newbarnfarm.com**

Six luxury cottages graded to four stars by the English Tourism Council. Exceptionally well equipped and sleeping 2-12 people. Glorious hilltop views of the South Devon countryside extending all the way to Dartmoor. Three miles to the nearest beach. Perfectly situated for the many tourist attractions in the Torbay and South Hams areas. Very peaceful and relaxing setting. Use of large indoor swimming pool, gymnasium, sauna and solarium (adjacent property half mile). On site six coarse fishing lakes, large games room, skittle alley. 40 acres of private pastures and woodland to roam. Dogs welcome in two of the cottages.

£ **Short Break details on request.**

## AMBER HOUSE HOTEL

**6 Roundham Road, Paignton TQ4 6EZ**
**Tel: 01803 558372**

Family-run licensed Hotel. Colour TV and tea/coffee making facilities in all rooms. En suite facilities and ground floor rooms. Good food, highly recommended. Large car park. Spacious suntrap garden and patio. Park and beach five minutes' walk. A warm welcome assured; pets by arrangement. Restricted smoking. We pride ourselves on our high standards. Details from Val and James Banks.

£ **Spring, Autumn and Winter breaks – four nights for the price of three. Bed and Breakfast from £18 per night.**

## SAND PEBBLES HOTEL & RESTAURANT

**Hope Cove, Near Salcombe TQ7 3HF**
**Tel: 01548 561673**
**website: www.sandpebbles.co.uk**

Small and friendly; all rooms en suite, with TV and beverage trays. 300 yards from sandy beaches and cliff top walks. Wonderful food, fine wines, peaceful and relaxing – "there's nowhere else quiet like it".

£ **Terms on request.**

See also Colour Advertisement on page 13

## AXEVALE CARAVAN PARK

✓✓✓

**Seaton EX12 2DF**
**Tel: 0800 0688816**
**website:www.axevale.co.uk**

A quiet, family-run park with 68 modern and luxury caravans for hire. The park overlooks the delightful River Axe Valley, and is just a 10 minute walk from the town with its wonderfully long, award-winning beach. Children will love our extensive play area, with its sand pit, paddling pool, swings and slide. Laundry facilities are provided and there is a wide selection of goods on sale in the park shop which is open every day. All of our caravans have a shower, toilet, fridge and TV. Also, with no clubhouse, a relaxing atmosphere is ensured.

£ **From £75 per week; reductions for three or fewer persons early/late season.**

## THE BEDFORD HOTEL

**1 Plymouth Road, Tavistock PL19 8BB**
**Tel: 01822 613221**

ETC ★★★

This splendid hotel, built on the site of a former Benedictine monastery, retains the charm and character of a more leisurely age, whilst providing the most up-to-date guest facilities. Here you can truly relax and enjoy the personal and attentive friendly service. Sample some of the West Country's finest food, using fresh local produce, in the delightful Woburn Restaurant. Situated in the historic and picturesque market town of Tavistock, on the edge of the Dartmoor National Park, there is simply so much to do and see on the doorstep. AA 2 Rosettes.

£ **Short Breaks from £45pp DB&B (based on two sharing); B&B £37.50pp. Special rates for January and February.**

## THE OLD COACH HOUSE HOTEL

**Ottery, Near Tavistock PL19 8NS**
**Tel: 01822 617515**

A lovely, small country Hotel on edge of tiny hamlet of Ottery, close to historic Tavistock and beautiful Dartmoor. Ideal base for visiting any part of Devon or Cornwall. Peaceful setting amid rolling farmland adjacent to Tamar Valley, designated an area of outstanding beauty. Super walking country, fishing and many National Trust houses and gardens nearby. Two golf courses within three miles and St. Mellion International Golf Club 20 minutes away, or just relax in our tranquil walled garden. All rooms en suite and have colour TV, tea/coffee making facilities, telephone and clock/radios. Adjacent self-catering cottage with two en suite bedrooms, sleeps 4. £200 low season, £260 mid season, £320 high season.

£ **Bargain Breaks from £70 to £98 for three nights DB&B.**

See also Colour Advertisement on page 10

## TORCROSS APARTMENTS

**Torcross TQ7 2TQ**
**Tel: 01548 580206 • Fax: 01548 580996**
**e-mail: enquiries@torcross.net • website: www.torcross.net**

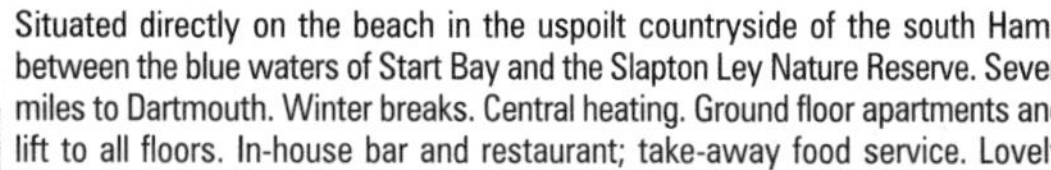

Situated directly on the beach in the uspoilt countryside of the south Hams between the blue waters of Start Bay and the Slapton Ley Nature Reserve. Seven miles to Dartmouth. Winter breaks. Central heating. Ground floor apartments and lift to all floors. In-house bar and restaurant; take-away food service. Lovely walks. Brochure with pleasure or visit our website.

£ **Short break details on request.**

See also Colour Advertisement on page 15

## PARKS HOTEL

**Rathmore Road, Torquay TQ2 6NZ**
**Tel: 01803 292420**
**e-mail: enquiries@parks-hotel.co.uk • website: www.parks-hotel.co.uk**

ETC ◆◆◆◆

A delightful, tastefully furnished hotel standing in its own grounds, situated in the parks surrounding the famous Torre Abbey. The position is quiet and on the level, 400 yards to the seafront, 300 yards to the Conference/Leisure Centre, and 300 yards to the rail station. All bedrooms en suite, with colour TV and tea/coffee making. Full central heating. Licensed bar. Ample private parking. Heated and secluded outdoor pool. Special breaks.

£ **Short break details on request. B&B from £21 to £28pppn.**

See also Colour Advertisement on page 11

## SUMMERDYNE HOLIDAY APARTMENTS

ETC ★★★

**Greenway Road, Chelston, Torquay TQ2 6JE**
**Tel: 01803 605439 • Fax: 01803 607441**
**e-mail: stay@summerdyne.co.uk • website: www.summerdyne.co.uk**

Summerdyne is an elegant Victorian villa, tastefully converted into 10 spacious self-contained apartments, all comfortably furnished, centrally heated and fully equipped to a high standard. Large gardens to play in or relax. Safe off-road parking. We are close to the beach, town centre and Cockington Country Park, making Summerdyne an ideal location for families and couples alike. Dale and Mandy Tanner, your resident hosts, will ensure you receive a very warm welcome and a pleasant stay at Summerdyne.

£ **Short Breaks from £70 per couple including central heating and bed linen. Weekly rates from £120 low season to £475 high season. Phone or e-mail for our information pack.**

See also Colour Advertisement on page 12

## CROWNDALE HOTEL

**18 Bridge Road, Torquay TQ2 5BA**
**Tel & Fax: 01803 293068**

Tom and Barbara are your friendly hosts at this 7-bedroom hotel which is situated in a quiet, tree-lined road, but which is close to all that Torquay has to offer. All our double or family rooms are en suite, well decorated and comfortable. All have central heating with thermostatic controls, colour TV, radio/alarm clock, hairdryer, and tea/coffee making facilities. There is a car park at the rear of the hotel and ground floor rooms are available. We welcome children and can supply a high chair, baby monitors, baby bath, changing mat and small steriliser for your convenience. Non-smoking.

£ **Terms available on request.**

See also Colour Advertisement on page 12

## GLENORLEIGH HOTEL

**26 Cleveland Road, Torquay TQ2 5BE**
**Tel: 01803 292135 • Fax: 01803 213717**
**e-mail: glenorleighhotel@btinternet.com • website: www.glenorleigh.co.uk**

Situated in a quiet residential area, Glenorleigh is 10 minutes' walk from both the sea front and the town centre. Delightful en suite rooms, with your comfort in mind. Good home cooking, both English and Continental, plenty of choice, with vegetarian options available daily. Bar leading onto terrace overlooking Mediterranean-style garden with feature palms and heated swimming pool. Discounts for children and Senior Citizens. Brochures and menus available on request. The hotel has featured on the BBC Holiday Programme.

£ **Short break details available on request.**

See also Colour Advertisement on page 12

## NORCLIFFE HOTEL

AA/RAC ★★

**Babbacombe Downs Sea Front, Torquay TQ1 3LF**
**Tel: 01803 328456 • Fax: 01803 328023**
**e-mail: manager@norcliffehotel.co.uk • website: www.norcliffehotel.co.uk**

The Norcliffe is a traditional family-run, licensed hotel. It has 28 bedrooms, all of which have en suite facilities, colour TV, radio, tea/coffee making facilities and telephone. The lounges are spacious and comfortable and the dining room is particularly attractive. Other facilities within the hotel include a heated indoor swimming pool, sauna and games room. Norcliffe is ideally situated on the Babbacombe Downs overlooking Lyme Bay to east Devon and Dorset, opposite the Cliff Railway down to Oddicombe Beach. The atmosphere is friendly and relaxed with emphasis on high standards and quality of service.

£ **Terms on request. Special breaks over Christmas and New Year.**

## GREEN PARK LICENSED HOTEL

**25 Morgan Avenue, Torquay TQ2 5RR**
**Tel: 01803 293618 • Fax: 01803 293618**
**e-mail: greenpark.torquay@cwcom.net**

Green Park is a small independent licensed hotel situated in a quiet road just 300 yards from the Town Centre and shops, leading onto Fleet Walk, Torquay's new shopping centre, and then down to the harbour and sea front. Green Park offers guests en suite rooms, colour TV, tea/coffee facilities, off-road car parking, large TV lounge, comfortable dining room and bar. Full central heating. Open all year including Christmas and New Year.

£ **Bed and Breakfast from £17.00, four-course optional Evening Meal by arrangement £10.00. Telephone Carole or Rowan for brochure.**

## PARKFIELD APARTMENTS

ETC ★★★

**Claddon Lane, Maidencombe, Torquay TQ1 4TB**
**Tel & Fax: 01803 328952**
**e-mail: enquiries@parkfieldapartments.co.uk • website: www.parkfieldapartments.co.uk**

June and Roy Lewis welcome you to Parkfield Luxury Apartments. Our 1,2 and 3 bedroom accommodation comes fully appointed, each with TV and video and its own patio, most have panoramic views over rolling countryside. Parkfield is set in an acre of landscaped grounds; children and dogs are most welcome. Parkfield offers children's play area, ample parking and kennels. This tranquil setting nestles at the gateway to the 'English Riviera' so we're just a short drive from beaches, coastal walks, traditional pubs, steam railways and other family attractions.

£ **Short Breaks available.**

See also Colour Advertisement on page 10

## ASHFIELD RISE

ETC ★★/★★★

**Ruckamore Road, Torquay TQ2 6HF**
**Tel: 01803 605156 • Fax: 01803 607373**
**website: www.ashfieldrise.co.uk**

Sleep 1-8. Apartments ideal for family holidays, some with sea view. Within walking distance of the sea front, Riviera Centre and the "old world" village of Cockington. Each apartment has modern kitchen and microwave, colour TV. Children and pets welcome; cots, high chair available. Secluded garden with large car park. All linen supplied free of charge; electricity metered. Couples, families and mature singles only. Ideal for conference delegates seeking the privacy and freedom of their own apartment. Please telephone or write for our free brochure. Members Torbay Self-Catering Association and WCTB.

£ **Terms from £95 to £450 per week. Bargain Breaks available October to May. Midweek bookings taken. Open all year.**

## RED HOUSE HOTEL

ETC/AA ★★

**Rousdown Road, Chelston, Torquay TQ2 6PB**
**Tel: 01803 607811 • Fax: 01803 605357**
**e-mail: stay@redhouse-hotel.co.uk • website: www.redhouse-hotel.co.uk**

We've joined together the friendly service and facilities of the 2 star Red House hotel for those wanting a traditional hotel atmosphere, with the privacy and freedom of Maxton Lodge's 24 self-contained holiday apartments. Two styles of accommodation sharing the same conveniently located grounds and superb range of facilities, so whether you're a working conference delegate or a fun loving family you'll find a style to suit you.

£ **Short break details on request**

See also Colour Advertisement on page 14

## DARTINGTON HALL

**Totnes, South Devon TQ9 6EL**
**Tel: 01803 847147; 01803 847107**
**e-mail: dhcc.ops@dartingtonhall.com • website: www.dartingtonhall.com**

The beautiful 14th century Medieval Courtyard at Dartington Hall is the perfect place to relax. Set amidst over 1000 acres of farmland and ancient deer park, there are many walks for you to enjoy, through the woodlands, along the river Dart and in the magnificent gardens surrounding the Hall. Dartington Hall is also an ideal base from which to explore Devon and Cornwall, including Dartmoor, the coast, The Eden Project and National Trust properties. Our White Hart Bar & Restaurant is located within the Courtyard and offers mouth watering meals, freshly prepared using the finest local ingredients, including organic produce from Dartington Hall's own market garden. Rosette Award for Food, "Which?" Guide to Country Pubs, Johansens, Les Routiers, AA The 'Pub Guide' 2002.

£ **£49.50 per person, D,B&B in single twin or double room (minumum stay 2 nights), stay 4 nights get 5th night free. Available January - June, or Mid-August to 22nd December.**

## SEA TROUT INN

ETC ★★

**Staverton, Near Totnes TQ9 6PA**
**Tel: 01803 762274 • Fax: 01803 762506**
**website: www.seatroutinn.com**

The Inn has two well-appointed bars with oak beams and real log fires, both pleasant places to relax and unwind after a day's walking or touring. 10 bedrooms, delightfully decorated in a comfortable cottage style, have private bathrooms, central heating, direct-dial telephone, tea/coffee making facilities and colour TV. Guests dining in the Hotel may choose from the award winning restaurant or the relaxing and leisurely atmosphere of the bars or, on warmer summer days, the attractive patio garden. An extensive menu ranges from light snacks to full meals, with vegetarian dishes always available. AA 2 Rosettes.

£ **B&B from £25pppn.**

See also Colour Advertisement on page 11

## THE RISING SUN INN

ETC/AA ★★

**Umberleigh EX37 9DU**
**Tel: 01769 560447 • Fax: 01769 560764**
**e-mail: risingsuninn@btinternet.com • website: www.risingsuninn.com**

Dating from the 13th century, the Rising Sun Inn is situated in the beautiful Taw Valley, ideal for visiting RHS Rosemoor Garden, Dartmoor, Exmoor and the North Devon coast. The inn offers traditional hospitality, excellent food and fine wines. Bedrooms are full of character and provide every modern comfort. There are facilities for golf, horse riding, cycling and walking the Tarka Trail, as well as exclusive salmon fishing on the River Taw. North Devon Food Pub of the Year.

£ **Short break details on request.**

## KITLEY HOUSE HOTEL & RESTAURANT

ETC ★★★★

**Kitley Estate, Yealmpton, PL8 2NW**
**Tel: 01752 881555 • Fax: 01752 881667**
**e-mail: sales@kitleyhousehotel.com • website: www.kitleyhousehotel.com**

Charming Devon Country House Hotel close to Plymouth, quiet location overlooking historic lake. Range of en suite accommodation available including suites, plus excellent, award-winning Restaurant and Bar. Pet friendly.

£ **Terms available on request.**

# Dorset

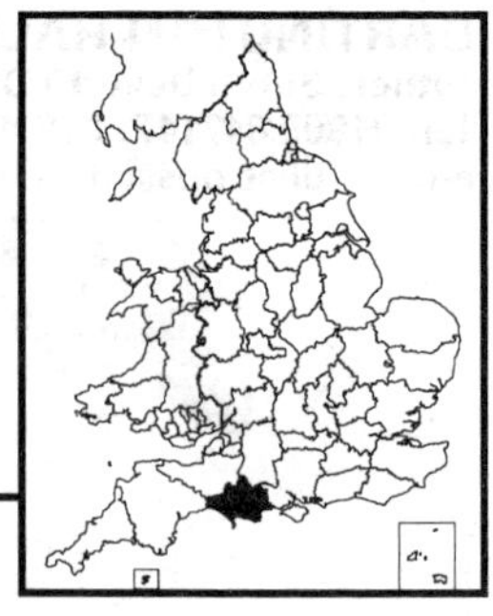

## DORSET COTTAGE HOLIDAYS

ETC ★★★/★★★★

**Tel: 01929 553443**
**e-mail: enq@dhcottages.co.uk • website: www.dhcottages.co.uk**

Delightful, graded self-catering accommodation throughout tranquil Dorset, just two hours from London. The coastline has been awarded World Heritage Site Status ranking it alongside the Grand Canyon. Come and see why. You and your family can relax on safe sandy beaches, explore rockpools, collect fossils and marvel at the dramatic rock formations. Wind down to the slower pace of rural life, wander through historic villages where time stood still. Superb walking area along extensive network of footpaths and open countryside, including nature reserves and common land, walk along the South West Coastal Path, the longest in Britain. Weekend/mid-week bookings taken. Last minute booking service. Credit Cards welcome. Pets go free. Open all year. Fully equipped.

£ **Terms from £105 per cottage for three nights.**

## ANVIL HOTEL AND RESTAURANT

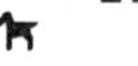

**Pimperne, Blandford DT11 8UQ**
**Tel: 01258 453431/480182 • Fax: 01258 480182**
**e-mail: info@anvilhotel.co.uk • website: www.anvilhotel.co.uk**

A long, low, thatched building set in a tiny village deep in the Dorset countryside, two miles from Blandford – what could be more English? And that is what visitors to the Anvil will find – a typical old English hostelry offering good, old-fashioned English hospitality. A mouth- watering menu with delicious desserts is available in the charming beamed restaurant with log fire, and in the two bars together with specials of the day. All bedrooms have private facilities with direct-dial telephone and Teasmaid. Ample parking. Pets welcome. Good Food Pub Guide, Les Routiers Silver Key Award for Food, Casserole Award for Housekeeping and Cleanliness.

£ **Double room from £75, single room from £55. Mini-break £120 for 2 people for 2 nights.**

## THE ELSTEAD HOTEL

ETC/AA/RAC ★★★

**12/14 Knyveton Road, Bournemouth BH1 3QP**
**Tel: 01202 293071 • Fax: 01202 293827**
**e-mail: enquiries@the-elstead.co.uk • www. the-elstead.co.uk**

Set in a quiet tree-lined avenue five minutes from the centre of Bournemouth, the Elstead is a very special hotel with a feel of warmth and elegance perfectly blended with superb facilities and caring professional staff. There are 50 en suite bedrooms, most of which have been recently refurbished. Each room has ironing facilities, hairdryer, satellite TV and voice mail. Non-smoking rooms are available. An elegant restaurant serves fresh, home-cooked food. For relaxation the Nordic Leisure Club offers a heated pool, sauna and steam room. The gym has impressive state-of-the-art exercise equipment and there is also a snooker and pool room. SEE ALSO ADVERTISEMENT ON THE INSIDE FRONT COVER.

£ **Terms and Short Break details available on request.**

See also Colour Advertisement on page 16

## SOUTHERNHAY HOTEL

**42 Alum Chine Road, Westbourne, Bournemouth BH4 8DX**
**Tel & Fax: 01202 761251**
**e-mail: enquiries@southernhayhotel.co.uk • web: www.southernhayhotel.co.uk**

The Southernhay Hotel provides warm, friendly, high standard accommodation with a large car park. All rooms have colour TV, tea/coffee making facilities, hairdryer and radio alarm clock. The hotel is ideally situated at the head of Alum Chine (a wooded ravine) leading down to the sea and miles of safe sandy beaches. The Bournemouth International Centre, cinemas, theatres, restaurants, clubs and pubs are all within easy reach; minutes by car or the frequent bus service. Seven bedrooms, five en suite. Open all year. Details from Tom and Lynn Derby.

£ **Bed and Breakfast from £18 to £25 per adult per night.**

---

## BRITMEAD HOUSE HOTEL

ETC/AA ◆◆◆◆

**West Bay Road, Bridport DT6 4EG**
**Tel: 01308 422941 • Fax: 01308 422516**
**e-mail: Britmead@talk21.com • website: www.britmeadhouse.co.uk**

An elegant Edwardian house, family-run and ideally situated between Bridport and West Bay Harbour with its beaches, golf course, Chesil Beach and the Dorset Coastal Path. We offer full en suite rooms (one ground floor), all with TV, tea/coffee making facilities and hairdryer. South-facing lounge and dining room overlooking the garden. Licensed. Private parking. Restricted smoking.

£ **B&B from £44-£64 for 2 nights; £72 to £84 for 3 nights. Rates for longer stays on request.**

---

## THE OLD RECTORY

ETC ◆◆◆◆

**Winterbourne Steepleton, Dorchester DT2 9LG**
**Tel: 01305 889468 • Fax: 01305 889737**
**e-mail: trees@eurobell.co.uk • website: www.trees.eurobell.co.uk**

Dating from 1850, the Old Rectory is situated in a quiet hamlet; grounds have croquet lawns, putting green, and children's swing. The four guest rooms are all individually furnished to a high standard, each with en suite facilities. No smoking. Breakfast is a delight, and private dining facilities are available on request for celebration dinners; special diets catered for. Alternatively local pubs and a large selection of restaurants both in Dorchester (six miles) and Weymouth (eight miles) are available. French spoken. Open all year except Christmas. Brochure available. ETC Silver Award.

£ **Bed and Breakfast from £25 per person.**

---

## EXPLANATION OF SYMBOLS

| | |
|---|---|
| ★ | Number of Stars (English Tourism Council/AA/RAC) |
| ◆ | Number of Diamonds (English Tourism Council/AA/RAC) |
| | Pets Welcome |
| | Reductions for Children |
| | Christmas Breaks |
| ♿ | Suitable for Disabled |

The symbols are arranged in the same order throughout the book so that looking down each page will give a quick comparison.

## CROMWELL HOUSE HOTEL

**ETC/AA/RAC ★★**

**Lulworth Cove BH20 5RJ**
**Tel: 01929 400253/400332 • Fax: 01929 400566**
**website: www.lulworthcove.co.uk**

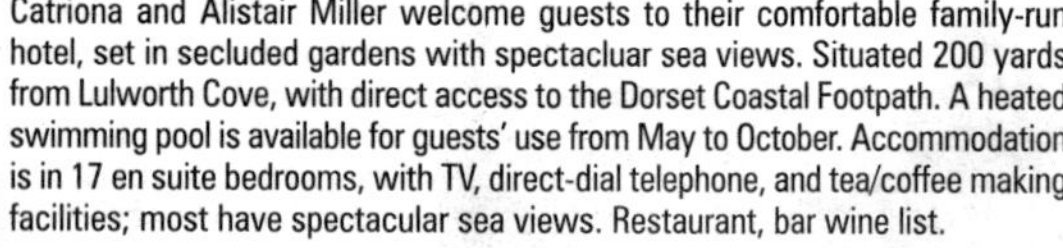

Catriona and Alistair Miller welcome guests to their comfortable family-run hotel, set in secluded gardens with spectacluar sea views. Situated 200 yards from Lulworth Cove, with direct access to the Dorset Coastal Footpath. A heated swimming pool is available for guests' use from May to October. Accommodation is in 17 en suite bedrooms, with TV, direct-dial telephone, and tea/coffee making facilities; most have spectacular sea views. Restaurant, bar wine list.

£ **Two nights Dinner, Bed and Breakfast (fully en suite) from £75. Off peak mid week breaks. All year except Christmas.**

See also Colour Advertisement on page 16

## LYME BAY HOLIDAYS

**ETC ★★★-★★★★★**

**44 Church Street, Lyme Regis DT7 3DA**
**Tel: 01297 443363 • Fax: 01297 445576**
**website: www.lymebayholidays.co.uk**

Over 130 self-catering cottages, houses and apartments - many in beautiful coastal and country locations. Lyme Regis and the surrounding areas are ideal destinations for short break holidays. There is much to explore in this Area of Outstanding Natural Beauty, as well as along the Jurassic coastline, now designated a World Heritage site. The picturesque seaside town of Lyme Regis with its famous Cobb harbour, offers a wide range of pubs, restaurants and cafes as well as an independent cinema and small theatre, making a weekend or midweek break a real treat. All properties are independently inspected by the English Tourism Council for quality assurance. Accommodate any number, from couples to large family groups. Short breaks available on many properties.

£ **3 nights over a weekend or 4 nights mid-week £115 - £1000.**

## THE POACHERS INN

**Piddletrenthide, Near Dorchester DT2 7QX**
**Tel: 01300 348358 • Fax: 01300 348153**
**website: www.thepoachersinn.co.uk**

Country Inn set in the heart of lovely Piddle Valley. Within easy reach of all Dorset's attractions. All rooms en suite with colour TV, tea/coffee, telephone; two rooms with four-poster beds. Full central heating. Restaurant. Half Board guests choose from à la carte menu at no extra cost. Send for brochure. Welcome Host.

£ **Bed and Breakfast £30 per person; Dinner, Bed and Breakfast £45 per person; 10% discount for 7 nights. Low season breaks: 2 nights Dinner, Bed and Breakfast £90 per person, 3rd night Dinner, Bed and Breakfast free. Available October to April.**

PLEASE MENTION THIS GUIDE WHEN YOU WRITE

OR PHONE TO ENQUIRE ABOUT ACCOMMODATION

IF YOU ARE WRITING, A STAMPED, ADDRESSED

ENVELOPE IS ALWAYS APPRECIATED

## THE OLD VICARAGE

ETC ◆◆◆◆◆

**Sherborne Road, Milborne Port, Near Sherborne DT9 5AT**

**Tel: 01963 251117 • Fax: 01963 251515**

**e-mail: theoldvicarage@milborneport.freeserve.co.uk • www.milborneport.freeserve.co.uk**

The Old Vicarage is a grand Gothic Victorian building furnished with antiques, set in three acres of well-kept grounds overlooking open country, next to a charming village and two miles from the historic town of Sherborne. On Fridays and Saturdays dinner is prepared by one of the owners, a highly acclaimed chef, using fresh ingredients from local farms. The cooking is based on French techniques with Far Eastern influences.

£ **Special weekend breaks for two people with dinner (four-course meals) on Friday and Saturday night are from £184 to £256 (2002) depending on the type of room and the time of year.**

See also Colour Advertisement on page 17

## THE KNOLL HOUSE

**Studland BH19 3AE**

**Tel: 01929 450450 • Fax: 01929 450423**

**e-mail: enquiries@knollhouse.co.uk • website: www.knollhouse.co.uk**

The Knoll House is a family-run country hotel in the wonderful coastal setting of a National Trust reserve overlooking three miles of golden beach and native heath. The hotel offers excellent facilities for all ages, with six fine lounges and restaurant, tennis courts, nine-acre golf course, and outdoor heated pool; Jacuzzi, sauna, steam room, plunge pool, and gym. For the children there is a restaurant, playroom, adventure playground, and two games rooms, as well as family suites of connecting rooms.

£ **£317 per person for five nights full board in double/twin room with washbasin; £799 for family suite with two adults and two children for five nights. Out of season.**

See also Colour Advertisement on page 16

## LULWORTH COUNTRY COTTAGES

**East Lulworth, Wareham**

Five family owned properties on historic 1200 acre estate. COASTGUARD COTTAGE is approximatley 400 yards from Lulworth Cove and sleeps 7, HOME FARM sleeps 7, ST MARY'S sleeps 10, 48 EAST LODGE sleeps 4 and 49 EAST LODGE sleeps 3. All cottages are well equipped with washing machine, tumble dryer, fridge/freezer, microwave, dishwasher and colour TV. Central heating, duvets with linen and electricity are inclusive. All have secure gardens and parking. We are situated in an area of exeptional natural beauty. Open throughout the year. SHORT BREAKS BY ARRANGEMENT. For brochure contact: Mrs E.S. Weld, Lulworth Castle House, East Lulworth, Wareham BH20 5QS (Tel & Fax: 01929 400100).

£ **Terms available on request.**

## EXPLANATION OF SYMBOLS

★ Number of Stars (English Tourism Council/AA/RAC)

◆ Number of Diamonds (English Tourism Council/AA/RAC)

Pets Welcome

Reductions for Children

Christmas Breaks

Suitable for Disabled

The symbols are arranged in the same order throughout the book so that looking down each page will give a quick comparison.

# Durham

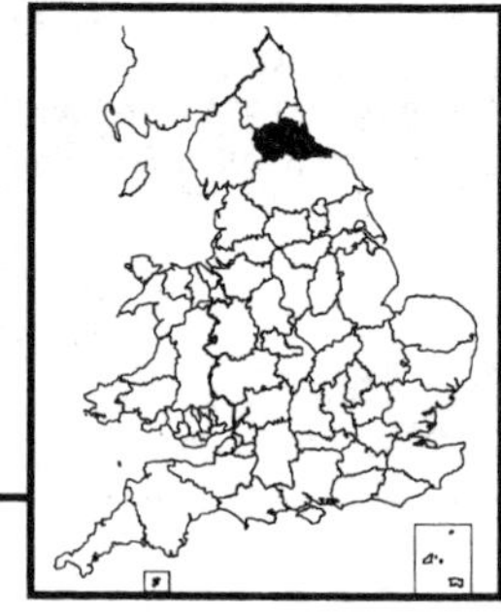

## DERWENT GRANGE FARM

ETC ★★/★★★

**Castleside, Consett DH8 9BN**
**Tel: 01207 508358**
**e-mail: ekelliot@aol.com**

Three adjoining self-contained units, two comprising one double and one twin bedroom, kitchen, bathroom and comfortable living area; the third has a double bedroom plus a studio couch in the living area. Colour TV, private garden and patio furniture, heating and linen are all included in the price. Just north of the village of Castleside on the A68 heading towards Corbridge with easy access to the Roman Wall, Durham City, the Metro Centre, Beamish Museum and lots more. Pass the Fleece Inn Pub on the north side of the village, take a left turn after a short distance, down a very steep hill, the road is signposted 'Derwent Grange', follow this and we are the farm on the right.

£ **Terms from £175 per week Low Season and from £250 per week High Season.**

See also Colour Advertisement on page 17

## THE NEW GRANGE HOTEL

ETC ★★★

**Southend Avenue, Darlington DL3 7HZ**
**Tel: 01325 365858/9 • Fax: 01325 487111**
**e-mail:enquiries@thenewgrangehotel.com • website: www.thenewgrangehotel.com**

The New Grange is a contemporary Grade II Listed townhouse hotel, situated in the bustling and fashionable west end of Darlington, within easy reach of Teesside International Airport and the A1 motorway. There are 45 bedrooms - all with modern amenities, conference and banqueting facilities for up to a hundred guests, a civil wedding licence, as well as fabulous landscaped gardens and complimentary car parking. Guests can enjoy a meal in Maxine's bar and restaurant where classic British cooking is given a modern twist.. Guests are also offered VIP use of Bannatyne's Health Club, a leisurely ten minute stroll from the hotel.

£ **Details of short breaks available on request.**

See also Colour Advertisement on page 17

## TEESDALE HOTEL

**Market Place, Middleton-in-Teesdale DL12 0QG**
**Tel: 01833 640264 • Fax: 01833 640651**
**website: www.freepages.co.uk/teesdale/**

Relax in our charming old world country inn, known for excellent food and wines. In an area of outstanding natural beauty with stunning scenery in every direction. High Force and Cauldron Snout waterfalls, wooded valleys, moorland and hills – wonderful walking country. Golf nearby. Close to Raby Castle, Bowes Museum, Beamish, Durham Cathedral, Metrocentre and the Lakes.

£ **Special 3 night break £99 per person dinner, bed and breakfast. All rooms en suite. Applicable 1st November to 31st March excluding Christmas and New Year. Single supplement £5 per person per night.**

# Gloucestershire

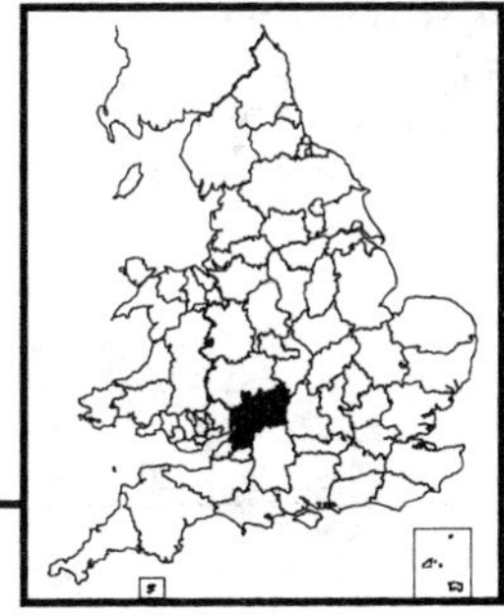

See also Colour Advertisement on page 18

## THE COMPASS INN

Tormarton, Near Badminton GL9 1JB
Tel: 01454 218242 • Fax: 01454 218741

Standing in its own grounds of six acres in the heart of the country, The Compass Inn has easy access to the M4 and M5; Heathrow one and a quarter hours by car. Ideally situated for visiting Bath, Bristol, Wells and the Cotswolds; easy access to the Wye Valley and the Royal Forest of Dean. Leisure activities which can be arranged locally include clay pigeon shooting, hot-air ballooning and horse riding. All guest rooms are en suite, with colour TV, direct-dial telephone and tea/coffee making. Restaurant and buffet open daily, bars offer a choice of real ales and a range of country wines. Unique enclosed Orangery, pleasant lawns and gardens.

£ **Short break details available on request.**

## BEECHMOUNT

ETC ◆◆◆

Birdlip GL4 8JH
Tel & Fax: 01452 862262

In the centre of Birdlip village, conveniently situated for many interesting places, picturesque views with lovely walks and an excellent base for touring the Cotswolds. Bedrooms are equipped to a high standard, all having washbasins; some en suite facilities; bathroom, separate shower; toilet. Children welcome at reduced rates, cot, high chair provided. Pets by arrangement. Open January to December. Choice of menu for breakfast. Small family-run guest house, highly recommended, and with competitive rates. Non-smoking.

£ **Bed and Breakfast from £19 per person; Evening Meal by prior arrangement, using home produce when available.**

## CHARLTON KINGS HOTEL

ETC/AA/RAC ★★★

London Road, Cheltenham GL52 6UU
Tel: 01242 231061 • Fax: 01242 241900
e-mail: enquiries@charltonkingshotel.co.uk • website: www.charltonkingshotel.co.uk

The ideal venue for Cheltenham and the Cotswolds. This pretty Victorian building began its life as a hotel only 10 years ago and is now firmly established, offering fine dining and excellent accommodation, with the kind of service only a small hotel can provide. It is ideally situated to tour the Cotswolds, only two miles from Cheltenham town centre, in an Area of Outstanding Natural Beauty. It has ample parking, so leave your car and enjoy one of the many local walks. All bedrooms are en suite and beautifully refurbished; most have views of the Cotswold Hills. Please do not hesitate to call for a brochure.

£ **A double en suite room from £47.50 per person for 1 night, £42.50 per person for 3 nights or £36.50pp for 5 nights inc. Full English Breakfast.**

## PARKVIEW

**4 Pittville Crescent, Cheltenham GL52 2QZ**
**Tel: 01242 575567**
**e-mail: jospa@tr250.freeserve.co.uk**

We offer accommodation in Cheltenham's nicest area but only ten minutes' walk from the centre. The bedrooms are large and airy and have TV, tea, coffee and provide views onto Pittville Park. This fine Regency house is inspected annually by the Tourist Authority; the RAC and "Which?" Bed and Breakfast Guide also inspect. Cheltenham is famous for horse racing and festivals of music and literature while nearby Prestbury is the most haunted village in England. The Cotswold villages stand in the surrounding hills while Stratford is one hour's drive. Tours can be arranged.

£ **Bed and Breakfast from £22 to £25 per person.**

## BELLS HOTEL

See also Colour Advertisement on page 18

**Lords Hill, Coleford GL16 8BE**
**Tel: 01594 832583 • Fax: 01594 832584**
**e-mail: enquiries@bells-hotel.co.uk • website: www.bellshotel.co.uk**

Family owned hotel established in 1971. Visit the beautiful Forest of Dean and Wye Valley. Close to Monmouth, Gloucester, National Birds of Prey Centre. Own 18 hole Golf Course - special Golf breaks available. Tennis court and bowling green all on site. 52 en suite bedrooms. Bar and restaurant open all day. Large car park.

£ **November 2002 to March 2003: Midweek Breaks from £40pppn; Bed and Breakfast from £35 per room; Half Board rates include complimentary golf. Weekend Breaks April to November 2003 from £140 including complimentary golf and Sunday lunch.**

## KILMORIE SMALLHOLDING

ETC ◆◆◆◆

**Gloucester Road, Corse, Staunton, Near Gloucester GL19 3RQ**
**Tel & Fax: 01452 840224**
**e-mail: sheila-barnfield@supanet.com**

Quality all ground floor accommodation,"Kilmorie" is Grade II Listed (c1848) within conservation area in a lovely part of Gloucestershire, deceptively spacious, yet cosy, tastefully furnished. Double, twin, family or single bedrooms all having tea trays, colour TVs, radios and H&C. Mostly en suite facilities. Very comfortable guests' lounge, traditional home cooking is served in the separate dining room, overlooking large garden where there are seats to relax, watch our free range hens (who provide excellent eggs for breakfast), or the wild birds and butterflies which we encourage to visit. Perhaps walk waymarked farmland footpaths which start here. Children may "help" with our child's pony and free range hens. Rural yet ideally situated to visit Cotswolds, Royal Forest of Dean, Wye Valley and Malvern Hills. Children over 5 years. Ample parking.

£ **3-course evening Dinner, Bed and full English Breakfast from £26. Bed and Breakfast from £18.**

## COURT FARM

See also Colour Advertisement on page 18

**Randwick, Stroud GL6 6HH**
**Tel: 01453 764210**
**e-mail: JohnETaylor@courfarm.freeserve.co.uk**

17th century beamed farmhouse with large en suite bedrooms, on small farm in the middle of the village. Large, pretty garden for guests to enjoy. From the Cotswold escarpment there are beautiful views over the Stroud valleys and the Severn Vale; NT woods above the village. Convenient overnight stop or good base for longer visits. Local attractions include Westonbirt Arboretum, Slimbridge Wildfowl Trust, Berkeley Castle, Gloucester Cathedral and Docks. Two village pubs can provide meals. We can arrange and advise on a wide range of walks. Non-smoking. Children and pets welcome. Please call for a brochure.

£ **Short break details on request.**

# Hampshire

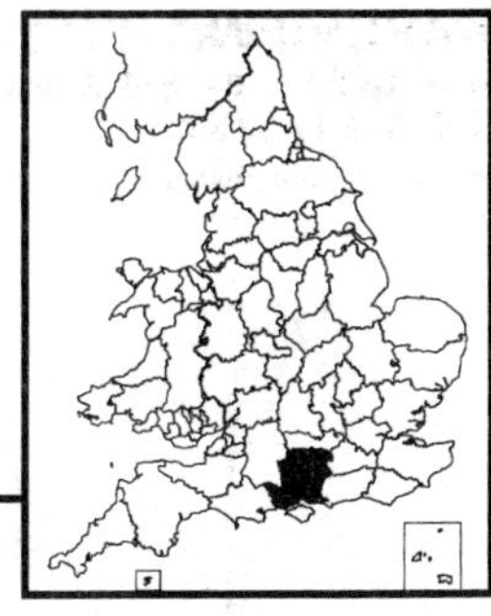

## THE WATERSPLASH HOTEL

**The Rise, Brockenhurst SO42 7ZP**
**Tel: 01590 622344 • Fax: 01590 624047**

Located in Brockenhurst, a New Forest village within easy reach of all that this 'Forest of Kings' has to offer. We provide all the comforts of a small family-run country house hotel in peaceful and secluded surroundings. A lovely swimming pool is set amidst the charming gardens. All of the 23 bedrooms are en suite, with colour TV, tea/coffee facilities and direct-dial telephones. Cuisine is fine English Fare, including trout and venison. Luxurious bar lounge with large selection of malts. Ample parking. Les Routiers, Ashley Courtenay.

£ **Terms on application.**

See also Colour Advertisement on page 19

## WHITE ROSE HOTEL

**ETC/AA ★★**

**Village Centre, Sway, Near Lymington SO41 6BA**
**Tel: 01590 682754 • Fax: 01590 682955**

An elegant Edwardian country house set on the fringe of the New Forest, the family-run White Rose stands in five acres of delightful grounds with an open air swimming pool. The hotel has thoughtfully planned accommodation on two floors linked by a lift. Guest rooms have en suite facilities, colour television, direct-dial telephone incorporating alarm call and baby listening features, and tea and coffee-making facilities. A most attractive lounge bar enjoys panoramic views over the gardens and is the ideal setting for an aperitif prior to consideration of a noteworthy à la carte and table d'hôte selection in the restaurant, vegetarian and special diets being willingly catered for.

£ **Short Break details on request.**

## "DOLPHINS"

**ETC ◆◆◆◆**

**6 Emsworth Road, Lymington SO41 9BL**
**Tel: 01590 676108/679545 • Fax: 01590 688275**
**website: www.DolphinsNewForestBandB.co.uk**

"Dolphins" is a very comfortable and homely Victorian cottage offering warm hospitality and the highest standard of accommodation. Single, twin, double and family rooms all with colour TV and tea/coffee making facilities; king-size or twin en suite available. Spacious sittingroom with open log fire (in winter) and colour satellite TV. Choice of breakfast; traditional home-cooked evening meals optional. Centrally located approximately 5 minutes' walk from railway/bus/coach stations, ferry and sea. Beautiful Forest walks, excellent cycle rides (mountain bikes with hats and maps available). Use of leisure club facilities, lovely beach chalet and mountain bikes. Children half price. Visa/Mastercard accepted. Please write, telephone or fax for brochure. Open all year.

£ **From £18.00 pppn; bargain Winter Breaks at greatly reduced prices.**

## PENNY FARTHING HOTEL

ETC/AA/RAC ◆◆◆◆

Romsey Road, Lyndhurst SO43 7AA
Tel: 023 8028 4422• Fax: 023 8028 4488
website: www.pennyfarthinghotel.co.uk

The Penny Farthing is a cheerful small Hotel ideally situated in Lyndhurst village centre, the capital of "The New Forest". The Hotel offers en suite single, double, twin and family rooms with direct dial telephones, tea/coffee tray, colour TV and clock radios. We also have some neighbouring cottages available as Hotel annexe rooms or on a self-catering basis. These have been totally refitted, much with "Laura Ashley", and offer a quieter, more exclusive accommodation. The hotel has a licensed bar, private car park and bicycle store. Lyndhurst has a charming variety of shops, restaurants, pubs, bistros and "The New Forest Information Centre and Museum".

£ **Terms on application.**

## BRAMBLE HILL HOTEL

ETC ★★

Bramshaw, Near Lyndhurst SO43 7JG
Tel: 023 8081 3165 • Fax: 023 8081 2126

Peacefully located in tranquil surroundings, this country house hotel is only three miles from Junction 1 of the M27 and is set in ancient woodland with 30 acres of glades, lawns and shrubbery to enjoy. Ideal for country walks and horse riding. A short drive from many places of interest including Salisbury, Stonehenge, Winchester and Beaulieu. All bedrooms have en suite bathrooms, and some have antique four-poster beds. Cosy public bar and restaurant. A warm friendly welcome and good home cooking assured.

£ **Three day Special Breaks, weekly terms, daily rates – please phone for details.**

See also Colour Advertisement on page 19

## BUSKETTS LAWN HOTEL

ETC/AA/RAC ★★

Woodlands, New Forest, Near Southhampton SO4O 7GL
Tel: 023 8029 2272/3417 • Fax: 023 8029 2487
e-mail: enquiries@buskettslawnhotel.co.uk • website: www.buskettslawnhotel.co.uk

A warm and comfortable, family-run country house in the delightful setting of the New Forest. All the well appointed bedrooms have en suite facilities, colour television, radio, direct dial telephone, hairdryer, trouser press and tea and coffee making facilities; all with mini fridges. Excellent food is offered in the restaurant, and service is friendly yet courteous. There is dancing at the hotel some weekends. Heated seasonal swimming pool, mini football pitch, putting and croquet, while riding, golf and fishing are nearby. Send for colour brochure. Established 1968.

£ **Special short breaks available all year round.**

See also Colour Advertisement on page 19

## THE WOODLANDS LODGE HOTEL

ETC/AA ★★★

Bartley Road, Woodlands, New Forest SO40 7GN
Tel: 023 8029 2257 • Fax: 023 8029 3090
e-mail: reception@woodlands-lodge.co.uk • website: www.woodlands-lodge.co.uk

The Woodlands Lodge Hotel is a luxuriously restored Georgian Country house, set within the beautiful New Forest, yet only 15 minutes from Southampton. Our attractive gardens have direct access to the forest, which are ideal for romantic walks. Golf, fishing and horse riding are available and the hotel is perfectly situated for touring the area. All bedrooms enjoy full en-suite facilities of whirlpool bath and separate shower and have king size beds, satellite TV, hairdryer, trouser press etc. Our four-course menu is changed daily to make use of fresh local produce and has two AA Rosettes for excellence. Woodlands Lodge – where a warm welcome awaits you.

£ **Two night break in a luxury room, breakfast and dinner, from £141 pp. Extra nights from £70. Discounted winter breaks; open Christmas and New Year.**

# Herefordshire

See also Colour Advertisement on page 20

## BELMONT LODGE & GOLF

Belmont, Hereford HR2 9SA
Tel: 01432 352666
e-mail: info@belmont-hereford.co.uk • website: www.belmont-hereford.co.uk

Belmont is situated along the beautiful River Wye, yet conveniently located just a few minutes' drive from the historic Cathedral City of Hereford - what better place to stay or play? The lodge offers 30 purpose-built hotel rooms with splendid views over the golf course and river. Whatever the standard of your golf, you will enjoy the 18 hole 6511 yard Par 72 Belmont Golf Course and its picture postcard scenery. A warm, friendly, personal service awaits you from our team of dedicated staff whose aim is to provide you with quality service - hotel, golf, meetings and functions, fishing, food and drink - all at affordable prices.

£ **Short break prices available on request.**

See also Colour Advertisement on page 20

## THE BOWENS COUNTRY HOUSE & RESTAURANT

ETC/AA ◆◆◆◆

Fownhope HR1 4PS
Tel & Fax: 01432 860430

Delightful Georgian house set in the peaceful Wye Valley village of Fownhope, midway between Hereford and Ross-on-Wye (on the B4224). Perfect centre for walking and touring - Wye Valley, Welsh Marches, Malverns, Brecon Beacons and Black and White Villages. Ten comfortable, well-appointed rooms, four of which are on the ground floor, all with full en suite facilities, TV, telephone and tea trays. Superb home cooked meals, vegetarians welcome. Fully licensed bar and good wine list. Large attractive garden with putting green and grass tennis court (summer months only). Ample private parking. Open all year.

£ **2 nights Bed and Breakfast from £65.00 per person; 2 nights Dinner, Bed and Breakfast packages available.**

## MAINOAKS FARM COTTAGES

ETC ★★★/★★★★

Goodrich, Ross-on-Wye
Tel: 01531 650448
website: www.mainoaks.co.uk

Set in 80 acres of pasture and woodland beside the River Wye in an area of outstanding natural beauty with an abundance of wildlife, this 15th century Listed farm has recently been converted to form six cottages of different size and individual character. All with exposed beams, pine furniture, heating, fully-equipped kitchens with microwaves, washer/ dryers, colour TV. Private gardens and barbecue area. Linen and towels provided. An ideal base for touring, beautiful walks, fishing, canoeing, pony trekking, bird-watching or just relaxing in this beautiful tranquil spot. Open all year. Pets by arrangement. Details from Mrs P. Unwin, Hill House, Chase End, Bromsberrow, Ledbury, Herefordshire HR8 1SE

£ **Short break details on request.**

## THE NEW PRIORY HOTEL

ETC ★★

**Stretton, Sugwas HR4 7AR**
**Tel: 01432 760264 • Fax: 01432 761809**
**e-mail: newprioryhotel@ukonline.co.uk • website: www.newprioryhotel.co.uk**

Originally built in the 18th century as a vicarage and situated just a short distance from the city of Hereford, The New Priory Hotel has a wide range of accommodation to suit everybody's needs, including twins, doubles, singles and family rooms, all en suite and with views of the surrounding countryside. The Priory Restaurant offers set meals or an à la carte menu to both residents and non-residents. There are also two bars which have open fires for winter warmth, a pool table, comfortable lounge with large TV and a large garden for children to play in.

£ **Terms available on request.**

## DOCKLOW MANOR

**Leominster HR6 0RX**
**Tel: 01568 760668**
**website: www.docklow-manor.co.uk**

Quietly secluded in five acres of garden and woodland, three delightful stone cottages have been simply but stylishly refurbished by the new owners. Guests are welcome to explore the extensive grounds, which enjoy superb westerly views towards the Black Mountains. Table tennis, croquet and trampolining are all available, with excellent fishing, golf and walking nearby. Dinners can be arranged at weekends or for special occasions, served in your own cottage or at the manor house. Docklow is ideally positioned for visiting the beautiful town of Ludlow, the Welsh border castles and market towns and the Malvern Hills.

£ **Open all year including Christmas and New Year. Short breaks low season. Terms on request.**

## COURT HOUSE

**Rowlestone, Pontrilas, Hereford HR2 0DW**
**Tel: 01981 240944**

Court House is a Tudor-style house where a very warm welcome awaits you, situated in the tiny hamlet of Rowlestone at the lower end of the Golden Valley. Tastefully furnished accommodation consists of one double bedroom with en suite and one twin with private bathroom. Both have oak beamed vaulted ceilings, TV, hairdryer, tea/coffee making facilities and extensive views to the Black Mountains. Wonderful walks with a wealth of gardens and historic churches to visit, or just listen to the dawn chorus. Central for Hereford, Ross-on-Wye and Hay-on-Wye with its abundance of secondhand bookshops. A perfect spot for the retired with a book or even a paint brush, with its wonderful scenic views.

£ **Short break details available on request.**

## EXPLANATION OF SYMBOLS

| | |
|---|---|
| ★ | Number of Stars (English Tourism Council/AA/RAC) |
| ◆ | Number of Diamonds (English Tourism Council/AA/RAC) |
| 🐕 | Pets Welcome |
| 🐴 | Reductions for Children |
| 🎄 | Christmas Breaks |
| ♿ | Suitable for Disabled |

The symbols are arranged in the same order throughout the book so that looking down each page will give a quick comparison.

# Isle of Wight

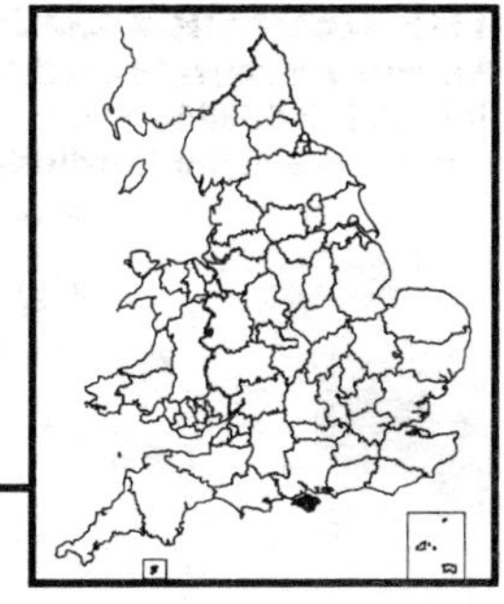

## ISLAND COTTAGE HOLIDAYS

**Tel: 01929 480080 • Fax: 01929 481070**
**e-mail: enq@islandcottageholidays.com**
**website: www.islandcottageholidays.com**

Charming individual cottages in lovely rural surroundings and close to the sea. Over 45 cottages situated throughout the Isle of Wight. Beautiful views – attractive gardens – delightful country walks. Some cottages on farms and some only a short walk from lovely sandy beaches. All equipped to a high standard and graded for quality by the Tourist Board. Sleep 1-14. For a brochure please contact: Mrs Honor Vass, The Old Vicarage, Kingston, Wareham, Dorset BH20 5LH (Tel 01929 480080; Fax: 01929 481070).

£ **Open all year. £132 – £1195 per week. Short Breaks available in low season (3 nights) £89 – £395.**

See also Colour Advertisement on page 20

## LAKE HOTEL

**Shore Road, Lower Bonchurch PO38 1RF**
**Tel: 01983 852613**

"Truly unbeatable value for money". This lovely country house hotel is set in a beautiful quiet two-acre garden on the seaward side of the olde worlde village of Bonchurch. Run by the same family for over 35 years, the hotel offers first class food and service, all in a relaxed and friendly atmosphere. All rooms are en suite with complimentary tea/coffee facilities and TV, and are decorated in the "Laura Ashley" style. We can offer an Isle of Wight car ferry inclusive price of just £160.00 for four nights' half board during March/April/May and October, and we really do believe that you will not find better value on our beautiful island.

£ **Terms on application.**

See also Colour Advertisement on page 20

## SOMERVILLE

**14 St George's Road, Shanklin PO37 6BA**
**Tel: 01983 862821**

The Somerville is a family-run hotel which offers a relaxed "home from home" atmosphere, with seven en suite bedrooms, all heated and with colour TV and beverage trays. There is also a licensed bar, a non-smoking lounge, dining room and off-road parking. The hotel is situated very close to cliff path, nearby town and beautiful Old Village and Keats Green. With a friendly atmosphere, comfortable bedrooms and excellent breakfasts, we are an ideal base from which to explore the island.

£ **Bed and Breakfast from £20 per night.**

See also Colour Advertisement on page 21

## THE BEDFORD LODGE HOTEL

ETC ◆◆◆◆

**4 Chine Avenue, Shanklin Old Village PO37 6AQ**
**Tel: 01983 862416 • Fax: 01983 868704**
**e-mail: mail@bedfordlodge.co.uk • website: www.bedfordlodge.co.uk**

Privately owned and personally-run, the Bedford Lodge is set in its own south-facing, private gardens, with sloping lawns, mature trees, flowering bushes and a sun terrace with views towards The Downs - a perfect setting to watch the world go by. All twelve of the en suite bedrooms are located on either the ground floor (some with direct access to the gardens), first or second floors and are equipped with tea and coffee making facilities, central heating, colour TV's and duvets. The licensed bar is open all day and is conveniently located on the ground floor. The breakfast room overlooks the garden and offers a choice of menu suitable for carnivores, vegetarians, healthy or unhealthy guests!

£ **Short break details available on request.**

## BRAEMAR HOTEL

RAC ◆◆◆

**1 Grange Road, Shanklin PO37 6NN**
**Tel & Fax: 01983 863172**

Tucked away in Shanklin's Old Village, this family-run licensed hotel is ideally located to offer all the pleasures of the Isle of Wight. From the moment you enter the Braemar, a happy, friendly atmosphere prevails, that makes for an unforgettable holiday. All 11 en suite bedrooms have colour TV, radio and tea/coffee making facilities; four-poster rooms, family and ground floor bedrooms also available. The bright dining room offers a comprehensive choice of menu (special diets catered for). Well-behaved dogs welcome.

£ **Short break details on request.**

## HAZELWOOD HOTEL

ETC ◆◆◆

**14 Clarence Road, Shanklin PO37 7BH**
**Tel & Fax: 01983 862824 • e-mail: barbara.tubbs@thehazelwood.free-online.co.uk**
**website: www.thehazelwood.free-online.co.uk**

Guests of all ages can enjoy the freedom of our family-run hotel with its home-from-home atmosphere and great value for money. Good home cooking with a choice of menu at dinner is served in our lovely dining room. Large TV lounge; all rooms are en suite, with family suites available; tea and coffee facilities at no extra cost; full central heating. Colour TV in all rooms. Family suites available. We also give over-55s and child reductions. Hazelwood is set in spacious grounds in a quiet tree-lined road close to the sea, station, shops and famous cliff path. Car ferry bookings can be arranged. Major credit cards accepted.

£ **Two nights B&B from £38 to £42, Evening Dinner available.**

See also Colour Advertisement on page 21

## FRENCHMAN'S COVE COUNTRY HOTEL

ETC/AA ◆◆◆

**Alum Bay Old Road, Totland PO39 0HZ**
**Tel: 01983 752227**
**website: www.frenchmanscove.co.uk**

Our delightful family-run guest house is set amongst National Trust downland, not far from the Needles and safe sandy beaches. Ideal for ramblers, birdwatchers, cyclists and those who enjoy the countryside. We have almost an acre of grounds. Cots and high chairs are available. All rooms are en suite, with colour TV and tea/coffee making facilities. Guests can relax in the cosy bar or in the attractive lounge. Also available is the Coach House, a delightfully appointed apartment (ETC 3 Stars) for two adults and two children. Please contact Sue or Chris Boatfield for details.

£ **Terms on request.**

# Kent

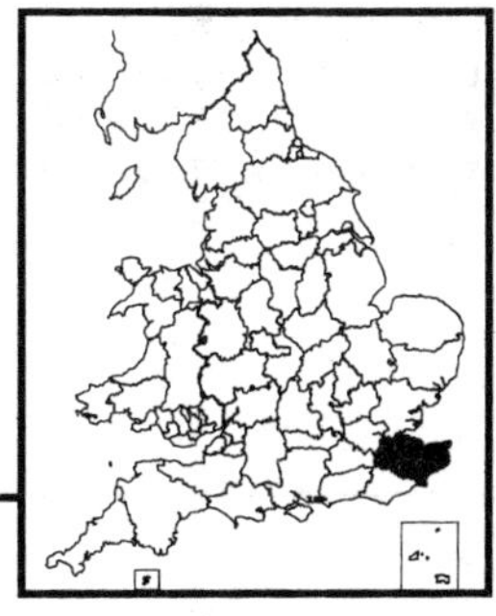

## BLERIOT'S

ETC ◆◆◆

**47 Park Avenue, Dover CT16 1HE**
**Tel: 01304 211394**

A Victorian residence set in a tree lined avenue, in the lee of Dover Castle. Within easy reach of trains, bus station, town centre, hoverport and docks. Channel Tunnel approximately 10 minutes' drive. Off-road parking. We specialise in one night 'stop-overs' and mini-breaks. Single, double, twin and family rooms with full en suite. All rooms have colour TV, tea and coffee making facilities, and are fully centrally heated. Full English breakfast served from 7am. Reduced rates for room only. Open all year. Mastercard and visa accepted.

£ **Bed & Breakfast £20 to £25. Mini-breaks £19.**

## PENNY FARTHING GUEST HOUSE

AA/RAC ◆◆◆

**109 Maison Dieu Road, Dover CT16 1RT**
**Tel: 01304 205563 • Fax: 01304 204439**
**e-mail: pennyfarthing.dover@btinternet.com • website: www.pennyfarthingdover.com**

Spacious and comfortable Victorian Guest House privately owned, minutes away from ferries, hoverport, trains and Tunnel. Ideally situated for restaurants, banks, shops and all other amenities. We cater for both overnight and short term stays offering a high standard at reasonable prices. All of our rooms feature en suite or with private shower, colour TV, tea/coffee making facilities. Guests have a wide choice of breakfasts, provision is made for early departures. Quotes for family rooms or 'room only' are available on request. Parking space available on the forecourt. Member of the White Cliffs of Dover Hotel & Guest House Group. Non-smoking establishment.

£ **Short Break details available on request.**

**FREE or REDUCED RATE entry to Holiday Visits and Attractions - see our READER'S OFFER VOUCHERS on pages 47 - 58**

# Lancashire

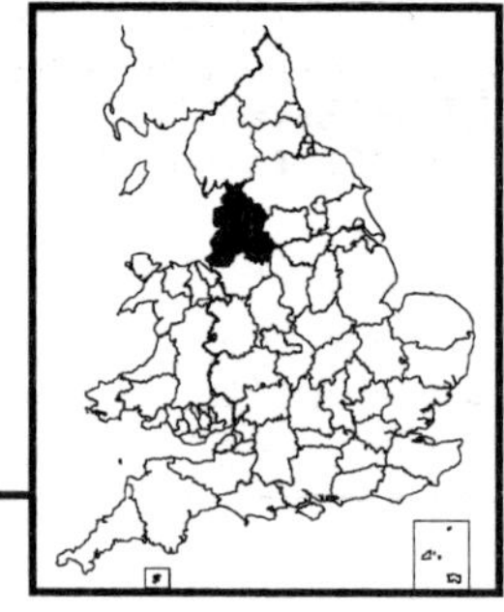

See also Colour Advertisement on page 21

## CASTLEMERE HOTEL

AA ◆◆◆

**13 Shaftesbury Avenue, North Shore, Blackpool FY2 9QQ**
**Tel: 01253 352430 • Fax: 01253 350116**
**e-mail: bookings@hotelcastlemere.co.uk • website: www.hotelcastlemere.co.uk**

The Castlemere is a licensed family run hotel. The resident proprietors Dave and Sue Hayward have been running the Castlemere for the past 11 years and have established an excellent clientele. The hotel is situated in the very pleasant North Shore area of Blackpool, adjacent to the delightful Queen's Promenade with its lovely views across the Irish Sea. The busy town centre, bus and train stations are convenient and a range of entertainment opportunities for all ages and tastes, including a Casino and Golf Course, are within an easy walk or a short tram ride. Blackpool is ideally situated for visiting the Dales, Lake District, "Bronte" Country and the Fylde Coast. Easy access to M55. All rooms are en suite with central heating, colour TV , alarm clock radios, tea-making facilities and hairdryers. Ironing facilities are also available. The Castlemere has a cosy bar, where evening snacks are available. Evening Dinner is optional. Open all year. Car Park. All major credit cards accepted. FHG Diploma winner.

£ **From £25 per day B&B. Winter Break terms on application.**

## RAKEFOOT FARM

ETC◆◆◆◆ ETC ★★★/★★★★

**Chaigley, Near Clitheroe BB7 3LY**
**Tel: (Chipping) 01995 61332/07889 279063 • Fax: 01995 61296**
**e-mail: info@rakefootfarm.co.uk • website: www.rakefootfarm.co.uk**

Family farm peacefully situated in the beautiful countryside of the Ribble Valley in the Forest of Bowland, with panoramic views. Ideally placed for touring Coast, Dales and Lakes. 8 miles M6 Junction 31a. Superb walks, golf and horse riding nearby, or visit pretty villages and factory shops. Warm welcome whether on holiday or business, refreshments on arrival. BED AND BREAKFAST or SELF-CATERING in 17th century farmhouse and traditional stone barn conversion. Wood-burning stoves, central heating, exposed beams and stonework. Most bedrooms en suite, some ground floor. Excellent home cooked meals, pubs/restaurants nearby. Indoor/outdoor play areas, gardens and patios. Dogs by arrangement. Laundry. NWTB AWARD FOR SELF-CATERING HOLIDAY OF THE YEAR 2000

£ **B&B £17.50 - £25. S/C four properties £80 - £507. Three can be internally interlinked.**

## COCKERHAM SANDS COUNTRY PARK

**Cockerham, Lancaster LA2 0BB**
**Tel: 01524 751387**

A family park situated on an inlet to the Irish Sea. Access to 15 miles of the new Lancashire Coastal Walk. Less than an hour to the Lake District, Morecambe or Blackpool. There is a heated swimming pool (June to September), shop, amusement arcade, launderette and the wonderful Cockerham Country Club with live entertainment at weekends. Modern four and six-berth fully equipped caravans for hire plus touring pitches with electric hook-up. Controlled dogs welcome. Write or telephone for brochure. Caravan Holiday Park of the Year 1999 (United Utilities/ NWTB Tourism Awards).

£ **Short Break details on request.**

## THE CHADWICK HOTEL

ETC/AA/RAC ★★★

**South Promenade, Lytham St Annes FY8 1NP**
**Tel: 01253 720061**
**website: www.thechadwickhotel.com**

Enjoy the luxury of this modern family-run 70-bedroom hotel which is renowned for good food and comfortable bedrooms, all of which have private facilities and colour TV with satellite. Many rooms with spa baths, also some with four-posters. Other facilities include an indoor swimming pool designed on an Ancient Greek theme and also a spa bath, sauna, Turkish room, solarium, games room, gym, soft play adventure area. North West Tourist Board Hotel of the Year Award 1999.

£ **Room and breakfast from £34.00pp; dinner, room and breakfast from £39.95pp.**

## BROADWATER HOTEL

ETC ◆◆

**356 Marine Road, East Promenade, Morecambe LA4 5AQ**
**Tel: 01524 411333**

The Broadwater is a small friendly hotel, situated on the select East Promenade with glorious views of Morecambe Bay and Lakeland Mountains. Only five minutes' walk from the town centre, shops and amusements. We offer every comfort and the very best of foods varied and plentiful with choice of menu. All rooms en suite with heating, colour TV and tea making facilities. A perfect base for touring, the Broadwater is only 45 minutes' drive away from Blackpool, Yorkshire Dales and Lake District, and 10 minutes from the historic city of Lancaster. Open all year. Dinner available.

£ **Bed and Breakfast from £18. Short Break details on request.**

## DALMENY HOTEL

ETC ★★★

**19-33 South Promenade, St Annes on Sea FY8 1LX**
**Tel: 01253 712236 • Fax: 01253 724447**
**e-mail: reservations@dalmeny.demon.co.uk**

Ideally situated on the seafront in St Annes overlooking the promenade and gardens, and within walking distance of the town centre. Accommodation includes 132 bedrooms – a choice of standard, premier or family suites for up to eight people. The hotel has a choice of three restaurants and also boasts an extensive leisure complex, indoor swimming pool and beauty salon. Family and children's entertainment is scheduled during the holiday periods and at weekends, and with the neighbouring resort of Blackpool with its many attractions only a short bus ride away, your stay can be as relaxing or as busy as you like.

£ **Short Break details on request.**

See also Colour Advertisement on page 21

## FERRARI'S COUNTRY HOUSE HOTEL & RESTAURANT

**Chipping Road, Thornley, Longridge, Preston PR3 2TB**
**Tel: 01772 783148**
**e-mail: info@ferrariscountryhouse.co.uk • website: www.ferrariscountryhouse.co.uk**

You can be assured of a warm welcome from Susan, Ginio and family at Ferrari's, in the heart of the Ribble Valley. The Country House offers 14 bedrooms, 5 of which are de luxe standard; some have jacuzzis and four-poster beds. As well as the main dining room which overlooks the beautifully laid out gardens, there are three further function rooms, a fully licensed bar and a residents' lounge. The proprietors pride themselves on satisfying the personal needs of their guests in a friendly and comfortable atmosphere. Whether for business or pleasure, Ferrari's will offer you the best in quality, service and value for money.

£ **Short break terms available on request.**

# Leicestershire

## including Rutland

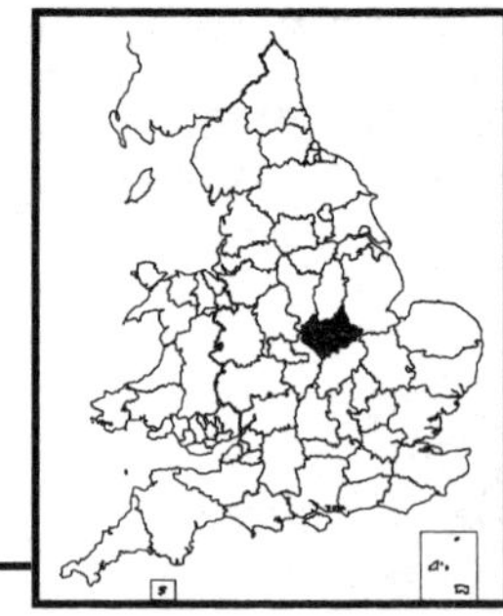

### THE HIGHBURY GUEST HOUSE

ETC ◆◆◆

**146 Leicester Road, Loughborough LE11 2AQ**
**Tel: 01509 230545 • Fax: 01509 233086**
**e-mail: emkhighbury@supanet.com • website: www.thehighburyhouse.co.uk**

The Highbury is set back from the road, has double glazing and is surrounded by a well-developed and cared for private garden which is frequently used in warm weather for sun bathing. The entrance hall is spacious. It is lightened by a leaded stained glass window at the top of the staircase.There's a pleasant conservatory type dining/sitting room. A large secluded car park is situated at the back of the house. Most bedrooms are fully en suite. All rooms offer remote-control TV, tea/coffee making facilities and wash-hand basin. Located half-a-mile from Loughborough town centre.

£ **Details on request.**

# Lincolnshire

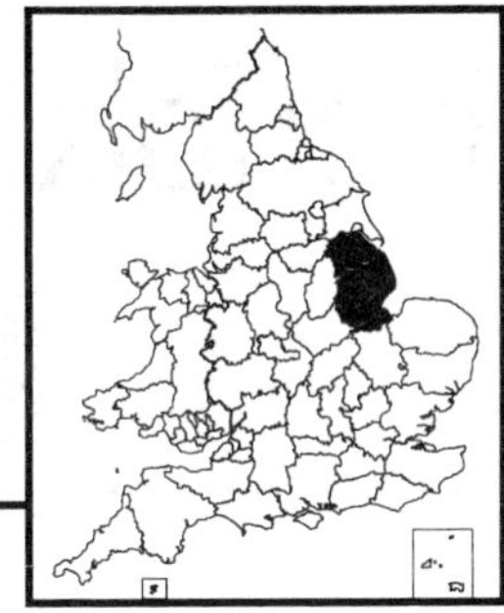

See also Colour Advertisement on page 22

## THE RED LION INN

**Main Road, Partney, Spilsby, Lincolnshire PE23 4PG**
**Tel: 01790 752271 • Fax: 01790 753360**
**e-mail: www.redlionpartney@onetel.net.uk**

Situated at the junction of the A16/A158 at Partney. Award-winning home-made food – over 20 dishes to choose from including vegetarian specials. Luxury en suite accommodation – three bedrooms, all with shower and toilet, radio, colour TV and beverage-making facilities. Ideally situated on the edge of the Lincolnshire Wolds, great for walking and sightseeing in Lincoln, Grimsby, Boston, Skegness, Horncastle and much more.

£ **Bed and full English breakfast £20pp sharing, £30 single occupancy; DB&B £45pppn or 3 nights for £110pp.**

## CLAREMONT GUEST HOUSE

**ETC/AA ◆◆**

**9-11 Witham Road, Woodhall Spa LN10 6RW**
**Tel: 01526 352000**

This traditional, unspoilt Victorian guest house in the centre of Woodhall Spa, Lincolnshire's unique resort, provides homely B&B. This is an excellent centre for touring, walking and cycling; off-street parking. Golf locally. En suite and family rooms; all rooms with tea/coffee making and TV. Good food close by.

£ **Special rates for short breaks from £15pppn.**

# Norfolk

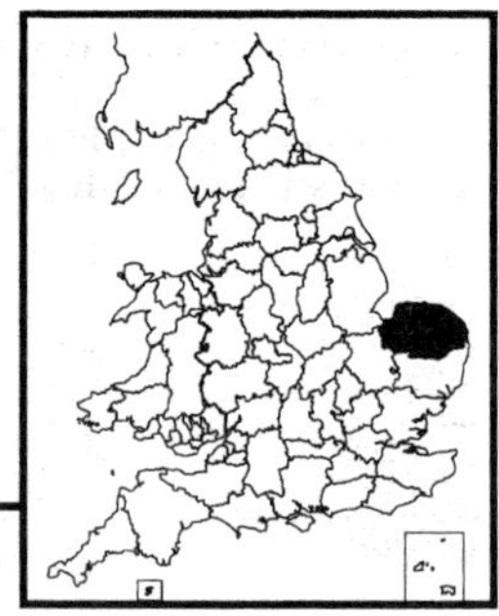

See also Colour Advertisement on page 23

## CAREFREE HOLIDAYS

Tel: 01493 732176
website: www.carefree-holidays.co.uk

Inexpensive 'live as you please' self-catering holidays in beautiful Norfolk. Chalets, bungalows and cottages near Great Yarmouth and the Norfolk Broads. The Laurels: superb bungalows close to beach, private car park; The Jasmines: lovely cottages, 100 yards to golden sandy beach; Belle-Aire: family chalets, clubhouse, free electricity. Debit/credit cards accepted. Superb value for 2003 season.

£ **Short Breaks of three/four nights available all season from £58. First pet £5, second pet free.**

See also Colour Advertisement on page 22

## BLUE RIBAND HOLIDAYS

**Caister-on-Sea/Hemsby, Great Yarmouth**
Tel: 01493 730445
website: www.BlueRibandHolidays.co.uk

Great short breaks! Spring, autumn and winter three/four nights. BELLE AIRE PARK, Hemsby – luxury chalets close to beach and amenities. SEA-DELL PARK, Hemsby – detached chalets on spacious park. CAISTER BEACH – caravans in unrivalled seafront position. PARKLANDS, Hemsby – detached bungalows on private estate. All accommodation is of a very high standard and is only a short drive from Great Yarmouth. Dogs are welcome on local beaches. Open all year including Christmas and New Year. Please phone for colour brochure (seven days). Debit/credit cards accepted.

£ **Short breaks from £14.50pp based on four sharing (minimum charge £58).**

## WINTERTON VALLEY HOLIDAYS

**Winterton-on-Sea, Near Great Yarmouth**
Tel: 01493 377175
website: www.wintertonvalleyholidays.co.uk

A selection of modern superior fully appointed holiday chalets in a choice of locations near Great Yarmouth. Enjoy panoramic views of the sea from WINTERTON, a quiet and picturesque 35-acre estate minutes from the beach, while CALIFORNIA has all the usual amenities for the more adventurous holidaymaker, with free entry to the pool and clubhouse. Pets are very welcome at both sites. Details from: 15 Kingston Avenue, Caister-on-Sea, Great Yarmouth NR30 5ET

£ **Terms and colour brochure on request.**

## STUART HOUSE HOTEL

ETC ★★

**35 Goodwins Road, King's Lynn PE30 5QX**
**Tel: 01553 772169; Fax: 01553 774788**
**e-mail: stuarthousehotel@btinternet.com • website: www.stuart-house-hotel.co.uk**

Quietly situated within its own grounds, the Hotel is just a short walk through the park from the medieval town centre and historic port of King's Lynn. Comfortable, individually-styled bedrooms. Superb restaurant and cosy "CAMRA – Good Beer Guide" Listed Bar. Ideally situated for Royal Sandringham, the Norfolk countryside and beach.

**£ Seasonal Bargain Breaks – the longer the stay, the better the bargain! Phone for details. From £25pppn.**

See also Colour Advertisement on page 23

## BEECHWOOD HOTEL

ETC/AA ★★

**Cromer Road, North Walsham NR28 0HD**
**Tel: 01692 403231**
**e-mail: info@beechwood-hotel.co.uk • website: www.beechwood-hotel.co.uk**

The combination of an elegant ivy-clad Georgian house dating back to 1800, surrounded by well-laid out gardens, with a lovely ambience generated by the proprietors' warm welcome and the attentive staff, has created a very special country house-style hotel in East Anglia. The bedrooms are delightful, with big windows and antique furniture. The atmosphere in the restaurant reflects the contentment of diners appreciating a menu that features fresh local produce and changes daily. It includes classic English dishes and Head Chef Steven Norgate's personal suggestions. ETC Gold Award, AA Two Red Stars.

**£ From 2 Feb-29 June & 2-30 Nov 2003 inclusive & on half-board Short Breaks of 2 nights, complimentary Sunday night accommodation & breakfast is available for a third night provided guests book a table in the restaurant for dinner.**

## SPIXWORTH HALL COTTAGES

ETC ★★★ and ★★★★ ♿

**Grange Farm, Buxton Road, Spixworth NR10 3PR**
**Tel: 01603 898190**
**e-mail: hallcottages@btinternet.com • website: www.hallcottages.co.uk**

Delightful 18th century coachman's cottage, Lodge Cottage and award-winning stable conversions in seclusion on our own farm. Ideal for exploring Norwich, the broads and countryside. Very well furnished and equipped, with central heating, log fires, secure gardens, games barn and children's play area, farm walks and fishing, tennis and space to unwind. We offer a warm welcome. Contact us for further details. National Accessibility Scheme, Level 4. CLA Farm Buildings Award. Broadlands Enhancement Award.

**£ Short Autumn to Spring weekend or midweek breaks from £150. Weekly rates from £220 to £640.**

## EXPLANATION OF SYMBOLS

| | |
|---|---|
| ★ | Number of Stars (English Tourism Council/AA/RAC) |
| ◆ | Number of Diamonds (English Tourism Council/AA/RAC) |
| 🐕 | Pets Welcome |
| (rocking horse) | Reductions for Children |
| (tree) | Christmas Breaks |
| ♿ | Suitable for Disabled |

The symbols are arranged in the same order throughout the book so that looking down each page will give a quick comparison.

## THE LIFEBOAT INN

**Ship Lane, Thornham PE36 6LT**
**Tel: 01485 512236 • Fax: 01485 512323**
**website: www.lifeboatinn.co.uk**

ETC ★★

A lovely 16th century traditional English inn, the Lifeboat is today some little way from the sea but the briny is still within sight in the distance. The bar with its low ceiling, pillars and uneven floor conjured up visions of the unhurried life of years gone by as we sampled an excellent pint of real ale and tucked into our fisherman's pie. Daily specials increase the choice of freshly prepared dishes available in the bar; or one may dine in the restaurant, where a frequently changing menu makes the best of local seasonal produce. All the comfortable bedrooms have en suite bathrooms and most enjoy views over the harbour to the sea. AA Rosette.

£ **Short break details on request.**

## THE BROADS HOTEL

**Station Road, Wroxham, Norwich NR12 8UR**
**Tel: 01603 782869 • Fax: 01603 784066**

Comfortable hotel renowned for its high standard cuisine. Owned and run by dog-loving family. Ideally situated for boating, fishing and exploring the beautiful Norfolk countryside and coastline. All rooms fully en suite with tea/coffee making facilities, colour TV etc. Please telephone for brochure.

£ **Winter Weekend Breaks and four-day Christmas House Party.**

# Northumberland

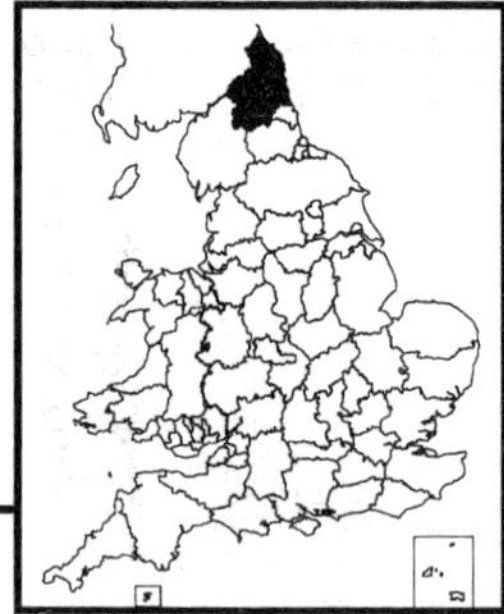

## THE HOPE & ANCHOR

**44 Northumberland Street, Alnmouth, Alnwick NE66 2RA**
**Tel: 01665 830363 • website: www.hopeandanchorholidays.co.uk**
**e-mail: debbiephilipson@hope&anchorholidays.fsnet.co.uk**

See also Colour Advertisement on page 24

A cosy coastal pub/hotel which is renowned for its friendly atmosphere and excellent freshly prepared home cooking. It has eight rooms, all en suite. Nearby there are beautiful beaches, golf courses and plenty of places for walking or cycling. Why not book the whole hotel, it is perfect for family get-togethers or for business conferences (special rates apply). Open all year.

£ **Short break details on request.**

# Oxfordshire

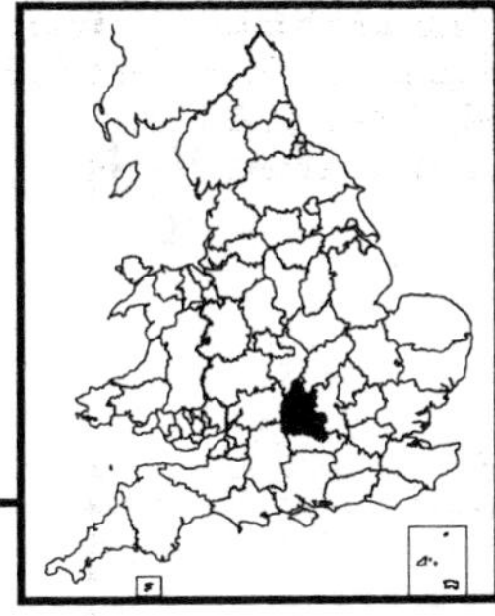

See also Colour Advertisement on page 24

## BANBURY HILL FARM

**Enstone Road, Charlbury OX7 3JH**
**Freephone 0800 0853474 • Tel: 01608 810314 • Fax: 01608 811891**
**e-mail: bookings@gfwiddows.f9.co.uk • website: www.charlburyoxfordaccom.co.uk**

At Banbury Hill Farm we offer single, twin/double en suite and family rooms en suite. A number of en suite rooms are also available on the ground floor in the converted Old Piggery. All rooms have tea/coffee facilities and colour TV. In the morning all guests come to the main farmhouse for breakfast. Also available are self-catering cottages, beautifully appointed with all modern facilities and extensive views of the Cotswold Hills.

£ **Short break details available on request.**

## FARINGDON HOTEL

**ETC ★★**

**1 Market Place, Faringdon SN7 7HL**
**Tel: 01367 240536 • Fax: 01367 243250**

Situated near the 12th century parish church, the Farringdon Hotel stands on the site of what is believed to have been the Palace of Alfred the Great. This old coaching inn, with 20 en suite bedrooms, has a reputation for comfort and hospitality. The hotel also provides an ideal touring base for Oxford and the Cotswolds. Situated in the Vale of the White Horse, off the A420 midway between Swindon and the famous University town of Oxford. The hotel also offers authentic Thai cuisine.

£ **Short break details on request.**

## KILLINGWORTH CASTLE INN

**Glympton Road, Wootton, Woodstock OX20 1EJ**
**Tel & Fax: 01993 811401**
**e-mail: wiggiscastle@aol.com • website: www.oxlink.co.uk/woodstock/kilcastle**

Built in 1637, this one-time coaching halt on the edge of a picturesque village. Now run by David and Susan Wiggins, the inn retains much of its original character. Acknowledged for the quality of its cask-conditioned ales, it is also known for the extensive à la carte meal selection available daily in the bar area. A small separate dining area caters for non-smokers and family parties. There is a games room and a pleasant lawned garden. Close to Blenheim Palace and the Cotswolds, this fine hostelry offers spacious en suite accommodation.

£ **Short break details on request.**

# Shropshire

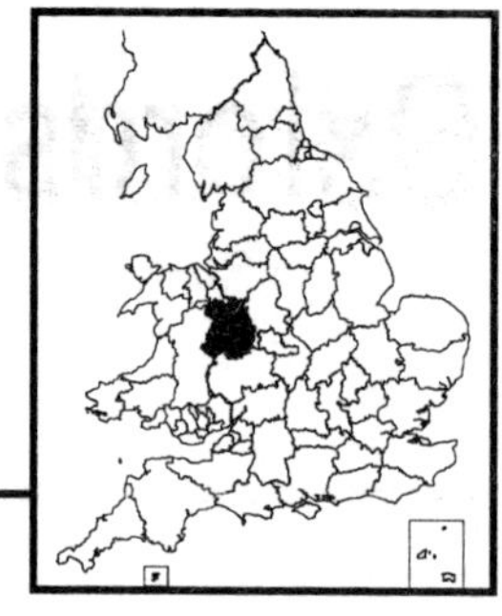

## MYND HOUSE HOTEL

**Ludlow Road, Little Stretton, Church Stretton SY6 6RB**
**Tel: 01694 722212**
**e-mail: info@myndhouse.co.uk • website: www.myndhouse.co.uk**

AA ★★

A small, family-run hotel at the foot of the Long Mynd, this Edwardian house is a great base for exploring the Stretton Hills, as well as local places of interest such as Ludlow, Ironbridge, Shrewsbury, Powis and Stokesay Castles. Comfortable en suite rooms with lovely views. The intimate restaurant serves excellent home-cooked meals, the cuisine being a fusion of East and West, using local ingredients; the bar offers a varied choice of wines. Dogs welcome free of charge.

£ **Short break details on request.**

## THE CROWN INN

**Hopton Wafers, Near Cleobury Mortimer DY14 0NB**
**Tel: 01299 270372 • Fax: 01299 271127**
**e-mail: desk@crownathopton.co.uk • website: www.crownathopton.co.uk**

ETC/AA ◆◆◆◆

It is difficult to decide whether to concentrate on cuisine, accommodation or the surroundings of this lovely old 16th century coaching inn – for all are appealing enough in themselves. Guest bedrooms have received the same loving attention to detail as public rooms, being decorated in a delightful country-cottage style and equipped with all practical necessities. Sandwiches, steaks and everything in between can be found on the excellent bar menu, and the light airy AA Rosette restaurant offers a delicious choice, prepared and presented with flair and imagination. ETC Silver Award.

£ **Short break details on request.**

## HARPER ADAMS UNIVERSITY COLLEGE

**Edgmond, Newport TF10 8NB**
**Tel: 01952 820280 • Fax: 01952 814783**
**e-mail: info@harper-adams.ac.uk • website: www.harper-adams.ac.uk**

Harper Adams is situated close to the north Shropshire / Staffordshire border in the village of Edgmond, three miles from the market town of Newport. The upper west wing of the magnificent main building is given over to eight charming guest suites, each with its own individual character. These suites are served by a private lounge and bathrooms and have superb views across Harper Adams' gardens and fields. Supplementing these suites are 180 en suite bedrooms, as well as 160 bedrooms with shared bathroom facilities. Guests are never more than a short walk away from numerous on-site facilities. Our team of domestic staff will be pleased to assist you in any way possible during your stay, and will ensure that rooms are serviced on a daily basis.

£ **Short break terms on request.**

# Somerset

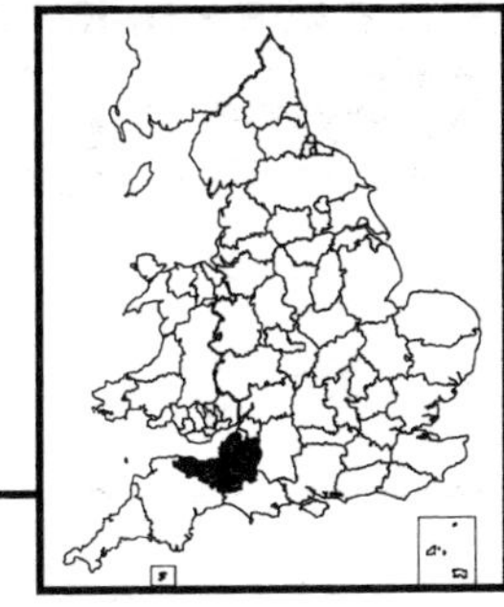

## WHITNELL FARM

**Binegar, Emborough, Radstock BA3 4UF**
**Tel: 01749 840277**

Delightful Manor House just off the B3139 Wells to Bath road. On the edge of a pretty Mendips village overlooking Cheddar Gorge, Wookey Hole. Very central for touring West Country - plenty to do and see. Garden and fields to relax in. Coast 20 miles, Bristol Airport 18 miles. 18-hole golf, fishing, riding. Ideal for a family holiday. Sleeps 2 to 8 persons. Sorry, no pets.

£ **Terms from £300 to £450 weekly.**

## THE OLD MALT HOUSE HOTEL

ETC/AA ★★

**Radford, Timsbury, Bath BA2 0QF**
**Tel: 01761 470106 • Fax: 01761 472726**
**e-mail: hotel@oldmalthouse.co.uk • website: www.oldmalthouse.co.uk**

See also Colour Advertisement on page 25

Built in 1835 as a malt house for the local brewery, this family-run country hotel is situated in a small village surrounded by beautiful countryside just 6 miles from the historic city of Bath. You will be greeted with a warm, friendly welcome and it will be our pleasure to ensure your stay is enjoyable and relaxing. There are 11 tastefully decorated bedrooms, all with en suite bath/shower rooms, colour TV, tea and coffee making facilities and stunning views across the countryside. Our restaurant serves home-cooked food using fresh local produce. Before or after your meal you may wish to enjoy a relaxing drink by the log fire in the lounge bar, where a good selection of wines and beers are served.

£ **Short break details on request.**

## PRIORS MEAD

**23 Rectory Road, Burnham-on Sea TA8 2BZ**
**Tel & Fax: 01278 782116 • Mobile: 07990 595585**
**e-mail: priorsmead@aol.com • website: www.priorsmead.co.uk**

See also Colour Advertisement on page 26

Peter and Fizz welcome guests to enjoy their enchanting Edwardian home set in half-an-acre of beautiful gardens with weeping willows, croquet and swimming pool. All three rooms have either twin or king-size beds, en suite/private facilities, washbasins, hospitality trays, colour TVs, etc. Peaceful location, walk to the sea, town, golf and tennis clubs. Ideal touring base for Bristol, Bath, Wells, Glastonbury, Wookey Hole, Cheddar and Dunster. A no-smoking home. Parking. Easy access to Junction 22 M5 for Wales, Devon and Cornwall. "Which?" Recommended.

£ **B & B from £20, singles £20. Reductions for three nights - £17pppn.**

See also Colour Advertisement on page 25

## SUNGATE HOLIDAY APARTMENTS

**Cheddar**
**Tel: 01934 842273 • Fax: 01934 741411**

In Cheddar village, close to Cheddar Gorge and the Mendip Hills, this Listed Georgian building has been thoughtfully converted into four non-smoking holiday apartments. Each apartment sleeps 2-4 and has lounge with sofa bed, TV, bedroom, bathroom, fully-equipped kitchen plus microwave. Linen supplied. Laundry facilities. Pets welcome with prior approval. Private parking. Swimming and leisure facilities nearby. Competitively priced for a short break, longer holiday or a short-term let. Bookings: Mrs Fieldhouse, "Pyrenmount", Parsons Way, Winscombe BS25 1BU.

£ **Details on request.**

## MANOR ARMS

**North Perrott, Crewkerne TA18 7SG**
**Tel & Fax: 01460 72901**

This handsome 16th century Grade II Listed building displays abundant character through its exposed stonework, inglenook fireplace and original oak beams, the bar warmed by a log fire in cool weather. Lovingly restored, the Inn has a reputation for its superb (and reasonably-priced) English fare. This is a tranquil area of picture-book villages and verdant, undulating countryside with the Dorset coast within 20 minutes' drive and a number of historic houses close at hand. Bed and Breakfast accommodation is available in both the Inn and the Coach House situated in the gardens in a quiet setting. All eight guest rooms have en suite showers and are comfortably furnished. The ideal venue for a quiet and rewarding break.

£ **B&B from £21. Special breaks available on request, including the 'Stay Free' Gourmet Break.**

See also Colour Advertisement on page 25

## LION HOTEL

AA ★★

**Bank Square, Dulverton TA22 9BU**
**Tel: 01398 323444 • Fax: 01398 323980**

The perfect headquarters for exploring the magic land of heather-clad moors, leafy lanes, nature trails, red deer and wild ponies of Exmoor, the attractive and comfortable Lion Hotel is set in the heart of the delightful little town of Dulverton, on Exmoor's southern fringe. Warm and friendly, the hotel takes great pride in the delicious home-cooked cuisine on offer in the charming restaurant. Alternatively, there is an extensive selection of meals available in the lounge bar. Full of character, guest rooms are fully en suite and have colour television, direct-dial telephone and beverage makers. Sporting activities available locally include riding, river and reservoir fishing, and golf.

£ **Details on request.**

## WESTERCLOSE HOUSE

**Withypool, Somerset TA24 7QR**
**Tel & Fax: 01643 831302**
**website: www.westerclose.f9.co.uk**

Cottages in The Exmoor National Park. Quality cottages, including bungalows, in the grounds of an old hunting lodge, overlooking the village and the beautiful Bark valley. Totally peaceful with superb views. So much to do locally - wonderful coast and countryside, and only one and a half hours from Bristol. Shop and pub three minutes away. Excellent walking and riding straight from your cottage. Very cosy with log burners and hand made furnishings. Dogs and horses most welcome. Individual gardens. Open all year. Sleep 2-7.

£ **Short Break details on request**

## SIMONSBATH HOUSE HOTEL

Simonsbath, Exmoor TA24 7SH
Tel: 01643 831259 • Fax: 01643 831557
website: www.SmoothHound.co.uk

AA ★★

The first house built on Exmoor in 1654 in the heart of the moor overlooking the River Barle and surrounded by moorland, making this the ideal location for long or short walks. Original features abound in the hotel - wood panelling and log fires to warm you on those chilly evenings. All bedrooms are en suite, with central heating, colour television, direct dial telephone, hospitality tray, hairdryer and some have four-posters. There is a relaxing lawned garden and ample off road parking. Relax and enjoy a four course evening dinner in our informal restaurant. Dogs are welcome to stay free of charge with you in your hotel bedroom or in one of our kennels with runs at the rear of the hotel. Open all year. Please telephone Andrew, Louise or Rob for our brochure or tariff. AA 74% and Red Rosette.

£ **Terms on request**

## MARSHFIELD HOTEL

Tregonwell Road, Minehead TA24 5DU
Tel: 01643 702517

ETC/AA ◆◆◆

A warm welcome is assured at this small, family-run hotel. Accommodation includes 10 en suite bedrooms each with TV, tea/coffee facilities, hair dryers, etc, and a ground floor en suite room suitable for disabled guests. Short breaks are available at certain times throughout the year, including all-inclusive golfing or riding holidays. Senior Citizens enjoy special rates. Home cooking, mainly using local produce, is served in our non-smoking dining room and special diets can be catered for on request. Wheelchair available. Exmoor National Park and a host of attractions are nearby.

£ **Bed and Breakfast £21.50pppn.**

## SEAPOINT

Porlock TA24 8QE
Tel: 01643 862289

ETC ◆◆◆◆

Comfortable Edwardian Guesthouse with spectacular views over Porlock Bay. Delicious traditional and vegetarian cuisine. Fine wines, log fires and candlelit dinners. Tastefully furnished bedrooms all en suite with colour TV, teamaking, hairdryers etc.

£ **Two-day Winter Breaks £49 per person DB&B – available November to February.**

## THE CASTLE HOTEL

Porlock TA24 8PY
Tel: 01643 862504

The Castle Hotel is a small, fully licensed family-run hotel in the centre of the lovely Exmoor village of Porlock. There are 13 en suite bedrooms, all fully heated, with colour TV and tea/coffee making facilities. The hotel offers everything from bar snacks to three-course meals which may be taken in the bar or the restaurant. Children and pets are most welcome. Good range of real ales; skittles, darts and pool.

£ **Special Breaks available – extremely good rates.**

See also Colour Advertisement on page 26

See also Colour Advertisement on page 26

## QUANTOCK ORCHARD CARAVAN PARK

ETC ★★★★★

**Flaxpool, Crowcombe, Near Taunton TA4 4AW**
**Tel: 01984 618618**
**e-mail: qocp@flaxpool.freeserve.co.uk • website: www.flaxpool.freeserve.co.uk**

The small, clean, friendly park for touring and camping. A small family-run touring park set in the beautiful Quantock Hills close to Exmoor and the coast in a designated Area of Outstanding Natural Beauty. We look forward to welcoming you to our five star park at any time of the year.

£ **Terms available on request.**

See also Colour Advertisement on page 24

## RALEGH'S CROSS INN

**Brendon Hill, Exmoor, Taunton TA23 0LN**
**Tel: 01984 640343 • Fax: 01643 851227**

Perched high in the beautiful Brendon Hills, Exmoor National Park, Ralegh's Cross Inn offers comfortable and tastefully refurbished en suite rooms (some with four-poster beds), all non-smoking with colour TV and hospitality tray. A full à la carte menu with freshly prepared starters, home-cooked main courses and home-made desserts is available daily. We're also famous locally for our tasty Farmer's Carvery. A walker's, rider's and fisherman's paradise with many nearby places of interest for the tourist too. Open all year. Colour brochure available. Awaiting inspection by ETC.

£ **Terms from £20 per night.**

See also Colour Advertisement on page 25

## CROFT HOLIDAY COTTAGES

ETC ★★★★

**The Croft, Anchor Street, Watchet TA23 0BY**
**Tel & Fax: 01984 631121**
**e-mail: croftcottages@talk21.com**

Situated in a quiet area of the harbour town of Watchet, a short walk from shops and harbour. The cottages and bungalow have the use of a heated indoor swimming pool, lawned area and children's play equipment. Sleep two to eight persons. Some units suitable for disabled guests. Each has central heating, bed linen, automatic washing machine, fridge, colour TV, radio, microwave, barbecue. Towels, cots and highchairs are available. Groceries may be ordered in advance. Watchet is an ideal centre for touring or walking the beautiful Exmoor, Brendon and Quantock Hills.

£ **Short Break Details on request.**

See also Colour Advertisement on page 24

## THE CROWN AT WELLS & ANTON'S BISTROT

ETC/AA ★★

**The Market Place, Wells BA5 2RP**
**Tel: 01749 673457 • Fax: 01749 679792**
**e-mail: reception@crownatwells.co.uk • website: www.crownatwells.co.uk**

A 15th century medieval coaching inn situated in the very heart of the historic City of Wells, within a minute's walk from the Cathedral and Bishop's Palace. An excellent base from which to tour Wells City and the many surrounding attractions in this wonderful part of Somerset. A range of comfortable, affordable en suite accommodation, including four-poster and family rooms. Private parking available. A variety of mouth-watering dishes is served in Anton's Bistrot, including delicious vegetarian options and tempting desserts. A buffet and tasty snacks are also available in the Penn Bar at lunchtimes and in the early evening. A warm welcome and friendly service in relaxed and comfortable surroundings.

£ **From £30pppn based on 2 sharing. Open all year.**

# Staffordshire

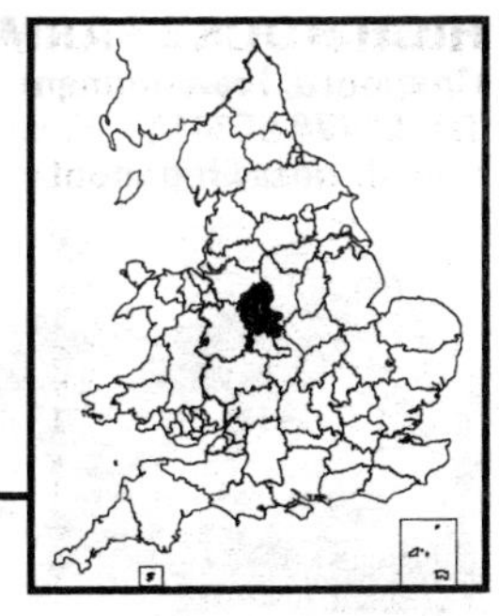

## PROSPECT HOUSE GUEST HOUSE

ETC ◆◆◆◆

334 Cheadle Road, Cheddleton, Leek ST13 7BW
Tel & Fax: 01782 550639
e-mail: prospect@talk21. com • website: www.prospecthouseleek.co.uk

Charming 19th century converted coach house. Beamed en suite rooms in a courtyard setting with independent access. All rooms have colour TV, hospitality tray, hairdryers, irons etc. There are two lounges, one overlooking the garden, and a children's play area. Delightful country and canalside walks. Close to Peak District National Park, Alton Towers, the historic market town of Leek and the Potteries. The Churnet Valley and Cheddleton Steam Railway are within easy walking distance. Open all year. Ample parking. French and German spoken. Ground floor rooms available.

£ **Bed and Breakfast from £21. Child discounts available.**

# Suffolk

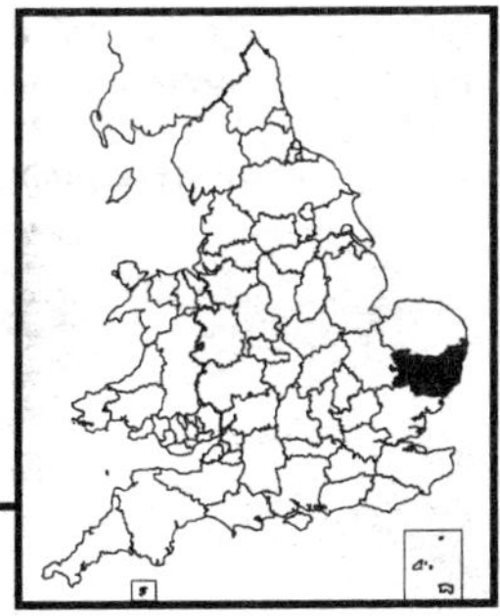

## FIDDLERS HALL

Cransford, Near Framlingham, Woodbridge IP13 9PQ
Tel: 01728 663729

Signposted on B1119, Fiddlers Hall is a 14th century, moated, oak-beamed farmhouse set in a beautiful and secluded position. It is two miles from Framlingham Castle, 20 minutes' drive from Aldeburgh, Snape Maltings, Woodbridge and Southwold. A Grade II Listed building, it has lots of history and character. The bedrooms are spacious; one has en suite shower room, the other has a private bathroom. Use of lounge and colour TV. Plenty of parking space. Lots of farm animals kept. Traditional farmhouse cooking.

£ **Bed and Breakfast terms from £23.00 per person.**

## HIGH HOUSE FARM

ETC ◆◆◆

**Cransford, Framlingham, Woodbridge IP13 9PD**
**Tel: 01728 663461 • Fax: 01728 663409**
**e-mail: b&b@highhousefarm.co.uk • website: www.highhousefarm.co.uk**

Beautifully restored 15th Century Farmhouse on family-run arable farm, featuring exposed oak beams and inglenook fireplaces, with spacious and comfortable accommodation. One double room en suite and one large family room with double and twin beds and private adjacent bathroom. Children's cots, high chairs, books, toys, and outside play equipment available. Explore the heart of rural Suffolk, local vineyards, visitor attractions and the Heritage Coast. Self catering available in three-bed Gamekeeper's House set in woodland.

£ **Bed and Breakfast from £22.50. Reductions for children and stays of three nights or more.**

See also Colour Advertisement on page 27

## 10 BANNER COURT

ETC ★★★

**Kirkley Court Cliff Road, Lowestoft NR33 0DB**
**Tel: 01502 511876**
**e-mail: aishakhalaf100@hotmail.com**

10 Banner Court is a large and graceful two-bedroomed property, which has been newly decorated and furnished. It is self-contained and positioned on the ground floor with a small garden. Located opposite a very repectable hotel, only. 3 minutes' walk to south beach and 15 minutes' walk along the promenade to town. Iron, washer and linen all provided, plus a welcome grocery pack. Outdoor drying facilities available. Numerous local events, including a summer carnival, French market and motor cycle cavalcade, are all sure to keep you busy and entertained.

£ **Details on request.**

See also Colour Advertisement on page 27

## WHITEHOUSE BARNS

ETC ★★★★

**Blythburgh, Near Southwold**

**e-mail: peneloperoskell@yahoo.co.uk • website: www.whitehousebarns.co.uk**

Two beautiful well-appointed barn conversions in spectacular peaceful location overlooking the Blyth estuary. In two acres of land with stunning views all around. They are ideal for families, walkers and birdwatchers. Southwold and Walberswick sandy beaches 4 miles. Wood-burning stoves and full central heating. Sleep 5/6 and 8/9. Spacious playbarn and babysitting service available. Contact Mrs P. Roskell-Griffiths, 61 Banthal Road, London N16 7AR Tel & Fax: 0208 806 5969.

£ **Prices from £260 to £680.**

## PUBLISHER'S NOTE

While every effort is made to ensure accuracy, we regret that FHG Publications cannot accept responsibility for errors, misrepresentations or omissions in our entries or any consequences thereof. Prices in particular should be checked because we go to press early. We will follow up complaints but cannot act as arbiters or agents for either party.

# Surrey

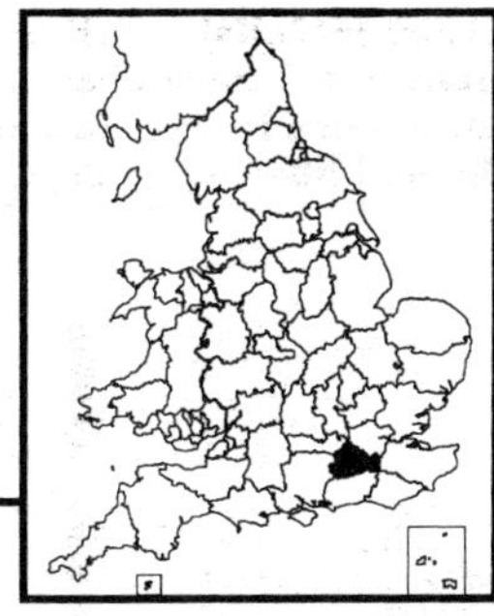

See also Colour Advertisement on page 27

## CHASE LODGE

**10 Park Road, Hampton Wick, Kingston-upon-Thames KT1 4AS**
**Tel: 020 8943 1862 • Fax: 020 8943 9363**

**ETC ★★★**

An award-winning hotel with style and elegance, set in tranquil surroundings at affordable prices. Quality en suite bedrooms. Full English breakfast. A la carte menu, licensed bar. Wedding receptions catered for; honeymoon suite. 20 minutes from Heathrow Airport; easy access to Kingston town centre and all major transport links. All major credit cards accepted. AA ★★★ *Gold Award*.

£ **Details on request.**

## LYNWOOD GUEST HOUSE

**50 London Road, Redhill RH1 1LN**
**Tel: 01737 766894 • Fax: 01737 778253**
**e-mail: lynwoodguesthouse@yahoo.co.uk • web: www.lynwoodguesthouse.co.uk**

**AA ◆◆◆**

Lynwood Guest House is five minutes away from town centre and train station. Gatwick Airport by car 15 minutes, by train 10 minutes. London by train 30 minutes. Easy access to M23 and M25. This large Victorian house offers a very friendly service. It is very clean and comfortable. All rooms have showers, tea/coffee making facilities, colour television, shaver points and heating. Some rooms have en suite facilities. There are eight allocated car parking spaces for customers.

£ **Bed and Breakfast from £20 per person sharing.**

PLEASE MENTION THIS GUIDE WHEN YOU WRITE

OR PHONE TO ENQUIRE ABOUT ACCOMMODATION

IF YOU ARE WRITING, A STAMPED, ADDRESSED

ENVELOPE IS ALWAYS APPRECIATED

# East Sussex

See also Colour Advertisement on page 28

## THE STAR INN

The High Street, Alfriston BN26 5TH
Tel: 0870 400 8102 • Fax: 01323 870922
e-mail: HeritageHotels_Alfriston.Star_Inn@forte-hotels.com

Prince Edward is among the guests who have visited this famous 14th century inn which was once a renowned meeting place for smugglers. Oak beams and open fires offer mellow reminders of the past and create an intimate atmosphere in the bar. There are 34 bedrooms, all en suite, with hairdryer, trouser press, tea-making facilities and direct-dial telephone with modem connection. Restaurant, bar and two lounges for relaxation and good food, with open fire in the winter. Set in the South Downs there are many fine walks, and the famous South Downs Way starts right at the door of the inn. Pets welcome at charge.

£ **Short Break details on request.**

See also Colour Advertisement on page 28

## MIRALEISURE SELF-CATERING HOLIDAYS

ETC ★★/★★★/★★★★

51 Marina, Bexhill-on-Sea TN40 1BQ
Tel: 01424 730298 • Fax: 01424 212500
e-mail: infomira@waitrose.com

MIRALEISURE
SELF CATERING HOLIDAYS

Fully equipped flats for one to six persons on or near Bexhill seafront, all conveniently situated for the beach, town centre and the famous De la Warr Pavilion. All properties are located in residential purpose-built blocks or houses and each provides an ideal base for quietly exhilarating holidays in Bexhill-on-Sea and for touring 1066 Country. Open all year.

£ **£175 - £425 per week. Short Breaks available off season.**

A useful index of towns and counties appears at the back of this book on pages 181 - 182. Refer also to Contents Page 43.

## "BRIGHTON" MARINA HOUSE HOTEL

**ETC/AA/RAC ◆◆◆**

**8 Charlotte Street, Brighton BN2 1AG**
**Tel: 01273 605349 • Fax: 01273 679484**
**e-mail: rooms@jungs.co.uk • website: www.brighton-mh-hotel.co.uk**

As a premier Bed and Breakfast, we offer our guests a unique and innovative experience during their stay with us. Pivotally located just off the sea front and walking distance from the major attractions. Luxuriously appointed rooms, unrivalled in their look and decor, are fully equipped for business and leisure with en suite facility. Our French, Swedish and Tudor-style rooms offer a fresh look in today's Bed and Breakfast for couples. We cater for families and are happy to provide cots and high chairs. In the Breakfast Room we are committed to creating the ultimate breakfast experience, catering for vegans, vegetarians, Continental and English cooked breakfast.

£ **Bed and Breakfast from £25–£49pppn.**

See also Colour Advertisement on page 28

## MA'ON HOTEL

**26 Upper Rock Gardens, Brighton BN2 1QE**
**Tel: 01273 694400**

This is a completely non-smoking Grade II Listed building run by proprietors who are waiting with a warm and friendly welcome. No children. Established over 20 years. Our standard of food has been highly recommended by many guests who return year after year. Two minutes from the sea and within easy reach of conference and main town centres. All nine bedrooms are furnished to a high standard and have colour TV, radio alarm clock, hospitality tray and hairdryer and most are en suite. A lounge with colour TV is available for guests' convenience. Diningroom. Full central heating. Access to rooms at all times.

£ **Terms from £30. Brochure on request with SAE.**

## THE CHERRY TREE HOTEL

**ETC ★★**

**15 Silverdale Road, Eastbourne BN20 7AJ**
**Tel: 01323 722406 • Fax: 01323 648838**
**e-mail: anncherrytree@aol.com • website: www.eastbourne.org/cherrytree-hotel**

Award-winning small, non-smoking, family-run hotel. Converted from an Edwardian residence it retains all its original charm, elegance and character. In a quiet residential area close to the sea front, theatres and downlands, the area benefits from unrestricted parking. All rooms are en suite and have colour TV, radio, hospitality tray and direct-dial telephone. Noted for its excellent traditional English cuisine and is licensed to residents. Open February to December, offering the highest standard of facilities and service which you would expect from a Two Star Silver Award Hotel.

£ **B&B from £28.00, DB&B from £41.00. Special Breaks and weekly terms on request**

## EXPLANATION OF SYMBOLS

|  |  |
|---|---|
| ★ | Number of Stars (English Tourism Council/AA/RAC) |
| ◆ | Number of Diamonds (English Tourism Council/AA/RAC) |
| | Pets Welcome |
| | Reductions for Children |
| | Christmas Breaks |
| ♿ | Suitable for Disabled |

The symbols are arranged in the same order throughout the book so that looking down each page will give a quick comparison.

## BEAUPORT PARK HOTEL

**Battle Road, Hastings TN38 8EA**
**Tel: 01424 851222**

ETC ★★★

This fine three-star country house hotel, standing in 33 acres of its own grounds, offers personal service from resident directors Kenneth Melsom and Stephen Bayes. All bedrooms are very well equipped, and are en suite. The hotel has a heated outdoor pool (summer), tennis courts, croquet, a putting green, French boules, outdoor chess and country walks, while squash, golf, and riding can all be enjoyed nearby. Country House Bargain Breaks available all year. AA.

**£ £128 to £140 per person for two nights, Friday to Sunday Dinner, Bed and Breakfast. £300 to £340 for four nights, Monday to Thursday Dinner, Bed and Breakfast. All year.**

## WESTWOOD FARM

**Stonestile Lane, Hastings TN35 4PG**
**Tel & Fax: 01424 751038 • Mobile: 0771 8055673**
**e-mail: york@westwood-farm.fsnet.co.uk**

ETC ◆◆◆

Farm with pet sheep, chickens, etc. Quiet rural location off country lane half-a-mile from B2093 approximately two miles from seafront and town centre. Golf course nearby. Central position for visiting places of interest to suit all ages. Elevated situation with outstanding views over Brede Valley. Double, twin, family rooms with en suite and private facilities. Colour TV and tea/coffee in all rooms. Two bedrooms on ground floor. Full English breakfast. Off-road parking. Also available six-berth self-catering caravan – details on request.

**£ Bed and Breakfast from £19 to £27 per person for two persons sharing. Reduced rates for weekly booking.**

See also Colour Advertisement on page 27

## DALE HILL HOTEl & GOLF CLUB

**Ticehurst, Wadhurst TN5 7DQ**
**Tel: 01580 200112**
**e-mail: info@dalehill.co.uk • website: www.dalehill.co.uk**

ETC ★★★★

Set in 350 acres of 'Outstanding Natural Beauty', the newly refurbished, four star Dale Hill Hotel offers an unmissable golfing experience. Dale Hill and Chart Hills have united under the Leaderboard Group providing a unique opportunity to play two championship courses. Dale Hill was designed by Ian Woosnam MBE, Chart Hills, the other, by Nick Faldo MBE. The latter has been described as the 'Best New Golf Course in England'. Packages involving accommodation and rounds of golf are available. For further details of offers or to request a brochure please contact the number above, or send an e-mail. AA Rosette.

**£ Details are available on request.**

PLEASE MENTION THIS GUIDE WHEN YOU WRITE

OR PHONE TO ENQUIRE ABOUT ACCOMMODATION

IF YOU ARE WRITING, A STAMPED, ADDRESSED

ENVELOPE IS ALWAYS APPRECIATED

# West Sussex

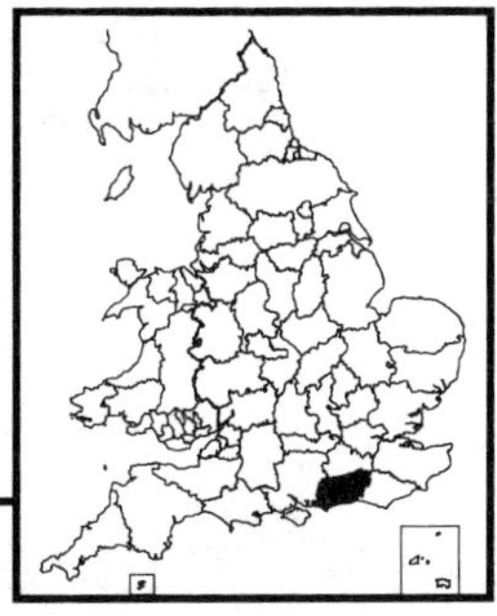

## THE HORSE AND GROOM

ETC◆◆◆◆

**East Ashling, Chichester PO18 9AX**
**Tel: 01243 575339 • Fax: 01243 575560**
**e-mail: horseand groomea@aol.com • website: www.horseandgroom.sageweb.co.uk**

One of the most attractive features of this delightful South Downs Village, The Horse and Groom presents a variety of options for a rewarding break. Superb walking, cycling and riding terrain is all around, and beautiful beaches can be reached in 20 minutes. Goodwood and Fontwell Park await the racing enthusiast and the city of Chichester and its famous harbour are close by. There are eleven bedrooms, all en suite with TV and beverage-making facilities. A first-rate choice of home-cooked fare is available each lunchtime and evening, augmented by traditional real ales and quality wines.

£ **Short Break details available on request.**

## HOLIDAY FLAT & COTTAGE

ETC ★★★

**New Hall, Small Dole, Henfield BN5 9YJ**
**Tel: 01273 492546**

New Hall, the Manor House of Henfield. stands in three-and-a-half acres of mature grounds, surrounded by farmland and footpaths. The holiday cottage is the original 1600s farmhouse, with one en suite bedroom, livingroom, dining room which could have two folding beds, and kitchen. The flat sleeps five in three bedrooms with lounge/diner, kitchen and bathroom. Both units comfortably furnished. Open all year round. Phone for details and availability.

£ **Short breaks £90 for 2 nights, £35 each additional night.**

See also Colour Advertisement on page 29

## HONEYBRIDGE PARK

ETC/AA ★★★★

**Honeybridge Lane, Dial Post, Near Horsham RH13 8NX**
**Tel & Fax: 01403 710923**
**e-mail: enquiries@honeybridgepark.co.uk • web: www.honeybridgepark.co.uk**

Delightfully situated in 15 acres, adjacent to woodlands, nestling within an Area of Outstanding Natural Beauty. An ideal location for touring, convenient for the South Coast resorts and ferry ports, as well as Brighton and Chichester, yet only one hour from London by train. Horsham is 10 miles north on the A24 and offers a wealth of historic and natural heritage. The park is maintained to the highest standards with generous-sized hard standing and grass pitches allowing comfort and privacy. Heated amenity block, storage, seasonal pitches; dogs welcome. Open all year. AA Four Pennants. David Bellamy Silver Award.

£ **Short Break details on request.**

See also Colour Advertisement on page 29

## ST ANDREWS LODGE

ETC/AA ◆◆◆◆

**Chichester Road, Selsey PO20 0LX**
**Tel: 01243 606899 • Fax: 01243 607826**
**e-mail: info@standrewslodge.co.uk**

Welcoming, family-run hotel with a reputation for an excellent hearty breakfast. Situated on the Manhood peninsula just south of Chichester, close to unspoilt beaches and countryside. Ten bedrooms, all en suite, with direct-dial telephones, TV, fridge and tea-making facilities; some on ground floor. Spacious lounges with log fire; friendly bar for residents only. Excellent Grade 1 (ETC Accessible Scheme) wheelchair access. Large secure car park. Evening meals by prior arrangement. Pets by arrangement. Apply for brochure and prices.

£ **Bed and Breakfast from £30pppn. Reductions on two/three night breaks.**

## WINDFALL COTTAGE

**29 Woodland Road, Selsey PO20 0AL**
**Tel: 01243 602205**

Guests are assured of a relaxed and friendly welcome at Windfall Cottage, which is situated just five minutes from the sea. Accommodation is available in two double and one twin bedroom, both with TV and tea/coffee making facilities. Just nine miles from historic Chichester, this is an ideal base for exploring the attractions of the South Coast, as well as for shopping and golf. Open all year.

£ **Bed and Breakfast from £18.50 (winter) to £22.00 (summer). Short break details on request from Mrs Margaret Pizzey.**

## PLEASE NOTE

All the information in this book is given in good faith in the belief that it is correct. However, the publishers cannot guarantee the facts given in these pages, neither are they responsible for changes in policy, ownership or terms that may take place after the date of going to press. Readers should always satisfy themselves that the facilities they require are available and that the terms, if quoted, still apply.

# Warwickshire

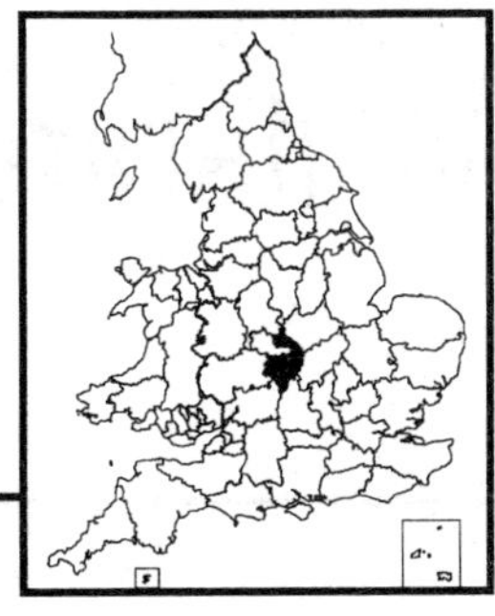

## THE GLOBE HOTEL

ETC ◆◆◆◆

**54 Birmingham Road, Alcester B49 5EG**
**Tel & Fax: 01789 763287**

A warm and friendly hotel in the historic market town of Alcester (seven miles from Stratford-upon-Avon). Stylish and spacious en suite bedrooms with remote control TV, radio alarm clocks, direct-dial telephones, modem connection and hospitality trays. Ideally placed for Stratford-upon-Avon, Warwick, M40/42 and M5 motorways, Airport/NEC (30 minutes) and touring the Cotswolds.Totally refurbished 2000.

£ **Short Break terms on application. Rooms from £35 to £65.**

## HOLLY TREE COTTAGE

**Birmingham Road, Pathlow, Stratford-upon-Avon CV37 0ES**
**Tel & Fax: 01789 204461**
**e-mail: john@hollytree-cottage.co.uk • website: www.hollytree-cottage.co.uk**

Period cottage dating back to the 17th century, with beams, antiques, tasteful furnishings and friendly atmosphere. Large picturesque gardens with extensive views over the countryside. Situated three miles north of Stratford towards Henley-in-Arden on A3400, convenient for overnight stops or longer stays, and ideal for theatre visits. Excellent base for touring Shakespeare country, Heart of England, Cotswolds, Warwick Castle and Blenheim Palace. Well situated for National Exhibition Centre. Double, twin and family accommodation with en suite and private facilities; TV and tea/coffee making facilities in all rooms. Full English Breakfast. Restaurant and pub meals nearby. Telephone for further details.

£ **B&B from £25 per person.**

## EXPLANATION OF SYMBOLS

| | |
|---|---|
| ★ | Number of Stars (English Tourism Council/AA/RAC) |
| ◆ | Number of Diamonds (English Tourism Council/AA/RAC) |
| | Pets Welcome |
| | Reductions for Children |
| | Christmas Breaks |
| ♿ | Suitable for Disabled |

The symbols are arranged in the same order throughout the book so that looking down each page will give a quick comparison.

# Wiltshire

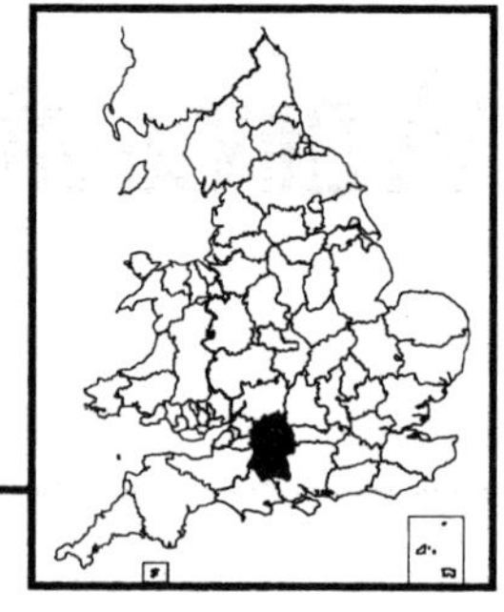

## MANOR FARM

**Burcombe, Salisbury SP2 0EJ**
**Tel: 01722 742177 • Fax: 01722 744600**
**e-mail: s.a.combes@talk21.com**

An attractive stone-built farmhouse with a lovely walled garden, set in a quiet village amid downland and water meadows, five miles west of Salisbury. The two bedrooms are very comfortable with en suite facilities, TV, tea tray and clock-radio. Large lounge and access to garden. This is an ideal location for Salisbury, Wilton and Stonehenge and easy access to many places of historic interest and gardens. For those seeking peace this is an idyllic place to stay with various walks and the local pub only a five minute stroll. Children welcome.

£ **Bed and breakfast from £22 to £23**

## SPINNEY FARMHOUSE

**Chapmanslade, Westbury BA13 4AQ**
**Tel: 01373 832412**

Off A36, three miles west of Warminster; 16 miles from historic city of Bath. Close to Longleat, Cheddar and Stourhead. Reasonable driving distance to Bristol, Stonehenge, Glastonbury and the cathedral cities of Wells and Salisbury. Pony trekking and fishing available locally and an 18 hole golf course within walking distance. Washbasins, tea/coffee-making facilities and shaver points in all rooms. Family room available. Guests' lounge with colour TV. Central heating. Children and pets welcome. Ample parking. Open all year. Farm fresh food in a warm, friendly, family atmosphere.

£ **Bed and Breakfast from £19 per night. Reduction after two nights. Evening Meal £11.**

## PUBLISHER'S NOTE

While every effort is made to ensure accuracy, we regret that FHG Publications cannot accept responsibility for errors, misrepresentations or omissions in our entries or any consequences thereof. Prices in particular should be checked because we go to press early. We will follow up complaints but cannot act as arbiters or agents for either party.

# Worcestershire

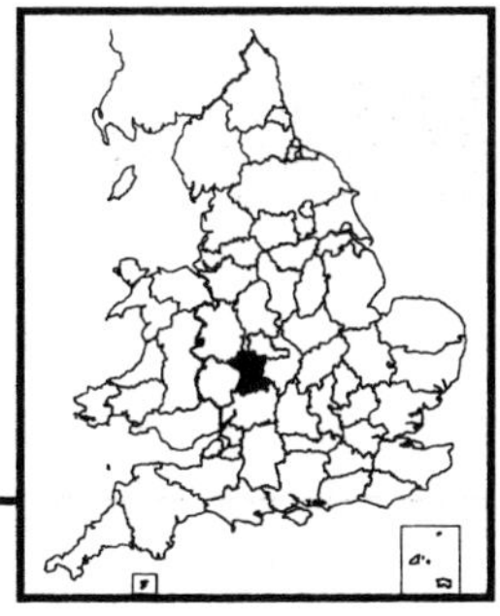

## MALVERN HILLS HOTEL

ETC/AA/RAC ★★

**Wynds Point, Malvern, Worcestershire WR13 6DW**
**Tel: 01684 540690 • Fax: 01684 540327**
**e-mail: malhilhotl@aol.com • website: www.malvernhillshotel.co.uk**

Nestling more than 800 feet up the majestic western slopes of the Malverns (on the site of a hostelry for travellers for more than half a millennium), this privately owned and run hotel is the ideal place for walking and enjoying the breathtaking views ('one of the goodliest vistas in England') from British Camp, the Iron Age hillfort and ancient earthworks which stand opposite the hotel. An oak-panelled lounge bar with seasonal open log fire offers excellent bar food and a fine selection of real ales (CAMRA recommended). Nightingales Restaurant provides candlelit dining complemented by a comprehensive wine list to suit all tastes. Open all year.

£ **Short break details available on request.**

## CROFT GUEST HOUSE

ETC ◆◆◆

**Bransford, Malvern WR6 5JD**
**Tel: 01886 832227 • Fax: 01886 830037**

16th-18th century part black and white cottage-style country house situated in the River Teme Valley, four miles from Worcester and Malvern. Croft House is central for visiting numerous attractions in Worcester, Hereford, Severn Valley and surrounding countryside. There is fishing close by and an 18-hole golf course opposite. Facilities include three en suite rooms (two double, one family) and two double rooms with washbasins, hospitality trays; TV in all bedrooms. Double glazing, central heating, residential licence and home-cooked dinners. There is a TV lounge for guests' use. A cot and baby listening service are provided. Credit and debit cards accepted.

£ **Bed and Breakfast from £22 to £30 single, £40 to £55 double. Festive Christmas and New Year Breaks available.**

## DEEPCROFT FARM HOUSE

**Newnham Bridge, Tenbury Wells WR15 8JA**
**Tel: 01584 781412**

Set in the Teme Valley, off the A456, on the borders of Worcestershire, Herefordshire and Shropshire this secluded old farmhouse, with five acres of garden and orchard, offers easy access to the Severn Valley Railway, the historic towns of Ludlow and Worcester as well as to the Welsh Marches and the Shropshire Hills. Ideal for fishermen, cyclists and tourists the accommodation comprises two twin-bedded and one single room, all with hand basins, shaver points, and tea/coffee making facilities. A comfortable sitting room with colour TV is also available for guests.

£ **Bed and full English breakfast from £20.**

# East Yorkshire

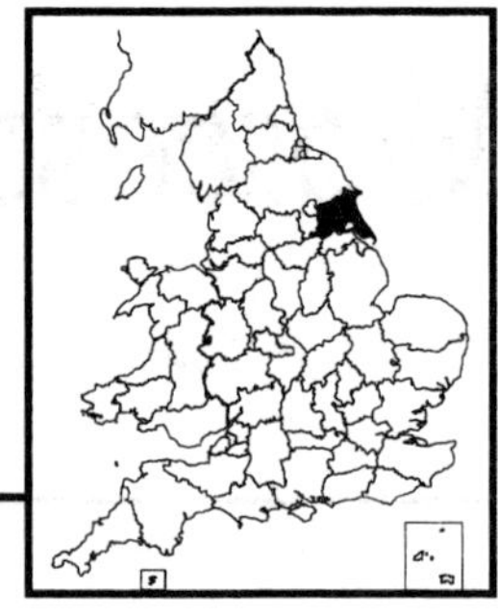

## ROSEBERY HOUSE

ETC ◆◆◆◆

**1 Belle Vue, Tennyson Avenue, Bridlington YO15 2ET**
**Tel: 01262 670336 • Fax: 01262 608381**
**e-mail: roseberyhouse@zexus.co.uk**

Grade II Listed Georgian house with character. It has a long sunny garden and superb views of the gardens and sea. Amenities are close by making it an ideal centre for walking, bird-watching, golfing, wind and sailboarding or touring the historic, rolling Wolds. A high standard of comfort, friendliness and satisfaction guaranteed. All rooms are en suite, centrally heated, have colour TV and tea/coffee facilities. Vegetarians are most welcome. Some car parking available. Open all year except Christmas and New Year.

£ **Bed and Breakfast from £19.50 per person.**

# North Yorkshire

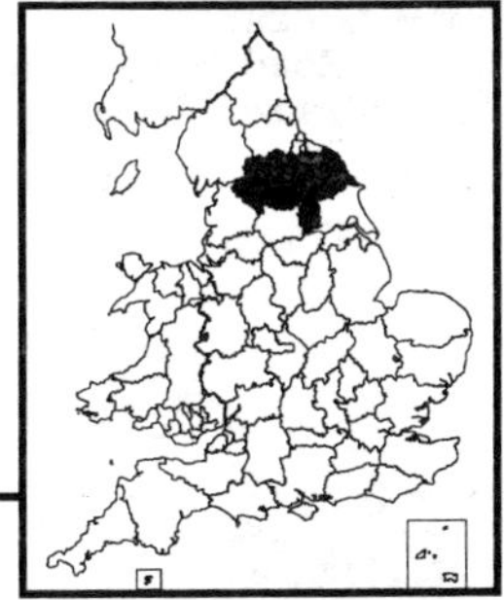

See also Colour Advertisement on page 29

## WHITE ROSE GOLF BREAKS

**Tel: 01943 609888**
**e-mail: golf@wrgb.legend.yorks.com • website: www.whiterosegolfbreaks.co.uk**

For your next golfing holiday visit Yorkshire's broad acres. Wide range of courses and hotels across East, West and North Yorkshire. For our brochure and information on bookings contact Peter Graham today

£ **Short break details available on request.**

See also Colour Advertisement on page 30

## THE BUCK INN

ETC/AA ★

**Thornton Watlass, Near Bedale, Ripon HG4 4AH**
**Tel: 01677 422461 • Fax: 01677 422447**

Friendly country inn overlooking the cricket green in a peaceful village just five minutes away from the A1. Refurbished bedrooms, most with en suite facilities, ensure that a stay at The Buck is both comfortable and relaxing. Delicious freshly cooked meals are served lunchtimes and evenings in the cosy bar and dining area. This is an ideal centre for exploring the Yorkshire Dales and moors. There is a children's playground in the secluded beer garden. Private fly fishing available on River Ure and five golf courses within 20 minutes' drive. Good Pub Guide, CAMRA Good Beer Guide, Room at the Inn, Good Pub Food Guide.

£ **Special rates for DB&B, minimum stay 2 nights.**

See also Colour Advertisement on page 29

## THE FOX & HOUNDS INN

ETC ◆◆◆◆

**Ainthorpe, Danby YO21 2LD**
**Tel: 01287 660218 • Fax: 01287 660030**

Residential 16th century Coaching Inn. Delicious meals served lunchtimes and evenings in both our dining room and cosy oak-beamed bar. Comfortable en suite bedrooms available. Enjoy our real ales or quality wines by the 14th century fireplace. Open all year. Situated between Castleton and Danby on the Fryup Road.

£ **Special mid-week breaks available.**

## SEA CABIN

ETC ◆◆◆

**16 Gap Road, Hunmanby Gap, Near Filey YO14 9QP**
**Tel: 01723 891368**

Warm & friendly hospitality plus good food at our well appointed twin bedroomed Granny annexe. En suite, own private lounge. Located on the cliff top, with easy access to the golden sands of Filey Bay. Private parking, quiet location, five minutes' drive from Filey town. Full English Breakfast. Bookings for Bed and Breakfast plus Evening Meal. Pet friendly beach and area. All year round bookings.

£ **Short break details available on request.**

## THE COPPICE

ETC ◆◆◆◆

**9 Studley Road, Harrogate HG1 5JU**
**Tel: 01423 569626 • Fax: 01423 569005**
**e-mail: coppice@harrogate.com • website: www.harrogate.com/coppice**

A high standard of comfortable accommodation awaits you at The Coppice, with a reputation for excellent food and a warm friendly welcome. All rooms en suite with telephones. Quietly located off Kings Road, five minutes' walk from the elegant shops and gardens of the town centre. Just three minutes' walk from the Conference Centre. Ideal location to explore the natural beauty of the Yorkshire Dales. Midway stop Edinburgh–London. Free Yorkshire touring map – ask for details.

£ **Single £30, double £48, family room from £58; Evening Meal £17.**

## GOWLAND FARM

ETC ★★★★

**Gowland Lane, Cloughton, Scarborough YO13 0DU**
**Tel: 01723 870924**
**website: www.gowlandfarm.co.uk**

Four charming converted stone barns situated within the beautiful North Yorkshire Moors National Park. The cottages have been furnished and fitted to a very high standard. They are fully carpeted, warm and cosy with central heating and double glazing. Electric fire and colour TV in all lounges. Well equipped kitchens. All linen and bedding provided (duvets). Large garden with plenty of car parking space. Garden furniture and laundry facilities. Sorry, no pets. Open all year. White Rose Award Self-Catering Holiday of the Year runner-up 1993.

£ **From £120 to £450 per week.**

## KILLERBY COTTAGE FARM

ETC ◆◆◆◆

**Killerby Lane, Cayton, Scarborough YO11 3TP**
**Tel: 01723 581236 • Fax: 01723 585465**
**e-mail: val@green-glass.demon.co.uk**

Simon and Val Green extend a warm Yorkshire welcome and invite you to share their charming farmhouse in the pleasant countryside between Scarborough and Filey. All our bedrooms are tastefully decorated and have en suite facilities, colour TV, and well-stocked beverage trays. Hearty breakfasts that will keep you going all day are served in the conservatory overlooking the lovely garden. Our 350-acre farm has diversified and we now have the Stained Glass Centre and tearoom which are open to visitors. Cayton offers easy access to Scarborough, Filey, Whitby, the North York Moors, and York.

£ **Short break details on request.**

See also Colour Advertisement on page 30

## NEW CLOSE FARM

Kirkby Malham, Skipton BD23 4DP
Tel: 01729 830240 • Fax: 01729 830179
e-mail: brendajones@newclosefarmyorkshire.net • www.newclosefarmyorkshire.co.uk

A supa dupa cottage on New Close Farm in the heart of Craven Dales with panoramic views over the Aire Valley. Excellent area for walking, cycling, fishing, golf and touring. Two double and one single bedrooms; bathroom. Colour TV and video. Full central heating and double glazing. Bed linen, towels and all amenities included in the price. Sorry, no young children, no pets. Non-smokers preferred. The weather can't be guaranteed but your comfort can. FHG Diploma Award Winner.

£ **Low Season £250, High Season £300; deposit required. Winter Short Breaks available.**

## GOLDEN FLEECE HOTEL

ETC/AA/RAC ★★

Market Place, Thirsk YO7 1LL
Tel: 01845 523108 • Fax: 01845 523996

Set in the heart of Herriot Country, the Golden Fleece Hotel is a 400-year-old coaching inn. This season's special "Mini Break" will provide you with local information on what to see and where to go around this delightful part of North Yorkshire. The Break is a dinner, bed and breakfast package and further information and current prices can be obtained by contacting the reception team at the hotel.

£ **DBB from £47.50pp off-peak; special offers for longer stays.**

## SYCAMORE HOUSE

ETC ◆◆◆

Danby, Whitby YO21 2NN
Tel: 01287 660125 • Fax: 01287 669122
e-mail: sycamore.danby@btinternet.com • www.SmoothHound.co.uk/hotels/sycamore1.html

Residents' lounge with TV. Bedrooms with TV and tea/coffee facilities. Stunning views from all rooms – with a choice of family, double, twin or single. Good walking and touring area, ideally placed for Heartbeat and Herriot country. Whitby, Scarborough, Middlesbrough, Pickering, York, Durham, Beamish and Hartlepool are all within easy reach. Too many places of interest to visit in just one week!. Reductions for children. Pets by arrangement. Please contact us for our brochure or visit our website.

£ **B&B from £22.50; weekly terms available. Optional Evening Meal £15.**

## NEWTON HOUSE

Neville Street, Haxby Road, York YO31 8NP
Tel: 01904 635627

Diana and John Tindall offer all their guests a friendly and warm welcome to their Victorian town house. A few minutes' walk from city centre, York's beautiful Minster, city walls and museums. Situated near an attractive park with good bowling greens. York is an ideal base for touring Yorkshire Moors, Dales and coast. Three double/twin en suite rooms, colour TV, tea/coffee tray, central heating. Car park. Non-smoking. Fire Certificate; Electrical Installation Certificate.

£ **Bed and Breakfast from £25pp.**

## BAILE HILL COTTAGE

ETC ★★★

**Bishophill, York**
**Tel: 01904 448670 • Fax: 01904 448908**
**e-mail: enquires@holiday-cottage.org.uk • website: www.holiday-cottage.org.uk**

This Victorian town cottage is in a peaceful area within the city centre with parking at the door. Sleeps four to five. Furnished and equipped to a very high standard including a fully fitted modern kitchen with microwave. The master bedroom has a four-poster bed, the second bedroom has twin single pine beds. The lounge has a cosy coal-effect gas fire and a colour teletext TV. The Victorian style bathroom has gold plated and dark mahogany fittings with an over bath shower. There is a private patio garden area, barbecue and utlilty room with an automatic washing machine and tumble dryer. Contact: Mrs Shirley Hodgson, Avalon, North Lane, Wheldrake, York YO19 6AY

£ **Short break details on request.**

## ORILLIA HOUSE

ETC ◆◆◆◆

**89 The Village, Stockton on Forest, York YO3 9UP**
**Tel: 01904 400600**
**website: www.orilliahouse.co.uk**

A warm welcome awaits you at Orillia House, conveniently situated in the centre of the village, three miles north east of York, one mile from A64. The house dates back to the 17th century and has been restored to offer a high standard of comfort with modern facilities yet retaining its original charm and character. All rooms have private facilities, colour TV and tea/coffee making facilities. Our local pub provides excellent evening meals. We also have our own private car park. Telephone for our brochure.

£ **Bed and Breakfast from £22.00.**

## KNAVESMIRE MANOR

ETC/AA/RAC ★★

**302 Tadcaster Road, York YO24 1HE**
**Tel: 01904 702941 • Fax: 01904 709274**
**e-mail: knavesmire@tiscali.co.uk • website: www.knavesmire.co.uk**

This fine Georgian house retains many original features and commands uninterrupted views across York's famous racecourse. The accommodation offers a choice of a motel-style garden room at ground level, or the more traditional rooms of the main building. Unwind in the beautiful tropical conservatory which has a heated pool with whirlpool spa. Superb cuisine is prepared in 'Restaurant 302' which enjoys an excellent local reputation. The ancient walled city of York has many attractions including the Minster, the Shambles, Jorvik Viking Centre, the National Rail Museum and the Castle Museum. AA Rosette for Food.

£ **Details on request.**

PLEASE MENTION THIS GUIDE WHEN YOU WRITE

OR PHONE TO ENQUIRE ABOUT ACCOMMODATION

IF YOU ARE WRITING, A STAMPED, ADDRESSED

ENVELOPE IS ALWAYS APPRECIATED

# Scotland

The Scott Monument, East Princes Street Gardens, Edinburgh

THE HIGHLANDS AND ISLANDS include much of what is often thought of as the 'real' Scotland. Stretching north from Fort William and Ben Nevis in the west to Inverness and the Moray Firth in the east, this unspoiled area contains some of Britain's most remote, least populated and most beautiful districts. Don't miss Loch Maree, Gairloch and Poolewe as you head northwards to Ullapool or picturesque Lochinver en route to lonely Durness. If time permits, a visit to the Western Isles, the Orkneys or Shetland will give you a taste of a different way of life, far removed from the bustle of towns and cities.

On the eastern borders of the Highlands lie Aberdeenshire and Moray, with their rugged peaks and rolling farmlands. Rich in fish, whisky, oil and castles, these counties boast 'Royal' Deeside, with Braemar and Balmoral as a tourist 'honeypot' and share with their neighbouring counties some of the most impressive scenery in Britain. Perth & Kinross and Angus offer a wealth of leisure activities: ski-ing in the glens, fishing on Loch Leven or Loch Earn, golf at Gleneagles or Carnoustie, climbing Lochnagar, pony trekking round Loch Tay, or sea-bathing at Arbroath or Montrose. The many attractive towns like Pitlochry, Aberfeldy, Crieff, Forfar etc and the busy cities of Perth and Dundee offer civilised shopping, eating and accommodation facilities.

Convenient road, rail and air links make Central and South-West Scotland a popular tourist destination. Argyll has a long, much indented coastline, looking out onto a scatter of islands such as Mull, Jura, Gigha and Islay. This is a popular outdoor resort area and has excellent hotels and a wide choice of

**SCOTTISH TOURIST BOARD**

**23 Ravelston Terrace,**
**Edinburgh**
**EH4 3EU**
**Tel: 0131-332 2433**
**Fax: 0131-332 9212**
**www.visitscotland.com**

**ANGUS & DUNDEE TOURIST BOARD**

**Castle Street**
**Dundee DD1 3AA**
**Tel: 01382 527527**
**Fax: 01382 527551**
**www.angusanddundee.co.uk**

**PERTHSHIRE TOURIST BOARD**

**Lower City Mills,**
**West Mill Street**
**Perth**
**PH3 1LQ**
**Tel: 01738 450600**
**www.perthshire.co.uk**

**HIGHLANDS OF SCOTLAND TOURIST BOARD**

**Peffery House**
**Strathpeffer**
**IV14 9HA**
**Tel: 0845 2255121**
**www.host.co.uk**

self catering accommodation. Oban is the principal centre and a busy port for the Inner and Outer Hebrides. The lively city of Glasgow is well worth a visit and has a growing reputation for its superb cultural, entertainment, shopping and sporting facilities. Ayrshire naturally means Rabbie Bums and Alloway, and also means golf – Prestwick, Troon and Turnberry are courses of international renown. Make time for a trip across to the lovely Isle of Arran – 'Scotland in miniature'.

Central Scotland is surprisingly rich in scenery and historic interest. The 'bonnie banks' of Loch Lomond, the Trossachs, Stirling Castle and Bannockburn are just some of the treasure stored here in the heart of Scotland. Excellent holiday centres with plenty of accommodation include Stirling itself, Killin, Aberfoyle, Callander, Lochearnhead and Dunblane. The rolling hills and fields of the Lothians, with Edinburgh at the heart, sweep down to the Forth as it enters the North Sea.

A short break in St Andrews and the Kingdom of Fife is the ideal escape from the pressures of everyday life. Curl up in a comfy chair by a roaring fire in an ancient castle hotel. Sample superb cuisine in gracious surroundings in a stately home. Or treat the family to a self-catering break in a house with a view. And no matter what time of year you choose to come, you can be sure that there will be plenty of things to see and do. With its dry climate, most sports, including golf, can be played throughout the year. And as the scenery changes character with each season, you will notice something new no matter how many times you return. It is, of course, golf that has placed Fife on the world stage. St Andrews is the "Home of

**AYRSHIRE & ARRAN TOURIST BOARD**

**15 Skye Road**
**Prestwick**
**KA9 2TA**
**Tel: 01292 678100**
**Fax: 01292 471832**
**www.ayrshire-arran.com**

**ABERDEEN & GRAMPIAN TOURIST BOARD**

**27 Albyn Place**
**Aberdeen**
**AB10 1YL**
**Tel: 01224 288828**
**www.agtb.org**

**ARGYLL & THE ISLES, STIRLING & TROSSACHS TOURIST BOARD**

**7 Alexandra Parade**
**Dunoon PA23 8AB**
**Tel: 01369 703785**
**www.scottish-heartlands.org**

**SCOTTISH BORDERS TOURIST BOARD**

**Shepherds Mill,**
**Whinfield Road**
**Selkirk**
**TD7 6DT**
**www.scot-borders.co.uk**

Golf", and the town, and Fife in general, boasts many fine courses which can be played all year round.

Edinburgh is the country's capital and a year-round tourist destination. It is always full of interest – the castle, the Palace of Holyrood, museums, galleries, pubs and entertainment – and Princes Street is one of the great scenic thoroughfares of the world. North Berwick and Dunbar are popular coastal resorts and this area, like Fife and Ayrshire, is a golfers' paradise. Opening onto the sea between the Lothians and Berwick-on-Tweed (which is technically in England), are the very attractive Scottish Borders. The ruined abbeys of Dryburgh, Jedburgh, Kelso and Melrose are a main attraction, as are the mills and mill-shops for the woollens which have made towns like Hawick and Galashiels famous.

For walkers, the Southern Upland Way runs from Cockburnpath on the east coast, through the Borders to Portpatrick, near Stranraer from where ferry services leave for Northern Ireland. We are now in Dumfries & Galloway whose hills and valleys run down to the Solway Firth within sight of the English Lake District. This is a popular touring and holiday region, with its green and fertile countryside, pleasant small towns and villages, and many attractions to visit. Scotland merits long acquaintance but Short Breaks provide an excellent sampler with the opportunity to enjoy its attractions at their own 'right' season.

*For further information, please contact the regional Tourist Boards.*

**GREATER GLASGOW & CLYDE VALLEY TOURIST BOARD**

**11 George Square**
**Glasgow**
**G2 1DY**
**Tel: 0141-204 4400**
**website: http://seeglasgow.com**

**DUMFRIES & GALLOWAY TOURIST BOARD**

**64 Whitesands,**
**Dumfries**
**DG1 2RS**
**Tel: 01387 253862**
**website: www.galloway.co.uk**

**KINGDOM OF FIFE TOURIST BOARD**

**Haig Business Park**
**Balgonie Park**
**Markinch**
**Fife KY7 6AQ**
**Tel: 01334 472021**
**www.standrews.com**

**EDINBURGH & LOTHIANS TOURIST BOARD**

**3 Princes Street**
**Edinburgh**
**EH2 2QP**
**Tel: 0845 2255121**
**website: www.edinburgh.org**

# The FHG Diploma

## HELP IMPROVE BRITISH TOURIST STANDARDS

You are choosing holiday accommodation from our very popular FHG Publications. Whether it be a hotel, guest house, farmhouse or self-catering accommodation, we think you will find it hospitable, comfortable and clean, and your host and hostess friendly and helpful.

Why not write and tell us about it?

As a recognition of the generally well-run and excellent holiday accommodation reviewed in our publications, we at FHG Publications Ltd. present a diploma to proprietors who receive the highest recommendation from their guests who are also readers of our Guides. If you care to write to us praising the holiday you have booked through FHG Publications Ltd. – whether this be board, self-catering accommodation, a sporting or a caravan holiday, what you say will be evaluated and the proprietors who reach our final list will be contacted.

The winning proprietor will receive an attractive framed diploma to display on his premises as recognition of a high standard of comfort, amenity and hospitality. FHG Publications Ltd. offer this diploma as a contribution towards the improvement of standards in tourist accommodation in Britain. Help your excellent host or hostess to win it!

---

We nominate ..............................................................................................................

..............................................................................................................................

Because

Your Name ..............................................................................................................

Address ..................................................................................................................

..............................................................................................................................

Telephone No...........................................

# Great Days Out – Visits and Attractions

**Scotland's Lighthouse Museum**
*Fraserburgh, Aberdeenshire • 01346 511022*
Discover the skill, the dedication, the science and the romance of this unique part of Scotland's maritime heritage. Explanatory displays, multi-screen technology and a trip to the top of Kinnaird Head Lighthouse.

**Culzean Castle and Country Park**
*Maybole, Ayrshire • 01655 884400*
*website: www.nts.org.uk/culzean.html*
Robert Adam's masterpiece set in beautifully landscaped gardens. Investigate the Eisenhower connection and visit the Interpretation Centre, swan pond and aviary. Restaurant and tea rooms, picnic areas.

**Shambellie Museum of Costume**
*Dumfries, Dumfriesshire • 01387 850375*
Step back in time and experience Victorian and Edwardian grace and refinement. Set in attractive wooded grounds, it offers visitors the chance to see period clothes in appropriate settings.

**Loch Lomond Shores**
*Balloch, Dunbartonshire • 01389 721500*
*website: www.lochlomondshores.com*
The gateway to Scotland's first National Park. At its heart is the stunning Drumkinnon Tower with state-of the-art visitor facilities. Shops and restaurants, outdoor play area, regular special events.

**Scotland's Secret Bunker**
*Near St Andrews, Fife • 01333 310301*
*website: www.secretbunker.co.uk*
An amazing labyrinth built 100ft below ground, from where the country would have been run in the event of nuclear war. The command centre with its original equipment can be seen, AV theatre and two cinemas.

**Glasgow Science Centre**
*Pacific Quay, Glasgow • 0141-420 5000*
*website: www.gsc.org.uk*
Scotland's flagship Millennium project, housed in 3 stunning buildings by the Clyde. Brings science and technology to life through hundreds of interactive exhibits.

**The Loch Ness Monster Visitor Centre**
*Drumnadrochit, Inverness • 01456 450342*
*website: www.lochness-centre.com*
All you ever wanted to know about the monster! Superb documentary, including eye-witness accounts. Shop with souvenirs.

**Gem Rock Museum**
*Creetown, Kirkcudbrightshire • 01671 82357*
*website: www.gemrock.net*
Award-winning collection of gems and minerals from around the world. Audio-visual programmes, Crystal Cave, exhibition workshop, tea rooms and gift shop.

**Royal Yacht Britannia**
*Leith, Edinburgh • 0131- 555 5566*
*website: www.royalyachtbritannia.co.uk*
One of the most famous ships in the world, serving the Royal Family for over 40 years and one million miles. A purpose-built visitor centre at Ocean Terminal tells its history.

**Scottish Mining Museum**
*Newtongrange, Midlothian • 0131- 663 7519*
Ex-miners take you on a tour of Scotland's most famous colliery, award winning talking tableaux, audio-visual presentation and new life-size reconstruction of coal-face. Tearoom.

**National Wallace Monument**
*Stirling, Stirlingshire • 01786 472140*
*website: www.stirling.co.uk/attractions*
Against the background of the events of 700 years ago when Scotland first struggled for independence, the story of William Wallace, freedom fighter and national hero. For a superb view, climb the 246 steps of the 220ft high tower.

**Talisker Distillery**
*Isle of Skye • 01478 640314*
The only distillery on the island, set in an area of great natural beauty. Talisker is one of the six 'classic malts"– friendly guides reveal some of the mysteries of its production, with a sample to taste before you leave.

# Aberdeenshire, Banff & Moray

## CAMBUS O'MAY HOTEL

**Ballater AB35 5SE**
**Tel & Fax: 013397 55428**
**website: www.cambusomayhotel.co.uk**

This family-run country house hotel is situated four miles east of Ballater overlooking the River Dee and its environs. The hotel prides itself on the old-fashioned standards of comfort and service it offers to its guests. Excellent food is available from the table d'hôte menu which changes daily and can be complemented by fine wines from the cellar. The 12 bedrooms have en suite facilities and the hotel is centrally heated throughout. The area affords a wealth of interests such as hill walking, golf, fishing, and shooting, and there are many historic sites including Balmoral Castle.

£ **Short break details available on request.**

## EXPLANATION OF SYMBOLS (Scotland and Wales)

| | |
|---|---|
| ★ | Number of Stars (STB/WTB/AA/RAC) |
| ◆ | Number of Diamonds (AA/RAC) |
| (dog symbol) | Pets Welcome |
| (rocking horse symbol) | Reductions for Children |
| (tree symbol) | Christmas Breaks |
| ♿ | Suitable for Disabled |

The symbols are arranged in the same order throughout the book so that looking down each page will give a quick comparison.

# Argyll & Bute

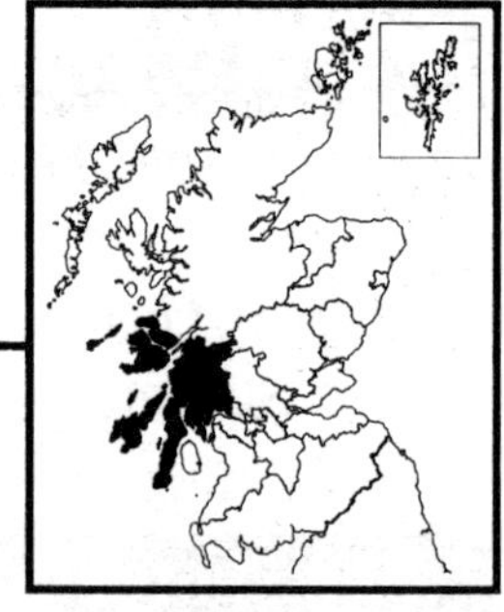

See also Colour Advertisement on page 32

## ROCKHILL WATERSIDE COUNTRY HOUSE

**Ardbrecknish, By Dalmally PA33 1BH**
**Tel: 01866 833218**

AA ◆◆◆

17th century guest house in spectacular waterside setting on Loch Awe with breathtaking views to Ben Cruachan, where comfort, peace and tranquillity reign supreme. Small private Highland estate breeding Hanoverian competition horses. 1200 metres free trout fishing. Five delightful rooms with all modern facilities. First-class highly acclaimed home cooking with much home-grown produce. Wonderful area for touring the Western Highlands, Glencoe, the Trossachs and Kintyre. Ideal for climbing, walking, bird and animal watching. Boat trips locally and from Oban (30 miles) to Mull, Iona, Fingal's Cave and other islands. Dogs' Paradise! Also Self-Catering Cottages.

£ **Short Break details on request.**

See also Colour Advertisement on page 32

## ARDANAISEIG HOTEL

**Kilchrenan, By Taynuilt, PA35 1HE**
**Tel: 01866 833333 • Fax: 01866 833222**
**e-mail: ardanaiseig@clara.net • website: www.ardanaiseig.hotel.com**

In a remote place of quiet tranquillity and almost surreal natural beauty, where the slopes of Ben Cruachan fall into the clear waters of Loch Awe, there is a small and wildly romantic old country house hotel. Ardanaiseig sits alone overlooking the mysterious islands and crannogs of the loch, in wooded grounds teeming with wildlife. Built in 1834, overlooking its own island, Ardanaiseig, with its own log fires, freshly-picked flowers, antique furniture and fine works of art, has a special stately and timeless atmosphere. It is ideally situated for visits to Argyll's many castles and sites of historic interest. The restaurant is noted for its imaginative use of fresh produce particularly seafood. Herbs from the walled garden enhance the subtle flavours created by the young, award-winning chef.

£ **Short Break details available on request.**

## PLEASE NOTE

All the information in this book is given in good faith in the belief that it is correct. However, the publishers cannot guarantee the facts given in these pages, neither are they responsible for changes in policy, ownership or terms that may take place after the date of going to press. Readers should always satisfy themselves that the facilities they require are available and that the terms, if quoted, still apply.

See also Colour Advertisement on page 32

## GIGHA HOTEL

STB ★★★ *Small Hotel*

Isle of Gigha PA41 7AA
Tel: 01583 505254 • Fax: 01583 505244
website: www.isle-of-gigha.co.uk

Situated in the Inner Hebrides, the community owned Isle of Gigha (God's Island) is surely one of Scotland's most beautiful and tranquil islands. Explore the white sandy bays and lochs. Easy walking, bike hire, birds, wildlife and wild flowers. Home to the famous Achamore Gardens with rhododendrons, azaleas and semi-exotic plants. Grass Airstrip, 9 hole golf course and regular ferry service (only 20 minutes from the mainland). We are dog friendly. Holiday cottages also available.

£ **Terms available on request.**

See also Colour Advertisement on page 32

## MELFORT PIER & HARBOUR

STB ★★★★★ *Self-catering*

Kilmelford, By Oban PA34 4XD
Tel: 01852 200333 • Fax: 01852 200329
e-mail: melharbour@aol.com • website: www.scotland2000.com/melfort

Take a relaxing and romantic short break in one of our luxury lochside houses, each with sauna, spa bath, satellite TV; some with sunbed, log fire. Clean air, tranquil surroundings, superb views. Watersports, riding, golf, fishing, hillwalking, castles. Bring your boat or use our small row boat/Canadian canoe. Ideal base for touring. Good restaurants, shopping and pubs nearby. Pets welcome.

£ **Call for Special Promotions. Start any day of the week. From £70 to £195 per house/night incl. all linen.**

## DARROCH MHOR CHALETS

Carrick Castle, Lochgoil PA24 8AF
Tel: 01301 703249 • Fax: 01301 703348

Chill out in Scotland's first National Park. Five self-catering chalets nestling on the shores of Lochgoil, each with superb lochside views and offering a peaceful and relaxing holiday in the heart of Argyll Forest Park. Each chalet has two bedrooms, livingroom with colour TV, fitted kitchen with fridge freezer, microwave, toaster etc and bathroom with bath and overhead shower. Car parking by each chalet. Great hill walking, ideal for pets, genuinely pet friendly. Open all year.

£ **Weekly rates £120 to £295, weekend and short breaks available all year round from £70, reductions for two persons, one pet free.**

## TORLOCHAN

STB ★★★ *Self-catering*

**Gruline, Isle of Mull PA71 6HR**
**Tel: 01680 300380 • Fax: 01680 300664**
**e-mail: diana@torlochan.sol.co.uk • web: holidaymull.org/members/torlochan.html**

Torlochan is situated in the centre of the Isle of Mull, with panoramic views over Loch na Keal. We are a small working croft, in which you can relax and enjoy the antics of our animals which include llamas, sheep, Jersey cows, goats, pigs and a variety of poultry. Eagles and wildlife in abundance, spotted from your door – come and see for yourself. We have two cottages, two log cabins for self-catering, and en suite bed and breakfast. A friendly welcome awaits you, your children and pets. Pets welcome free of charge. More information and brochure available from Diana McFarlane.

£ **Self-catering from £205 per week; short breaks (s/c) £45 per night. B&B from £20pp. Short Breaks November to April; Christmas/New Year Breaks in cottages only. Details on request.**

## ASKNISH COTTAGE

**Arduaine, By Oban PA34 4XQ**
**Tel: 01852 200247**
**e-mail: elspeth@arduaine.org.uk**

A warm welcome from Elspeth at Asknish Cottage. Arduaine, with panoramic views towards Shuna, Scarba, Luing and Jura is half-way between Oban, 18 miles to the north, and Lochgilphead to the south. Ideally placed to take advantage of the many local activities, boat trips, dinghy and sailing boat hire, fishing and diving or visiting the main islands by ferry; this is good walking country either energetic or leisurely; horse riding or trekking. Argyll has many gardens and historic sites. There are a number of good restaurants in hotels and inns within six miles of the cottage, one within walking distance. Pets welcome. Wild garden, tame owner.

£ **Terms from £17 to £18 per person per night.**

## VICTORIA HOTEL

**Barmore Road, Tarbert, Loch Fyne PA29 6TW**
**Tel: 01880 820236 • Fax: 01880 820638**

This recently refurbished hotel enjoys a superb harbourside location. Delicious bar meals are available, as well as candlelit dinners served in the new restaurant. Accommodation is in one twin, one double and three twin bedrooms, all en suite, with a choice of cooked or Continental breakfast.

£ **Short break details on request.**




A useful index of towns and counties appears at the back of this book on pages 181-182. Refer also to Contents Page 43.

# Borders

## WILLIAMHOPE

**Near Clovenfords, Galashiels TD1 3LL**
**Tel: 01896 850243**

**STB ★★★** ***Guest House***

Situated 8 miles from Galashiels at the head of a spectacular valley of about 2200 acres. An ideal centre for hill and forest walks or cycling with plenty to interest the naturalist. Fishing on the nearby lochs can be arranged. Williamhope has been converted into a homely, comfortable and well-equipped guest house. It has also been tastefully furnished to maintain its character. The garden is a place where you can sit and enjoy the peace and quiet. There is a good selection of dishes for breakfast with home-made preserves. Also on offer is an excellent three course dinner using fresh local produce. Packed lunches are available on request. A high standard of bed and breakfast accommodation is on offer at Williamhope, with attention to cleanliness and comfort being paramount.

£ **Terms available on request.**

## THE GLENBANK HOUSE HOTEL

**Castlegate, Jedburgh TD8 6RD**
**Tel: 01835 862258 • Fax: 01835 863697**
**e-mail: enquiries@glenbankhotel.co.uk • website: www.glenbankhotel.co.uk**

Glenbank is set in its own grounds with ample private car parking. Guests can relax in one of the en suite bedrooms which are all comfortably furnished with central heating, television and tea/coffee making facilities. We have a cosy well-stocked lounge bar with an extensive selection of malt whiskies, wines, liqueurs, spirits, beers and soft drinks. Bar lunches and evening meals are served in our 30-seater à la carte restaurant. The menus are extensive and use local produce according to season. Jedburgh offers an attractive setting in which to spend a well-deserved break. With town trails, riverside walks, renovated buildings, Mill shops, Visitor Centres as well as numerous castles and abbeys nearby - there is certainly plenty to keep you occupied!

£ **Short Break details on request.**

## MILLARS HOTEL

**Market Square, Melrose TD6 9PQ**
**Tel: 01896 822645 • Fax: 01896 823474**
**e-mail: carle2@btinternet.com • website: www.millarshotel.co.uk**

**STB ★★★** ***Small Hotel***

See also Colour Advertisement on page 33

Award winning, traditional townhouse hotel situated at foot of Eildon Hills and ideally located for walking, fishing, golf at Borders' 21 courses, or just relaxing in Melrose, the Borders' premier town. Millars Hotel offers quality accommodation and award-winning service and food; all rooms ensuite and non-smoking with colour TV, telephone, complimentary tray, hairdryer, trouser press and radio alarm. Non-smoking dining areas. We specialise in short breaks. Taste of Scotland, Welcome Host, Green Tourism Bronze Award, Walkers and Cyclists Awards, Visit Scotland Food Award.

£ **Seasonal packages available from £45pp Dinner Bed & Breakfast. Please phone for full details.**

# Dumfries & Galloway

See also Colour Advertisement on page 33

## CRAIGADAM

STB ★★★★ AA/RAC ◆◆◆◆◆

**Castle Douglas DG7 3HU**
**Tel & Fax: 01556 650233**
**website: www.craigadam.com**

A family-run 18th century farmhouse situated in the hills looking across Galloway. All bedrooms are en suite and there is a lovely oak-panelled dining room which offers Cordon Bleu cooking using local produce such as venison, pheasant, salmon. Oak-panelled billiards room. Come home in the evening to comfort, warmth and good Scottish hospitality. Fish on our own trout loch. The area offers much to the traveller with its lovely beaches, hill and forest walks, sailing, fishing, bird watching, pony trekking, golfing, as well as many places of historic and local interest. Please telephone Richard or Celia for further details. Taste of Scotland winner 2001, RAC and Little Gem Award, AA Premier Collection.

£ **Short break details on request.**

See also Colour Advertisement on page 33

## CREETOWN CARAVAN PARK

STB ★★★★ *Holiday Park*

**Silver Street, Creetown DG8 7HU**
**Tel & Fax: 01671 820377**
**e-mail: Beatrice.Mcneill@btinternet.com • website: www.creetown-caravans.co.uk**

Situated just off the A75, 6 miles east of Newton Stewart and three miles from the Galloway Forest Park, an ideal base for exploring this scenic area. Village shops and hotels only a two-minute walk. Selection of de luxe six-berth caravans to let, all of an excellent standard and fully-equipped. Heated outdoor swimming pool (seasonal), children's play area, games room with video games and pool tables. Creetown is part of the local designated cycle route. Facilities for touring caravans and tents.

£ **Terms available on request.**

See also Colour Advertisement on page 33

## MABIE HOUSE HOTEL

★★★ *Hotel*

**Mabie, Dumfries DG2 8HB**
**Tel: 01387 263188 • Fax: 01387 249696**
**e-mail: niki@mabiehouse.co.uk • website: mabiehouse.co.uk**

Set in beautiful gardens which are in turn set in the heart of Mabie Forest, this 18th century Listed building is being carefully restored to its former glory. It is an impressive sandstone-built two-storey building with original stained glass windows and grand entrance hall. Since taking over the hotel three years ago we have completely refurbished all the ground floor rooms and bedrooms. We have a bar lounge, a function room, an intimate dining room, eight bedrooms and a luxury suite. Whether it is the quiet outdoors you seek or an active weekend break, Mabie House is ideal for you.

£ **Terms on request.**

# Edinburgh & Lothians

See also Colour Advertisement on page 34

## BLENHEIM HOUSE HOTEL

**14 Westgate, North Berwick EH39 4AF**
**Tel: 01620 892385 • Fax: 01620 894010**
**e-mail: mail@blenheimhousehotel.com • website: www.blenheimhousehotel.com**

The Blenheim House Hotel is ideally situated in the main street of the picturesque seaside town of North Berwick, offering an excellent base for discovering the surrounding beauty spots. The area is a golfers' paradise, with 14 courses within half an hour's drive, including the famous Muirfield. It is a family-run hotel open throughout the year, with 11 en suite bedrooms, all with tea/coffee making facilities and colour TV. We offer freshly-prepared home-cooked food using local produce. Savour a glass of wine from our varied and interesting wine list whilst enjoying the splendid views to the sea, or take advantage of our sun patio and large garden with access to the putting greens and beach.

£ **Short break details on request.**

## NIRVANA COTTAGE

STB ★★★ *Self-Catering*

**Tyninghame, Lothians**
**Tel: 01620 860217 (local manager)**
**e-mail: info@nirvanacottage.com • website: www.nirvanacottage.com**

Unwind and relax at peaceful Nirvana cottage. Delightful semi-detached cottage in quiet conservation village, is perfect for a family holiday or a relaxing weekend retreat. Ideal for exploring safe, sandy beaches, wild and deserted hills plus historic and dynamic Edinburgh (25 miles). Enjoy cycling, swimming, fishing, riding, golf, hiking or birdwatching (Scottish Seabird Centre). Garden and patio with barbecue and garden furniture. Private parking. Carefully modernised, fully equipped with central heating. Books, games, TV. Sleeps 2/6. No pets. Non-smoking. Brochure from Mrs S.P Green, 32 Tenison Avenue, Cambridge CB1 2DY Tel & Fax: 01223 356038.

£ **Prices from £300 per week inclusive of linen and electricity. Short breaks £60 per night, 3 nights minimum. Available all year.**

## EXPLANATION OF SYMBOLS (Scotland and Wales)

| | |
|---|---|
| ★ | Number of Stars (STB/WTB/AA/RAC) |
| ◆ | Number of Diamonds (AA/RAC) |
| [dog] | Pets Welcome |
| [rocking horse] | Reductions for Children |
| [tree] | Christmas Breaks |
| ♿ | Suitable for Disabled |

The symbols are arranged in the same order throughout the book so that looking down each page will give a quick comparison.

# Fife

See also Colour Advertisement on page 34

## THE PEAT INN

STB ★★★★★ *Restaurant with Rooms*

Peat Inn, Cupar KY15 5LH
Tel: 01334 840206 • Fax: 01334 840530
e-mail: reception@thepeatinn.co.uk

Situated just six miles from St Andrews in the village named after the Inn. 'The Residence', eight luxurious suites, offers peace and comfort. The Restaurant has earned an international reputation over 30 years, offering fresh Scottish produce, creativity and value. AA 2 Red Stars and 3 Rosettes.

£ **3 nights for the price of 2 – £210pp. Includes three nights accommodation in one of our suites, three-course set dinner each evening followed by breakfast in the morning, and VAT. From October 2002 to 30th April 2003, subject to availability.**

## DUNCLUTHA GUEST HOUSE

STB ★★★★ *Guest House*

16 Victoria Road, Leven KY8 4EX
Tel: 01333 425515 • website: www.dunclutha-accomm.demon.co.uk
Fax: 01333 422311 • e-mail: pam.leven@dunclutha-accomm.demon.co.uk

This quiet Victorian former rectory provides the ideal location for touring. Ideal base for golf enthusiasts, within easy reach of 26 golf courses and only 14 miles from St Andrews. 40 minutes from Edinburgh Airport and Perth, 35 minutes from Dundee. Three en suite rooms – one double, one twin, one family (sleeps 3/4), one family (sleeps 3) with private bathroom. Colour TV and tea/coffee facilities in all rooms; cot available. Visitors' lounge with TV. Most credit cards accepted. Non-smoking. Open all year.

£ **Terms from £25pppn.**

## PLEASE NOTE

All the information in this book is given in good faith in the belief that it is correct. However, the publishers cannot guarantee the facts given in these pages, neither are they responsible for changes in policy, ownership or terms that may take place after the date of going to press. Readers should always satisfy themselves that the facilities they require are available and that the terms, if quoted, still apply.

# Greater Glasgow

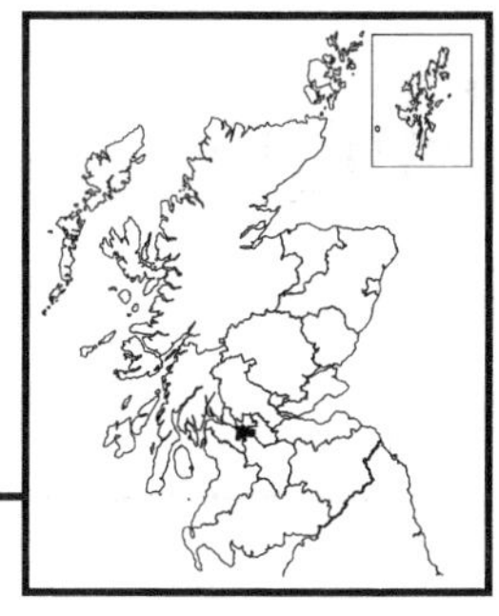

## ARGYLL HOTEL

STB ★★★ *Hotel*

**973 Sauchiehall Street, Glasgow G3 7TQ**
**Tel: 0141-337 3313 • Fax: 0141-337 3283**
**e-mail: info@argyllhotelglasgow.co.uk • website: www.argyllhotelglasgow.co.uk**

The Argyll Hotel is ideally located half-a-mile west of the city centre, within a few minutes' walk of the SECC, Glasgow University, Kelvingrove Art Gallery and the Kelvin Hall International Sports Arena. This private Georgian terrace hotel has been refurbished to a very high standard, and each of the 38 en suite bedrooms (single, double, twin and family) has its own charm and individuality. Sutherlands Restaurant and Bar serves fresh Scottish produce cooked in traditional style. A warm welcome awaits at the Argyll Hotel.

£ **B&B from £48, from £31pp sharing twin/double.**

---

# Highlands

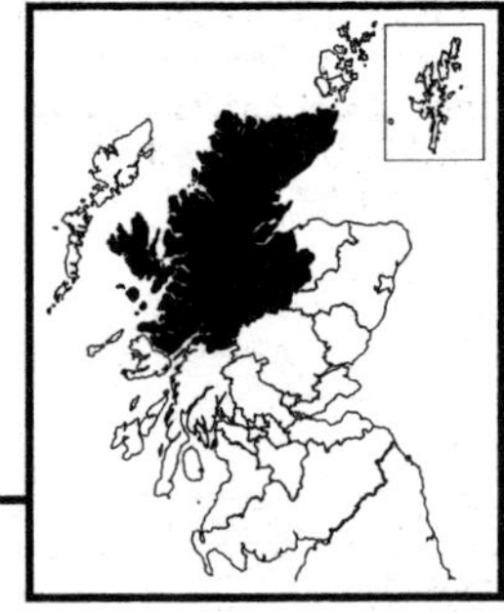

## THE ISLES OF GLENCOE HOTEL & LEISURE CENTRE

STB ★★★ *Hotel*

**Ballachulish PH49 4HL**
**Tel: 01855 821582 • Fax: 01855 821463**
**website: www.freedomglen.co.uk/ig**

"A really friendly place to go with a great, relaxed family atmosphere. The pool and leisure centre make it perfect!' Almost afloat, nestling on the side of the loch, this breathtaking new hotel offers everything of which you dream on holiday, spacious loch and mountain-view bedrooms and a relaxed, convivial ambience. The sparkling waters of the heated pool entice to the delights of the Leisure Centre: jacuzzi, sauna, steam room, exercise room and solarium. Enjoy the casual surroundings of the magnificent lochside conservatory restaurant or the lively and informal Bistro Bar. Special children's menu and early dinner.

£ **Special offer breaks: £99 for 3 nights B&B; Dinner from £15 per person. All prices per person and subject to availability.**

See also Colour Advertisement on page 34

## NETHER LOCHABER HOTEL

STB ★★ *Hotel*

**Onich, Fort William PH33 6SE**
**Tel: 01855 821235 • Fax: 01855 821545**

An ideal centre from which to explore Lochaber, the Ardnamurchan Peninsula and Glencoe. Traditional home cooking goes hand in hand with homely service, comfortable accommodation and private facilities. The inn stands on the shores of beautiful Loch Linnhe at Corran Ferry.

£ **Details on request.**

## CLAN MACDUFF HOTEL

★★ *Hotel*

**Achintore, Fort William PH33 6RW**
**Tel: 01397 702341 • Fax: 01397 706174**

This family-run hotel overlooks Loch Linnhe, two miles south of Fort William. Situated in its own grounds in a quiet and peaceful location, it is an ideal base for touring and experiencing the rugged mountains and enchanting coastline of the West Highlands. All rooms have colour TV, hairdryer, hospitality tray and private facilities. Small, well-behaved pets are always welcome. Please write or phone for a colour brochure.

£ **B&B from £20pppn, 3 nights DB&B from £89. Spring and Autumn special offers.**

See also Colour Advertisement on page 34

## LOCH LEVEN HOTEL

Onich, By Fort William, Inverness-shire PH33 6SA
Tel: 01855 821236 • Fax: 01855 821550
e-mail: lochlevenhotel@lineone.net. • website: www.lochlevenhotel.co.uk

The Loch Leven Hotel was originally built more than 300 years ago. It now combines the best of old and new. It is owned and run by Hilary and John who provide comfort in an informal setting. All 10 rooms are en suite and most have magnificent views. Our Loch View Restaurant looks out to the loch and the magnificent mountains beyond. There is an extensive menu and a daily-changing set meal, all freshly prepared using the best Scottish produce. Most evenings you can also indulge in our own Oriental menu. The comfortable lounge bar offers an impressive display of around 75 malts, and the public bar has a real fire and lots of atmosphere! There is a family/games room for more relaxed dining.

£ **B&B from £25-£50pppn**

## LINNHE LOCHSIDE HOLIDAYS

STB ★★★★ *SC*/★★★★★ *Holiday Park*

Corpach, Fort William PH33 7NL
Tel: 01397 772376 • Fax: 01397 772007
e-mail: holidays@linnhe.demon.co.uk • web: www.linnhe-lochside-holidays.co.uk

Almost a botanical garden and stunningly beautiful. Wonderful views and ideal for touring or simply relaxing and soaking up the scenery. Licensed shop, private beach and free fishing. Colour brochure sent with pleasure. "Best Park in Scotland 1999 Award", David Bellamy Silver Award.

£ **De luxe pine chalets from £55 per night (minimum 3 nights), £325 per week. Luxury holiday caravans from £35 per night (minimum 2 nights), £180 per week.**

## INVERGARRY HOTEL

★★★ *Small Hotel*

Invergarry PH35 4HJ
Tel: 01809 501206 • Fax: 01809 501400
e-mail: hotel@invergarry.net • website: www.invergarry.net/hotel

Set in a small village amidst the beautiful scenery of the Scottish Highlands, The Invergarry Hotel has ten comfortable en suite rooms in a distinctive Victorian building. The restaurant features fine Scottish produce and the well-stocked bar has a range of over 30 malts.

£ **Short break details on request.**

## EAST LODGE HOTEL

Strathconon, By Marybank, Muir of Ord IV6 7QQ
Tel: 01997 477222 • Fax: 01997 477243
e-mail: elh@btinternet.com

Situated in one of Scotland's last unspoilt glens, this former Victorian sporting lodge is now a comfortably appointed hotel of typical Highland character. The en suite bedrooms have tea/coffee making facilities, colour TV and telephone. The fully licensed restaurant offers a varied menu of traditional home cooking and the wood-panelled residents' lounge is a tranquil setting to relax. This is an excellent location for fly fishing, birdwatching, walking, cycling, climbing, pony trekking, golf and touring. Inverness main line rail and airport connections 45 minutes. Families welcome. Pets by arrangement.

£ **Short break details on request.**

# Perth & Kinross

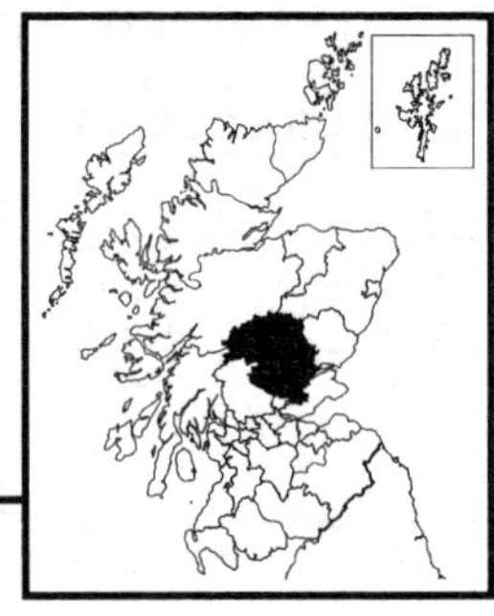

See also Colour Advertisement on page 35

## THE FOUR SEASONS HOTEL

**St Fillans PH6 2NF**
**Tel: 01764 685333 • Fax: 01764 685444**
**e-mail: info@thefourseasonshotel.co.uk • website: www.thefourseasonshotel.co.uk**

**RAC/AA ★★★**

The finest lochside location in the Southern Highlands. Meall Reamhar Restaurant and Tarken Rum offer imaginative cuisine using only the best fresh Scottish produce whilst considering both the adventurous and the traditional diner. All spacious rooms are en suite, many with loch views. We are well placed to offer a tremendous variety of day trips including the Earthquake House in Comrie, Loch Tay Crannog, a steam train trip to Mallaig, the oldest Yew tree in Europe at Fortingall, Rob Roy's grave at Balquhidder, and much more. Over 35 golf courses within an hour, to suit all standards. This part of Scotland has infinite variety of walking, from woodland walks to wide-open spaces seen from a conquered Munro. Come and relax with us. AA 2 RED ROSETTES, TASTE OF SCOTLAND, WHICH? GOOD HOTEL GUIDE, JOHANSENS, BEST LOVED HOTELS.

£ **Short Break terms on request.**

## COIRE BUIDHE

**Strathyre FK18 8NA**
**Tel: 01877 384288**
**e-mail: coirebuidhe@amserve.net • website: www.coirebuidhe.co.uk**

**STB ★★**

Coire Buidhe sits in the beautiful valley of Strathyre, nine miles from Callander, an excellent base for touring Loch Lomond, Trossachs, Stirling and Edinburgh, with both east and west coasts within easy reach. Accommodation comprises two double en suite, one triple en suite, one single, one twin and one family room all with tea making facilities. Sitting and dining rooms. Parking. Children welcome at reduced rates - cot, highchair and babysitting offered. All water sports and shooting available, plus trekking, tennis, hill walking, golf and putting. Bed and Breakfast from £17, special diets catered for. Bar and restaurant meals available 50 yards. Full Fire Certificate. Garden patio available for guests' use. Open all year.

£ **Short Break terms on request.**

## EXPLANATION OF SYMBOLS (Scotland and Wales)

| | |
|---|---|
| ★ | Number of Stars (STB/WTB/AA/RAC) |
| ◆ | Number of Diamonds (AA/RAC) |
| (dog symbol) | Pets Welcome |
| (rocking horse symbol) | Reductions for Children |
| (tree symbol) | Christmas Breaks |
| ♿ | Suitable for Disabled |

The symbols are arranged in the same order throughout the book so that looking down each page will give a quick comparison.

# Stirling & The Trossachs

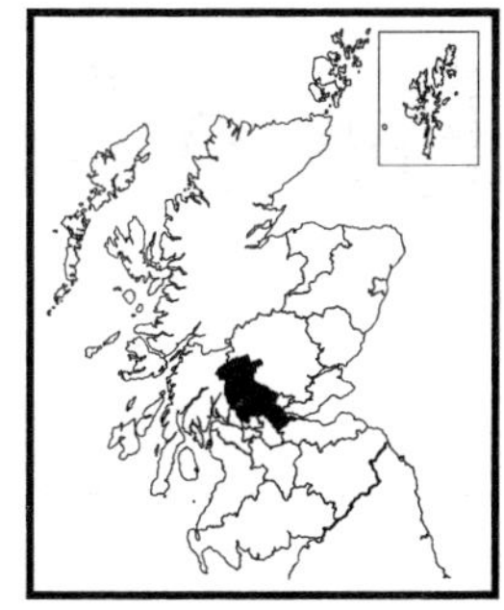

See also Colour Advertisement on page 35

## RIVERVIEW HOUSE

STB ★★★ *Guest House*

**Leny Road, Callander FK17 8AL**
**Tel: 01877 330635 • Fax: 01877 339386**
**e-mail: auldtoll@aol.com • website: www.nationalparkscotland.co.uk**

Excellent value-for-money accommodation in the Trossachs area which forms the most beautiful part of Scotland's first National Park. Ideal centre for walking and cycling holidays, with cycle storage available. In the guest house all rooms are en suite, with TV and tea-making. Private parking. Also available self-catering stone cottages, sleep 3 or 4. Sorry, no smoking and no pets. Call Drew or Kathleen Little for details.

£ **B&B from £21, dinner by arrangement from £12. Low season and long stay discounts available. Self-catering cottages from £225 per week (STB ★★★★)**

See also Colour Advertisement on page 35

## THE HARVIESTOUN

STB ★★★ *Hotel*

**Dollar Road, Tillicoultry FK13 6PQ**
**Tel: 01259 752522 • Fax: 01259 752523**
**e-mail: harviestounhotel@aol.com • website: www.harviestouncountryhotel.com**

A sympathetically converted Listed building at the foot of the Ochil Hills. Off the A91, ideal central location for tourists or business travellers.11 bedrooms, all en suite and non-smoking; many with superb views of the hills. All day dining in colourful courtyard restaurant. Conferences, weddings and social functions catered for. Many attractions and leisure amenities in the area, including horse riding, fishing and golf (some discounted green fees can be arranged).

£ **Terms available on request. Special rates for 2 nights Dinner, Bed and Breakfast.**

PLEASE MENTION THIS GUIDE WHEN YOU WRITE

OR PHONE TO ENQUIRE ABOUT ACCOMMODATION

IF YOU ARE WRITING, A STAMPED, ADDRESSED

ENVELOPE IS ALWAYS APPRECIATED

# Isle of Skye

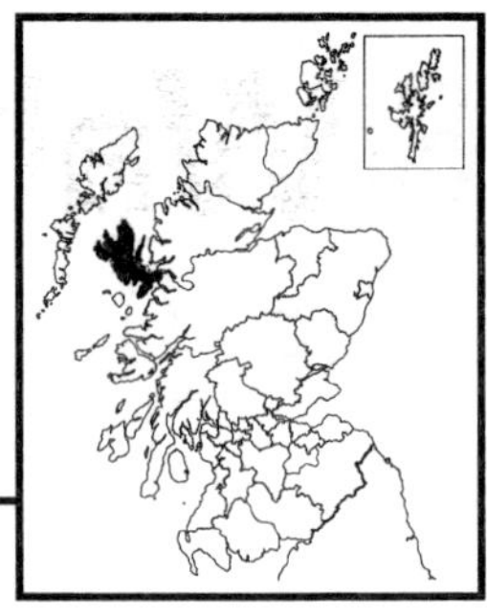

## SKEABOST COUNTRY HOUSE HOTEL

AA ★★★

**Skeabost Bridge, Portree IV51 9NP**
**Tel: 01470 532202 • e-mail: reception@skeabostcountryhouse.com**
**Fax: 01470 532454 • website: www.skeabostcountryhouse.com**

Skeabost Country House is a historic period Victorian hunting lodge on the shores of Loch Snizort amidst 25 acres of mature landscaped grounds. Indulge yourself and enjoy our warm, professional hospitality, log fires and exquisite fine dining in our baronial-style dining room. Superb individual rooms, service and six course dining. Cosy and romantic, relaxing and refined. Breathtaking sunsets and autumn northern lights. 9 hole, 18 tee, par 62, picturesque lochside golf course. 8 miles of salmon and trout fishing on the river Snizort. Rod/golf club hire, friendly resident ghillie service. AA two Rosettes.

£ **From £105pp for a three night B&B break (based on 2 sharing a double/twin room). Includes free fishing and golf. Available 1st October 03 to 31st March 04. Excludes Christmas and New Year.**

## • • *Some Useful Guidance for Guests and Hosts* • •

Every year literally thousands of holidays, short breaks and overnight stops are arranged through our guides, the vast majority without any problems at all. In a handful of cases, however, difficulties do arise about bookings, which often could have been prevented from the outset.

*It is important to remember that when accommodation has been booked, both parties – guests and hosts – have entered into a form of contract. We hope that the following points will provide helpful guidance.*

**GUESTS:**

- When enquiring about accommodation, be as precise as possible. Give exact dates, numbers in your party and the ages of any children.
- State the number and type of rooms wanted and also what catering you require – bed and breakfast, full board etc. Make sure that the position about evening meals is clear – and about pets, reductions for children or any other special points.
- Read our reviews carefully to ensure that the proprietors you are going to contact can supply what you want. Ask for a letter confirming all arrangements, if possible.
- If you have to cancel, do so as soon as possible. Proprietors do have the right to retain deposits and under certain circumstances to charge for cancelled holidays if adequate notice is not given and they cannot re-let the accommodation.

**HOSTS:**

- Give details about your facilities and about any special conditions. Explain your deposit system clearly and arrangements for cancellations, charges etc. and whether or not your terms include VAT.
- If for any reason you are unable to fulfil an agreed booking without adequate notice, you may be under an obligation to arrange suitable alternative accommodation or to make some form of compensation.

*While every effort is made to ensure accuracy, we regret that FHG Publications cannot accept responsibility for errors, omissions or misrepresentations in our entries or any consequences thereof. Prices in particular should be checked because we go to press early. We will follow up complaints but cannot act as arbiters or agents for either party.*

# Wales

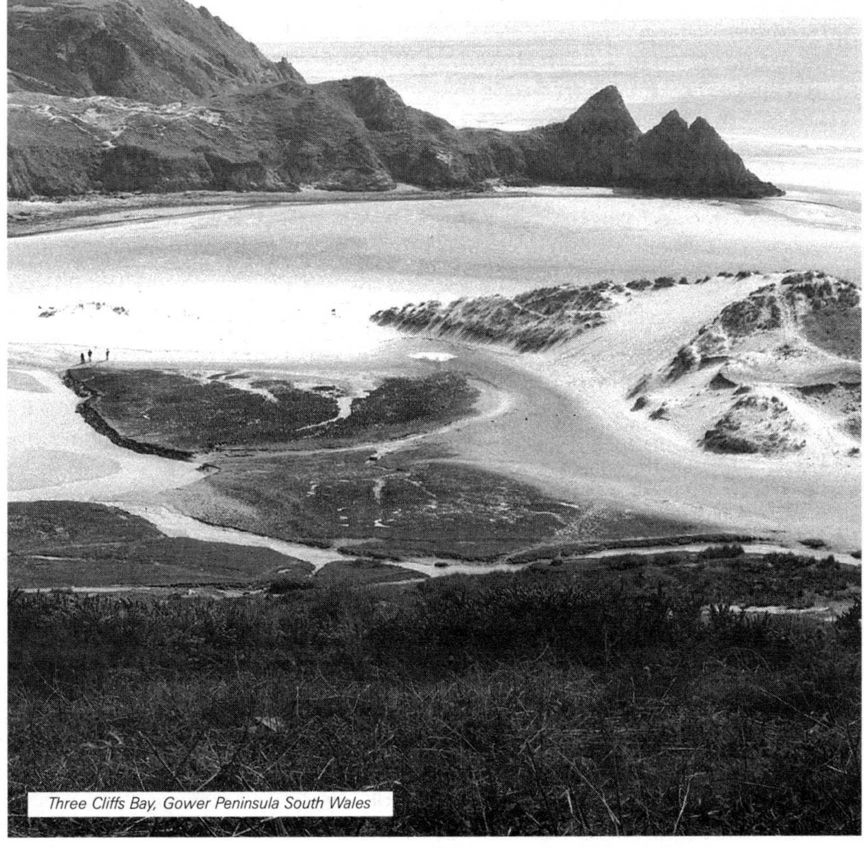

*Three Cliffs Bay, Gower Peninsula South Wales*

SCENERY, history and the quality of life are the main ingredients of a holiday in Wales, which makes this a perfect destination for a Short Break holiday.

You can't go far in Wales without a view of mountains or the sea. And you can't go far in Wales without being in a National Park! Wales has three of these, each with its own special character. In the north, the Snowdonia National Park has mountains, moors, lakes and wooded valleys, dominated of course by Snowdon, the highest peak in England and Wales. At its northern edge is Anglesey and the North Wales Coast resorts, all popular tourist areas. But the atmosphere of the National Park is best experienced in the small towns and villages at its heart, such as Llanberis, Beddgelert, Betws-y-Coed and Capel Curig.

Approximately 100 km to the south and east is the Brecon Beacons National Park. From Llandeilo by the Black Mountain in the west, through the Brecon Beacons themselves to the Black Mountains and Hay-on-Wye on the border with England, here are grassy, smooth hills, open spaces, bare moors, lakes and forests. All that is lacking is the sea – and it's the sea which has made the Pembroke Coast National Park possible. From Tenby in the south to Cardigan in the north, the park offers every kind of coastal scenery: steep cliffs, sheltered bays and harbours, huge expanses of sand and shingle, rocky coves and quiet wooded inlets.

But 'scenery' doesn't end with the national parks. Wales also has five areas nominated officially as being of 'Outstanding Natural Beauty'. The Gower Peninsula, west of Swansea, is a scenic jewel – small but sparkling! The Wye Valley from Chepstow to Monmouth includes the ruined Tintern Abbey and many historic sites including Chepstow itself, Raglan and Caerleon.

The Isle of Anglesey, apart from its quiet beauty, claims the world's longestplacename, Llanfairpwllgwyn gyllgogerychwyrndrobwllllantysiliog ogogoch – usually: shortened to Llanfair PG! The Llyn Peninsula, west of Snowdon is perhaps the most traditionally Welsh part of Wales and finally, the Clwydian Range behind Rhyl and Prestatyn, where St Asaph has the smallest cathedral in Britain.

Wales welcomes its visitors all year round and can provide them with the highest standards of hotels and self-catering, guest-houses and well-run caravan sites. Home-grown produce like succulent Welsh lamb, tasty seafood, cheeses and garden vegetables make up a healthy Welsh larder. Little wonder the Welshman enjoys singing for his supper!

**WALES TOURIST BOARD**
2 Fitzalan Road
Cardiff
CF24 0UY
Tel: 08701 211251
Fax: 08701 211259
website: www.visitwales.com

**NORTH WALES TOURISM**
77 Conwy Road
Colwyn Bay
North Wales
LL29 7LN
Tel: 01492 531731 or
08705 168767
www.nwt.co.uk

**MID & WEST COAST WALES TOURISM**
Treowain Enterprise Park
Llanidloes Road, Machynlleth
Powys SY20 8EG
Freephone: 0800 273747
Fax: 01654 703855

**SOUTH WALES TOURISM**
Charter Court,
Enterprise Park
Swansea
SA7 9DB
Tel: 01792 781212
Fax: 01792 781300

*The fantasy village of Portmeirion, near Porthmadog, North Wales*

# Great Days Out – Visits and Attractions

**Gwynfynydd Gold Mine**
*Dolgellau, Gwynedd • 01341 423332*
Explore the underground workings of the only operational gold mine in Wales open to the public. Compare today's mining with past methods and see how gold ore is smelted. Pan for gold – any you find is yours to keep!

**Erddig**
*Near Wrexham, North Wales • 01978 313333*
Has been described as the "most evocative upstairs-downstairs house in Britain". Visit below stairs and see what it was like to work and live in a country house.

**Penmachno Woollen Mill**
*Betws-y-Coed, North Wales • 01690 710545*
Learn about the fascinating process of power loom weaving and visit the mill shop which offers excellent quality knitwear and the traditional rugs.

**Welsh Woollen Industry Museum**
*Llandyssul, Carmarthenshire • 01559 370929*
Housed in old former mills, demonstrations of hand carding, spinning, weaving and dyeing. Gift shop and cafe.

**Vale of Rheidol Railway,**
*Aberystwyth, Cardiganshire • 01970 625819*
An unforgettable journey by narrow gauge steam train , climbing over 600 feet in 12 miles from Aberystwyth to Devil's Bridge.There are many sharp turns and steep gradients, and the journey affords superb views of the valley.

**Marine Life Centre**
*St David's, Pembrokeshire •01437 721665*
All-weather attraction giving a unique insight into the undersea world. Simulation of underwater caves, shipwreck tank and touch tanks; gift shop, refreshments, play areas.

**Pembroke Castle**
*Pembroke, Pembrokeshire • 01646 681510*
The birthplace of Henry VII, this is the oldest castle in West Wales, dating back to the 13th century, with a fine five-storey circular keep. Exhibitions, displays, videos and tableaux give a fascinating insight into history and heritage.

**Powis Castle and Garden**
*Near Welshpool, Powys • 01938 554336*
Perched on a rock above gardens of great historical and horticultural importance, the medieval castle contains a superb collection of paintings and furniture and a collection of treasures from India.

**King Arthur's Labyrinth**
*Machynlleth, Powys • 01654 761584*
*website: www.kingarthurslabyrinth.com*
A boat ride along a beautiful subterranean river takes you to the Labyrinth, carved from rock, where the tales of King Arthur are re-told. New 'Bard's Quest' challenges you to go in search of the lost legends hidden in the Maze of Time.

**Rhondda Heritage Park**
*Trehafod, South Wales • 01443 682036*
*www.netwales.co.uk/rhondda-heritage*
A living testament to the coal mining valleys of the Rhondda, and to the spirit of the people who dug for "Black Gold". Special effects and life-like models bring to life this unique story.

**Carreg Cennen Castle**
*Near Landeilo, South Wales • 01558 822291*
*website: www.cadw.wales.gov.uk*
In a spectacular location in the Brecon Beacons National Park, this 'eagle's nest' of a castle is an adventure below and above ground, with passageways cut into the cliff face leading to natural caves.

**Cefn Coed Colliery Museum**
*Neath. South Wales • 01639 750556*
Housed in the buildings of what was once the deepest anthracite mine in the world, giving a vivid portrayal of the working conditions endured by the miners.

**Centre for Visual Arts**
*Cardiff, South Wales • 029 20394040*
Wales' largest gallery with regularly changing exhibitions and 'Fantasmic', an interactive gallery with over 100 hands-on exhibits to push, pull, touch and see

# DISCOVER SOUTH WALES WITH NEATH PORT TALBOT HOTELIER'S ASSOCIATION

Aberavon Beach Hotel

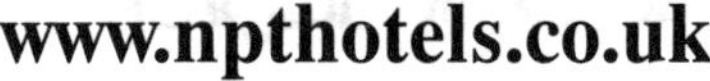

Ty'n-y-Caeau

Bwthyn-y-Saer & Hafod y Wenol

Tree Tops Guest House

www.npthotels.co.uk

Castle Hotel

Pen-yr-Allt inn

www.npthotels.co.uk

Cwmbach Cottages & Cwmbach Lodge

Lletty Piod Farm

Drws Nesaf

Gelli Farmhouse

Green Lanterns Guest House

**For an exciting range of self-catering cottages and lodges, guest houses, farm-houses, inns and hotels just visit www.npthotels.co.uk and discover a county full of beauty and culture.**

**For further information on attractions and activities in Neath Port Talbot please contact Pont Nedd Fechan Tourist Information Centre Tel 01639 721795 Quoting "FHG 2003"**

**Neath Port Talbot County Borough Council**
**Cyngor Bwrdeistref Sirol Castell-nedd Port Talbot**

# BRYNBRAS CASTLE

CHRISTMAS BREAKS

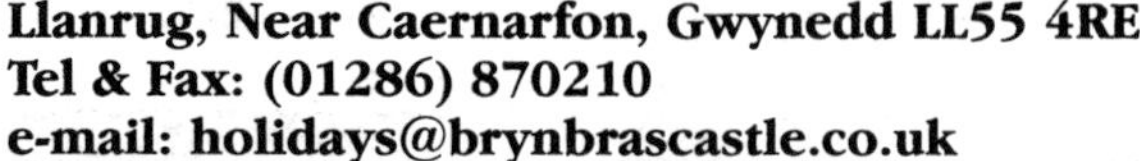

**Llanrug, Near Caernarfon, Gwynedd LL55 4RE**
**Tel & Fax: (01286) 870210**
**e-mail: holidays@brynbrascastle.co.uk**
**website: www.brynbrascastle.co.uk**

Welcome to elegant Tower-House and enchanting Castle Apartments within a romantic Regency Castle of timeless charm. (Listed Building of Architectural/Historic interest). Centrally situated in gentle Snowdonian foothills for enjoying North Wales' magnificent mountains, beaches, resorts, heritage and history. Many local restaurants and inns nearby. (Details available in our Information Room). A delightfully unique selection for 2-4 persons of fully self-contained, beautifully appointed, spacious, clean and peaceful accommodation, each with its own distinctive, individual character. Generously and conveniently equipped from dishwasher ....to fresh flowers. Inclusive of central heating, hot water, linen, toiletries, welcome tray. All WTB Highest Grade. 32 acres of truly tranquil landscaped gardens, sweeping lawns, woodland walks and panoramic hill-walk overlooking sea, Anglesey and Snowdon. The comfortable, warm and welcoming Castle in serene surroundings is open all year, including for short breaks, offering privacy and relaxation — ideal for couples. Regret young children not accepted.

**Please contact Mrs Marita Gray-Parry directly any time for a brochure/booking**

*Self catering Apartments*

e.g. 2 persons for 2 nights from £170 incl "Romantic Breaks"

# Anglesey & Gwynedd

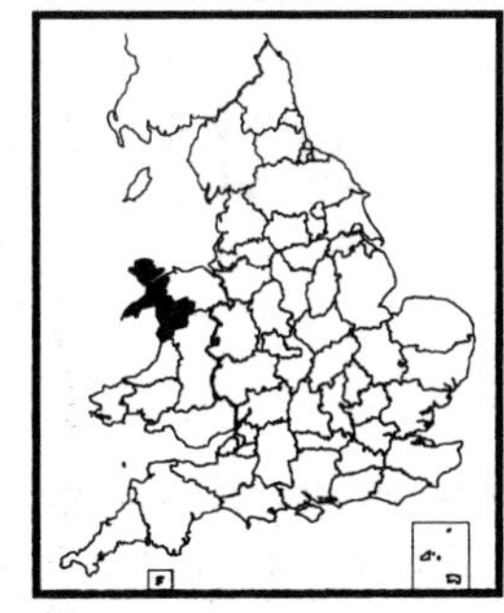

See also Colour Advertisement on page 36

## BONTDDU HALL COUNTRY HOUSE HOTEL,

Bontddu, Near Dolgellau, Gwynedd LL40 2UF
Tel: 01341 430661 • Fax: 01341 430284

WTB ★★★★ *Hotel*
AA/RAC ★★★

This historic Gothic mansion stands in 14 acres of landscaped gardens with breathtaking views of Cader Idris. First-class accommodation is offered in tastefully appointed bedrooms, each one with en suite facilities, colour television, clock radio, direct-dial telephone and tea and coffee-makers; there are also several luxury suites. The Restaurant is well noted for its gourmet specialities: regional and classical dishes are carefully prepared using the best of local produce. There is a wide variety of things to see and do in the vicinity and the historic castles of Caernarvon and Harlech are within easy reach. AA two Rosettes.

£ **Terms available on request.**

## GWESTY MINFFORDD HOTEL

Talyllyn LL36 9AJ
Tel: 01654 761665 • Fax: 01654 761517
e-mail: hotel@minffordd.com • website: www.minffordd.com

★★★ *Hotel*

Small 17th century Drover's Inn at the base of Cader Idris (2697ft), ideal for 'walkies' or as a centre for touring. For the two-legged guest – enjoy a Minffordd dinner, cooked on an Aga using local Welsh produce, organic vegetables, Welsh flavouring. Residential and restaurant licence. Seven bedrooms all en suite, two ground floor; non-smoking. Pets welcome; no children under 12. Dolgellau six miles, Machynlleth eight. AA ★★, Founder Member Taste of Wales, Good Food Guide 2000.

£ **Short break details on request from hosts, Gordon and Michelle Holt.**

## PUBLISHER'S NOTE

While every effort is made to ensure accuracy, we regret that FHG Publications cannot accept responsibility for errors, misrepresentations or omissions in our entries or any consequences thereof. Prices in particular should be checked because we go to press early. We will follow up complaints but cannot act as arbiters or agents for either party.

# North Wales

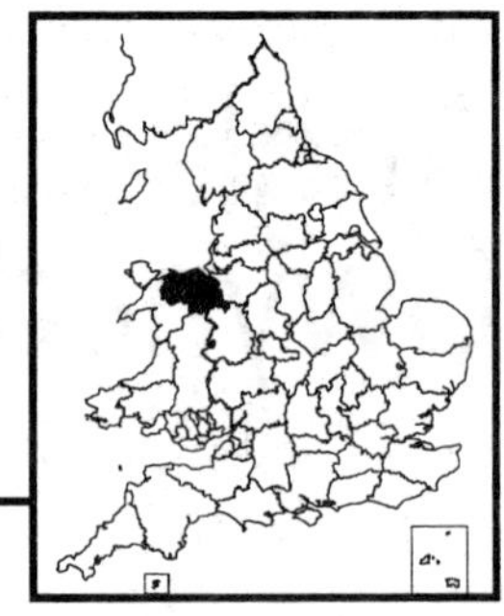

## MORETON PARK LODGE

WTB/AA/RAC ★★★ *Hotel*

**Gledrid, Chirk, Wrexham LL14 5DG**
**Tel: 01691 776666• Fax: 01691 776655**
**e-mail: reservations@moretonpark.com • website: www.moretonpark.com**

Moreton Park Lodge is a centrally located purpose-built complex on the Welsh–Shropshire border, within easy reach of Oswestry, Wrexham, Shrewsbury, Llangollen and Chester. It has a wide variety of rooms, all with en suite bathrooms and a choice of double or twin beds; other amenities include hot drinks facilities, hairdryer, direct-dial telephone and central heating. There are also luxurious split-level suites with additional features. There is ample parking, and the Lodge is only a one-minute walk from the Lord Moreton Pub and Restaurant.

£ **Short break details on request.**

See also Colour Advertisement on page 36

## CASTLE BANK HOTEL & LICENSED RESTAURANT

**Mount Pleasant, Conwy LL32 8NY**
**Tel: 01492 593888**
**e-mail: contact@castle-bank.co.uk • website: www.castle-bank.co.uk**

Set in its own grounds overlooking the River Conwy and yet close to the town centre, Conwy Golf Club and the harbour, Castle Bank is the ideal centre for your visit to North Wales. All bedrooms have private toilet and shower and every room has tea/coffee facilities, TV and hairdryer. Before dining relax in our well stocked bar where our wine list offers a selection for all tastes. The Restaurant offers an imaginative and varied menu with great emphasis placed on quality. Ample parking. We are a non-smoking establishment

£ **Two-day break: B&B £50pp.**

See also Colour Advertisement on page 36

## THE LODGE

**Tal-y-Bont, Conwy LL32 8YX**
**Tel: 01492 660766 • Fax: 01492 660534**

Nestling in the lovely rolling hills of the beautiful Conwy Valley, our family-run hotel has all the ingredients for a wonderful holiday. Enjoy peace and quiet, superb food, and attention from our friendly and efficient staff. We have ten Classical Suite rooms, two Premier Rooms and two super Cottage Suites, in a rural garden setting, all extremely well appointed, with extra little touches to make you feel at home. All major attractions are within easy reach, including Bodnant Gardens. Large private car park; extensive established grounds.

£ **Bed and Breakfast from £30 to £60pppn; 2 nights Dinner, Bed and Breakfast from £88 to £100. Weekly terms on request.**

## WELLINGTON HOTEL ★★

12 North Parade, Llandudno LL30 2LP

Tel: 01492 876709 • Fax: 01492 871160 • website: www.thewellingtonhoteluk.com

e-mail: chrisandpamela@thewellingtonhoteluk.com

Set between the Great and Little Ormes in Llandudno Bay, opposite the Victorian pier, is the Wellington Hotel, offering fully en suite rooms, with evening meals on request. Come and enjoy the splendour of this fully licensed hotel which offers a warm welcome all year round. Rooms have TV, radio alarms and much more. Enjoy the local attractions or explore the surrounding areas such as Snowdonia. A warm welcome is assured from Chris and Pamela Collings. Llandudno Hotels Association member.

£ **Bed and Breakfast from £25 per person per night. Four-course evening meal £12.50. Special rates for 7-day bookings.**

## THE GOLDEN PHEASANT HOTEL WTB/AA ★★★

Glyn Ceiriog, Near Llangollen LL20 7BB

Tel: 01691 718281 • Fax: 01691 718479

e-mail: goldenpheasant@micro-plus-web.net • website: www.goldenpheasanthotel.co.uk

See also Colour Advertisement on page 36

Situated in the heart of the Ceiriog Valley, one of the most picturesque in North Wales. This 18th century hotel offers peace and tranquillity. All rooms en suite, some with whirlpool baths and four-poster beds. Excellent restaurant, olde worlde charm bar with open fire, comfortable lounges, garden, patios and large car park. Pets welcome in all rooms except restaurants and lounge.

£ **2 nights D,B&B from £100pp.**

## HAFOD COUNTRY HOTEL WTB ★★★ *Hotel* AA ★★

Trefriw, Near Llanrwst, North Wales LL27 0RQ

Tel: 01492 640029* • Fax: 01492 641351

e-mail: hafod@breathemail.net • website: http://www.hafodhouse.co.uk

Excellent food, a warm welcome and relaxed informality, combined with an individual sense of style, many antiques, oak panelled bar and, in winter, a log fire, are the ingredients Chris and Rosina Nichols use to create the atmosphere of their country home hotel. Yr Hafod (the summer dwelling) overlooks its own grounds and the lush Conwy Valley, while behind, the village of Trefriw nestles into the heavily wooded eastern flank of Snowdonia. Hafod is an ideal base for the discerning visitor to relax and enjoy all that this fascinating, historic and varied corner of Britain has to offer. AA 2 Star 71%.

£ **Short Breaks from £50pppn for Dinner, Bed and Breakfast.**

## EXPLANATION OF SYMBOLS (Scotland and Wales)

| | |
|---|---|
| ★ | Number of Stars (STB/WTB/AA/RAC) |
| ◆ | Number of Diamonds (AA/RAC) |
| [dog] | Pets Welcome |
| [rocking horse] | Reductions for Children |
| [tree] | Christmas Breaks |
| ♿ | Suitable for Disabled |

The symbols are arranged in the same order throughout the book so that looking down each page will give a quick comparison.

# Pembrokeshire

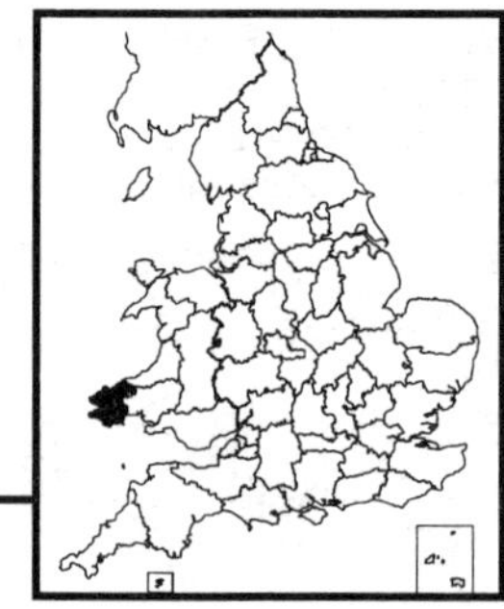

See also Colour Advertisement on page 37

## HEATHFIELD MANSION

**Letterston, Near Fishguard SA62 5EG**
**Tel: 01348 840263**
**e-mail: angelica.rees@virgin.net**

**WTB ★★★** *Country House*

A Grade II Listed Georgian country house in 16 acres of pasture and woodland, Heathfield is the home of former Welsh rugby international, Clive Rees and his wife Angelica. This is an ideal location for the appreciation of Pembrokeshire's many natural attractions. There is excellent golf, riding and fishing in the vicinity and the coast is only a few minutes' drive away. The accommodation is very comfortable and two of the three bedrooms have en suite bathrooms. The cuisine and wines are well above average. This is a most refreshing venue for a tranquil and wholesome holiday.

£ **Bed & Breakfast from £25 to £27 per person; Dinner by arrangement. Short Breaks available.**

See also Colour Advertisement on page 37

## GWARMACWYDD FARM

**Llanfallteg, Whitland SA34 0XH**
**Tel: 01437 563260 • Fax: 01437 563839**
**e-mail: info@a-farm-holiday.org • website:www.a-farm-holiday.org**

**WTB ★★★★** *Self-catering*

Gwarmacwydd is a country estate of over 450 acres, including two miles of riverbank. Come and see a real farm in action, the hustle and bustle of harvest, newborn calves and lambs. Children are welcomed. On the estate are five character stone cottages. Each has been lovingly converted from traditional farm buildings, parts of which are over 200 years old, and each is fully furnished and equipped with all modern conveniences. All electricity and linen included. All cottages are heated for year-round use. Colour brochure on request.

£ **Short Breaks available Friday–Friday or Friday–Monday except Christmas/New Year/Easter/Spring Bank Holiday/July and August.**

# Powys

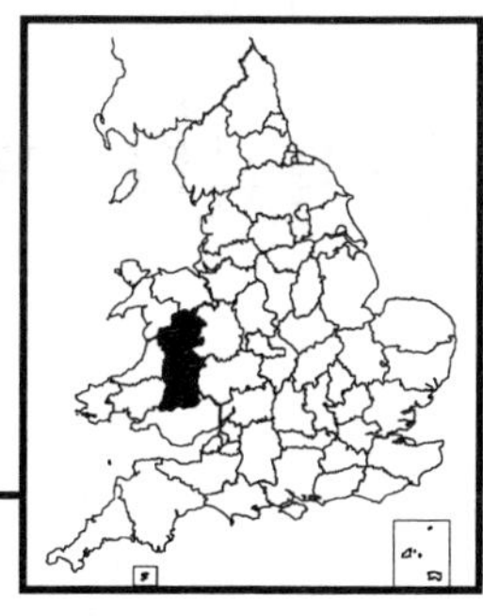

## FOREST CABIN BARGAIN BREAKS

**Tel: 02920 754887**
**website: www.business.virgin.net/victoria.wells**

Arguably as like the Canadian Rockies as you will find in this country. High in the majestic mountains and forests of Mid-Wales. Enjoy the sheer exhilaration of mountain air so pure it sparkles like champagne! Pets very welcome. Special discounts for seven-day and three/four person bookings. Reductions for children.

£ **As low as £65 for three nights. Includes cabin, breakfast and dinner.**

## OAK WOOD LODGES

**Llwynbaedd, Rhayader, Powys LD6 5NT**
**Tel: 01597 811422**

Self-catering Log Cabins. Superb Norwegian log cabins situated at approximately 1000ft above sea level with spectacular views of the Elan Valley and Cambrian Mountains. Enjoy pursuits such as walking, pony trekking, mountain biking, fishing, and bird watching in the most idyllic of surroundings. Excellent touring centre. Dogs welcome. Short breaks as well as full weeks. Open all year round. Please phone for more details and brochure.

£ **Short break details on request.**



A useful index of towns and counties appears at the back of this book on pages 181-182. Refer also to Contents Page 41.

# South Wales

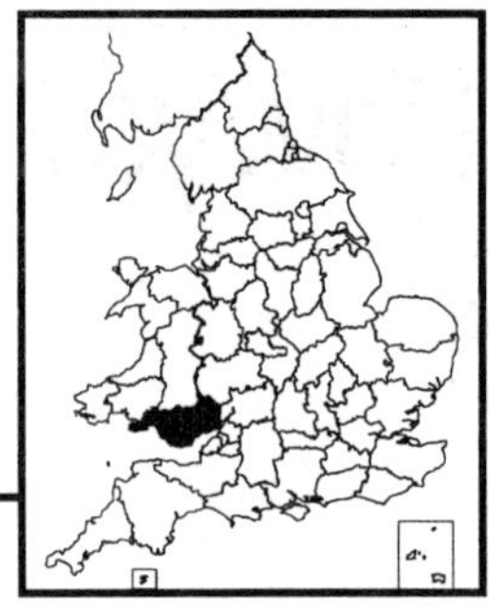

## WELSH INSTITUTE OF SPORT

WTB ★ *Conference Centre*

**Sophia Gardens, Cardiff CF11 9SW**
**Tel: 02920 300500 • Fax: 02920 300600**
**e-mail: wis@scw.co.uk • website: www.sports-council-wales.co.uk**

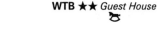

The Institute is ideally situated in a beautiful 'green belt' area overlooking the River Taff, and within a few minutes' walk of the centre of Cardiff. Nearby attractions include the Millennium Stadium, County Cricket Ground, Cardiff Castle, National Museum of Wales, St David's Hall, shopping centre, Cardiff Bay, and New Theatre. Leisure facilities include swimming pool, sauna, squash courts, tennis courts and a weights room. Whatever functions you are planning, you will find that our flexible approach will make this a popular venue, which is endorsed by a number of well-known organisations.

£ **Bed and Breakfast £24.75 per person per night; Half Board with lunch £25.75; Half Board with supper £27.00. Available all year.**

## PLAS LLANMIHANGEL

WTB ★★ *Guest House*

**Llanmihangel, Near Cowbridge CF71 7LQ**
**Tel: 01446 774610**
**e-mail: plasllanmihangel@ukonline.co.uk**

Plas Llanmihangel is the finest medieval manor house in the beautiful Vale of Glamorgan. We offer a genuine warmth of welcome, delightful accommodation, first-class food and service in our wonderful home. The baronial hall, great log fires, the ancient tower and acres of beautiful historic gardens intrigue all who stay in this fascinating Grade 1 Listed house. Its long history and continuous occupation have created a spectacular building in romantic surroundings, unchanged since the sixteenth century. A great opportunity to experience the ambience and charm of a past age (featured in the Consumer Association's 'Which? Good Bed & Breakfast Guide'). Three double rooms. High quality home-cooked evening meal on request.

£ **Bed & Breakfast from £28.**

## PLEASE NOTE

All the information in this book is given in good faith in the belief that it is correct. However, the publishers cannot guarantee the facts given in these pages, neither are they responsible for changes in policy, ownership or terms that may take place after the date of going to press. Readers should always satisfy themselves that the facilities they require are available and that the terms, if quoted, still apply.

## CULVER HOUSE HOTEL

WTB ★★ *Hotel*

**Port Eynon, Gower SA3 1NN**
**Tel: 01792 390755**
**website: www.culverhousehotel.co.uk**

An idyllic location 100 yards from the beautiful "Blue Flag" beach at Port Eynon on the breathtaking Gower Peninsula. We pride ourselves on taking thoughtful care of our guests. Our restaurant is of an exceptionally high standard. Interesting menus provide for all tastes including a wide vegetarian choice, focusing on freshly prepared dishes using local produce. We welcome singles and do not charge a supplement. All bedrooms are en suite or have private facilities, most have sea views. Ground floor rooms available. We are non-smoking.

£ **Short Break details on request.**

See also Colour Advertisement on page 37

## THE INN AT THE ELM TREE

WTB ★★★★★ *Inn*
AA/RAC ◆◆◆◆◆

**St Brides, Wentlooge, Near Newport, South Wales NP10 8SQ**
**Tel: 01633 680225 • Fax: 01633 681035**
**e-mail: inn@the-elm-tree.co.uk • website: www.the-elm-tree.co.uk**

A hidden retreat between two cities - Cardiff and Newport – just two miles from the M4 and a different world away. Originally an early 19th century barn, now transformed from a celebrated restaurant to an inn, The Elm Tree keeps the spirit of timeless hospitality alive, but with all the most modern appointments. Comfort epitomised, attention to detail paramount, relaxation assured, The Inn at The Elm Tree is the perfect retreat for a week or weekend, a special night stay, or simply a drink. The Restaurant has a long-standing reputation as one of the most distinguished in the area, using Wales' best natural produce. Bedrooms are individually designed to the highest standards, some with Jacuzzi, four posters and waterbeds. AA Rosette, Which? Good Hotel Guide. Gold Welcome Host, Taste of Wales, Johansen Recommended.

£ **Short Break details on request.**

See also Colour Advertisement on page 37

## THE RAT TRAP

WTB ★★★

**Old Chepstow Road, Llangeview, Near Usk, Monmouthshire NP15 1EY**
**Tel: 01291 673288**
**e-mail: info@rattraphotel.com • website: www.rattraphotel.com**

The Rat Trap Restaurant and Hotel is a family-run business, specialising in personal service. Situated in the heart of the Usk vale and adjacent to the Wye Valley, just one mile from the picturesque town of Usk - centrally located for business or pleasure; Newport, Cwmbran, Pontypool and Cardiff are all less than half an hour's drive away. Activities in the area include golf, gliding, grass skiing, horse riding, clay pigeon shooting, wind surfing and the surrounding countryside provides for some beautiful walks and cycle rides. All rooms in the hotel are furnished and maintained to a high standard, modern, bright and fully-equipped with colour television, direct dial telephone, tea coffee making and en suite facilities.

£ **Short Break details on request.**

## EXPLANATION OF SYMBOLS (Scotland and Wales)

| | |
|---|---|
| ★ | Number of Stars (STB/WTB/AA/RAC) |
| ◆ | Number of Diamonds (AA/RAC) |
| 🐕 | Pets Welcome |
| (rocking horse) | Reductions for Children |
| (tree) | Christmas Breaks |
| ♿ | Suitable for Disabled |

The symbols are arranged in the same order throughout the book so that looking down each page will give a quick comparison.

# Isle of Man

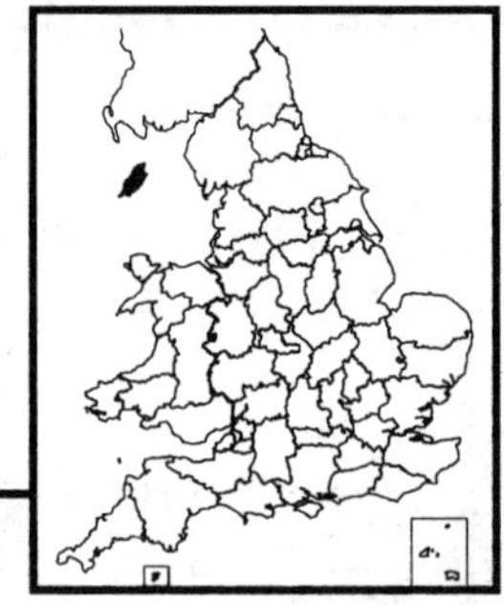

See also Colour Advertisement on page 30

## CASTLETOWN GOLF LINKS HOTEL

**ETC★★★**

**Fort Island, Derbyhaven, Isle of Man**
**Tel: 01624 822201 • Fax: 01624 824633**
**e-mail: golflinks@manx.net • website: www.golfiom.com**

Whatever you might be looking for, from a holiday to remember and cherish to a great golfing experience, or a wonderful choice for a conference venue, a fabulous wedding destination with a honeymoon suite to dream about, we have it. In fact the Castletown Golf Links Hotel caters happily and easily for all our guests' needs and occasions. This character-filled hotel is situated on Fort Island with breathtaking views across the Irish Sea, and panoramic views over the championship course. Only five minutes away from the airport, comfortable bedrooms, excellent restaurants, with leisure facilities such as heated swimming pool, sauna and two snooker tables. So what are you waiting for, get on the phone, the fax or the e-mail and find out what you have been missing.

£ **Terms on request.**

It has been said that the Isle of Man combines the best features of England, Scotland, Ireland and Wales, and Manxmen will tell you that you have not seen the best of the British Isles until you have been there. Perhaps this is why for many years the ancient kingdom of Mann has been a favourite destination for thousands of British visitors who come to a place with its own laws, its own language and even its own currency. Some visitors reckon that it is the nearest thing to going abroad without actually leaving the British Isles. Another bonus is that you can drive on the left and sterling is acceptable tender.The island is full of history. In fact legend has it that when the giant Finn McCooll had created the Giant's Causeway in Antrim he hurled a clod of earth into the Irish Sea and created the Isle of Man. There are many attractions for all ages here, from the modern pleasure of the island's capital, Douglas, to beautiful countryside and pretty little towns and villages for those who wish a more tranquil holiday.The Isle of Man really does have something for everyone, not least of which is its accessibility from all parts of Britain.

**PO Box 292, Douglas, Isle of Man IM99 2PT (01624 665371/662264**
**www.isle-of-man.com**

# INDEX OF TOWNS & COUNTIES – please also refer to Contents Page 43

# OTHER FHG TITLES FOR 2003

FHG Publications have a large range of attractive holiday accommodation guides for all kinds of holiday opportunities throughout Britain. They also make useful gifts at any time of year. Our guides are available in most bookshops and larger newsagents but we will be happy to post you a copy direct if you have any difficulty. POST FREE for addresses in the UK. We will also post abroad but have to charge separately for post or freight.

The original
**Farm Holiday Guide to COAST & COUNTRY HOLIDAYS** in England, Scotland, Wales and Channel Islands. Board, Self-catering, Caravans/Camping, Activity Holidays.

**BED AND BREAKFAST STOPS**
Over 1000 friendly and comfortable overnight stops. Non-smoking, Disabled and Special Diets Supplements.

**BRITAIN'S BEST HOLIDAYS**
A quick-reference general guide for all kinds of holidays.

Recommended
**WAYSIDE AND COUNTRY INNS** of Britain
Pubs, Inns and small hotels.

Recommended
**COUNTRY HOTELS**
of Britain
Including Country Houses, for the discriminating.

**PETS WELCOME!**
The original and unique guide for holidays for pet owners and their pets.

**CHILDREN WELCOME!** ☐
Family Holidays and Days Out guide.
Family holidays with details of amenities for children and babies.

**The GOLF GUIDE – Where to play Where to stay** ☐
In association with GOLF MONTHLY. Over 2800 golf courses in Britain with convenient accommodation. Holiday Golf in France, Portugal, Spain,USA, South Africa and Thailand.

**SELF-CATERING HOLIDAYS** ☐
in Britain
Over 1000 addresses throughout for self-catering and caravans in Britain.

The FHG Guide to **CARAVAN & CAMPING HOLIDAYS,** £4.49 ☐
Caravans for hire, sites and holiday parks and centres.

Tick your choice and send your order and payment to

FHG PUBLICATIONS, ABBEY MILL BUSINESS CENTRE, SEEDHILL, PAISLEY PA1 1TJ
TEL: 0141- 887 0428; FAX: 0141- 889 7204
e-mail: fhg@ipcmedia.com

FHG

Deduct 10% for 2/3 titles or copies; 20% for 4 or more.

Send to: NAME ..........................................

ADDRESS ..........................................

..........................................

..........................................

POST CODE ..........................

I enclose Cheque/Postal Order for £ ..........................................

SIGNATURE..........................DATE ..........................

Please complete the following to help us improve the service we provide. How did you find out about our guides?:

☐ Press ☐ Magazines ☐ TV/Radio ☐ Family/Friend ☐ Other

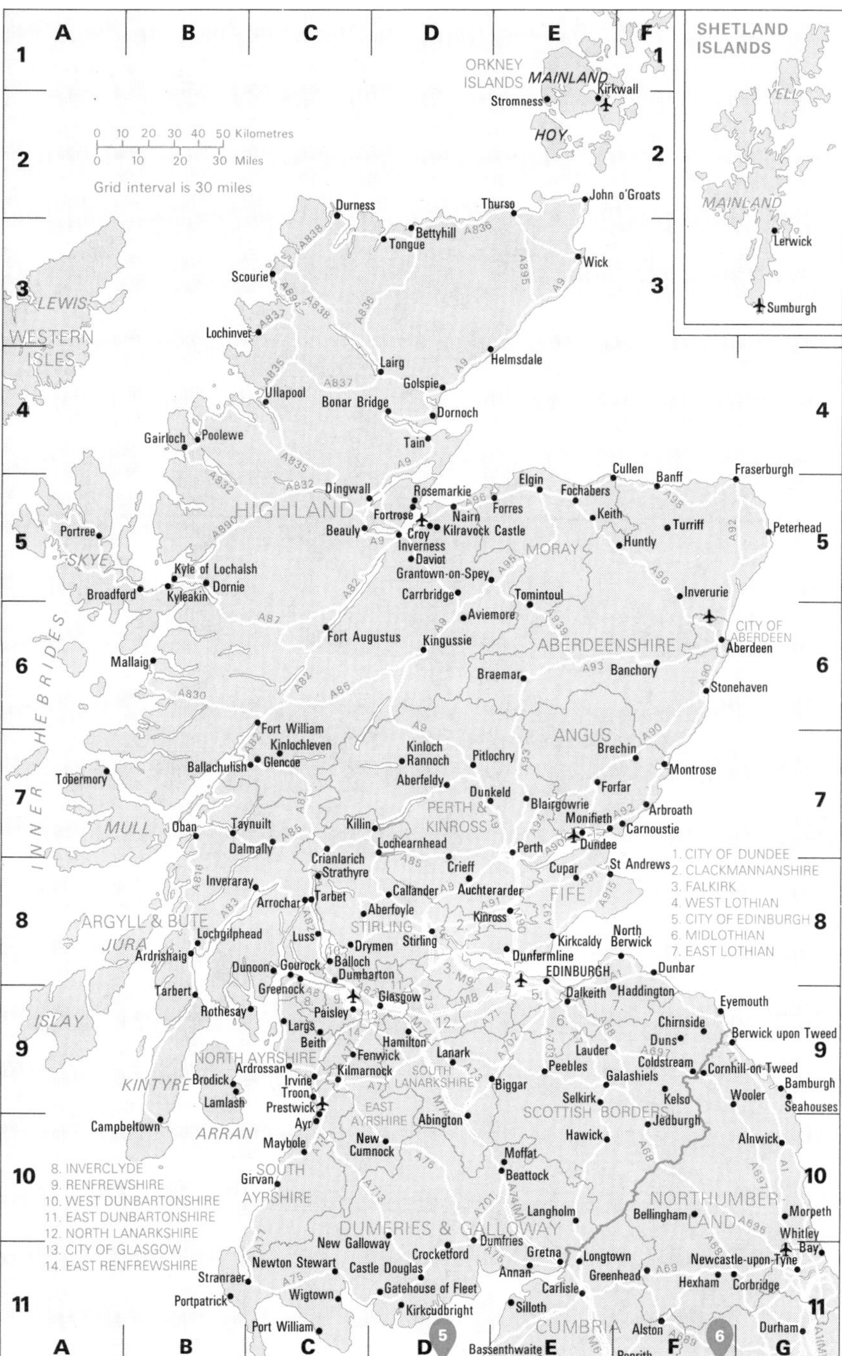
SHETLAND ISLANDS
YELL
MAINLAND
Lerwick
Sumburgh
ORKNEY ISLANDS
MAINLAND
Kirkwall
Stromness
HOY
0 10 20 30 40 50 Kilometres
0 10 20 30 Miles
Grid interval is 30 miles
John o'Groats
Thurso
Durness
Bettyhill
Tongue
Wick
Scourie
LEWIS
WESTERN ISLES
Lochinver
Helmsdale
Lairg
Golspie
Ullapool
Bonar Bridge
Dornoch
Gairloch
Poolewe
Tain
Cullen
Banff
Fraserburgh
Dingwall
Rosemarkie
Elgin
Fochabers
HIGHLAND
Fortrose
Nairn
Forres
Keith
Turriff
Peterhead
Portree
Beauly
Croy
Kilravock Castle
Inverness
Daviot
MORAY
Huntly
SKYE
Kyle of Lochalsh
Dornie
Broadford
Kyleakin
Grantown-on-Spey
Carrbridge
Tomintoul
Inverurie
Aviemore
CITY OF ABERDEEN
Fort Augustus
Kingussie
ABERDEENSHIRE
Aberdeen
Mallaig
Braemar
Banchory
Stonehaven
INNER HEBRIDES
Fort William
Kinlochleven
ANGUS
Brechin
Ballachulish
Glencoe
Kinloch Rannoch
Pitlochry
Montrose
Tobermory
Aberfeldy
Dunkeld
Forfar
PERTH & KINROSS
Blairgowrie
Arbroath
MULL
Oban
Taynuilt
Killin
Monifieth
Carnoustie
Dalmally
Lochearnhead
Perth
Dundee
Crianlarich
Strathyre
Crieff
Cupar
St Andrews
Inveraray
Auchterarder
FIFE
Arrochar
Tarbet
Callander
Aberfoyle
Kinross
ARGYLL & BUTE
STIRLING
Lochgilphead
Luss
Stirling
Kirkcaldy
North Berwick
JURA
Drymen
Dunfermline
Ardrishaig
Dunoon
Gourock
Balloch
Dumbarton
EDINBURGH
Dunbar
Greenock
Glasgow
Dalkeith
Haddington
Tarbert
Eyemouth
Rothesay
Paisley
ISLAY
Largs
Chirnside
Beith
Hamilton
Lauder
Duns
Berwick upon Tweed
NORTH AYRSHIRE
Fenwick
Lanark
Coldstream
Cornhill-on-Tweed
Ardrossan
Kilmarnock
SOUTH LANARKSHIRE
Peebles
Galashiels
Bamburgh
Brodick
Irvine
Biggar
KINTYRE
Troon
EAST AYRSHIRE
Selkirk
Kelso
Wooler
Seahouses
Lamlash
Prestwick
Abington
SCOTTISH BORDERS
Ayr
Jedburgh
Campbeltown
ARRAN
Hawick
New Cumnock
Alnwick
Maybole
Moffat
SOUTH AYRSHIRE
Beattock
Girvan
NORTHUMBERLAND
Langholm
Bellingham
Morpeth
DUMFRIES & GALLOWAY
Whitley Bay
New Galloway
Crocketford
Dumfries
Gretna
Longtown
Newton Stewart
Castle Douglas
Annan
Newcastle-upon-Tyne
Stranraer
Greenhead
Hexham
Corbridge
Gatehouse of Fleet
Carlisle
Portpatrick
Wigtown
Kirkcudbright
Silloth
CUMBRIA
Port William
Alston
Durham
Bassenthwaite
Penrith
1. CITY OF DUNDEE
2. CLACKMANNANSHIRE
3. FALKIRK
4. WEST LOTHIAN
5. CITY OF EDINBURGH
6. MIDLOTHIAN
7. EAST LOTHIAN
8. INVERCLYDE
9. RENFREWSHIRE
10. WEST DUNBARTONSHIRE
11. EAST DUNBARTONSHIRE
12. NORTH LANARKSHIRE
13. CITY OF GLASGOW
14. EAST RENFREWSHIRE
A
B
C
D
E
F
G
1
2
3
4
5
6
7
8
9
10
11

# Map 1

A
B
C
D
E
F
1
2
3
4
0 10 20 30 40 50 Kilometres
0 10 20 30 Miles
Grid interval is 30 miles
1. BRIDGEND
2. RHONDDA CYNON TAFF
3. MERTHYR TYDFIL
4. CAERPHILLY
5. BLAENAU GWENT
6. TORFAEN
7. SOUTH GLOUCESTERSHIRE
8. BRISTOL
9. NORTH WEST SOMERSET
10. BATH & NORTH EAST SOMERSET
Dolgellau
Barmouth
Tywyn
Aberdovey
Machynlleth
Welshpool
Montgomery
Newtown
Llanidloes
Aberystwyth
CARDIGANSHIRE
POWYS
SHROPSHIRE
Stafford
Shrewsbury
Wellington
Wolverhampton
Church Stretton
Wentnor
Bridgnorth
Bishop's Castle
Craven Arms
Ludlow
Kidderminster
Knighton
Rhayader
Presteigne
Droitwich
Aberaeron
New Quay
Llandrindod Wells
Tregaron
Leominster
Kington
HEREFORD AND WORCESTER
Worcester
Builth Wells
Painscastle
Llanwrtyd Wells
Lampeter
Cardigan
Newcastle Emlyn
Llandyssul
Llandovery
Hay-on-Wye
Felton
Malvern
Hereford
Ledbury
Fishguard
Tewkesbury
Brecon
St David's
CARMARTHENSHIRE
PEMBROKESHIRE
Carmarthen
Llandeilo
Ross-on-Wye
Cheltenham
Gloucester
Haverfordwest
Broad Haven
Narberth
Symonds Yat
Abergavenny
Monmouth
Coleford
Cinderford
GLOUCESTERSHIRE
Milford Haven
Saundersfoot
Merthyr Tydfil
MONMOUTH-SHIRE
NEATH & PORT TALBOT
Stroud
Lydney
Pembroke
Tenby
Llanelli
Pontypool
Swansea
Neath
Pontypridd
Chepstow
Wotton-under-Edge
SWANSEA
Port Talbot
Caerphilly
Newport
NEWPORT
Malmesbury
Tormarton
CARDIFF
Porthcawl
Bridgend
Cardiff
VALE OF GLAMORGAN
Clevedon
Bristol
Chippenham
Barry

## Map 2

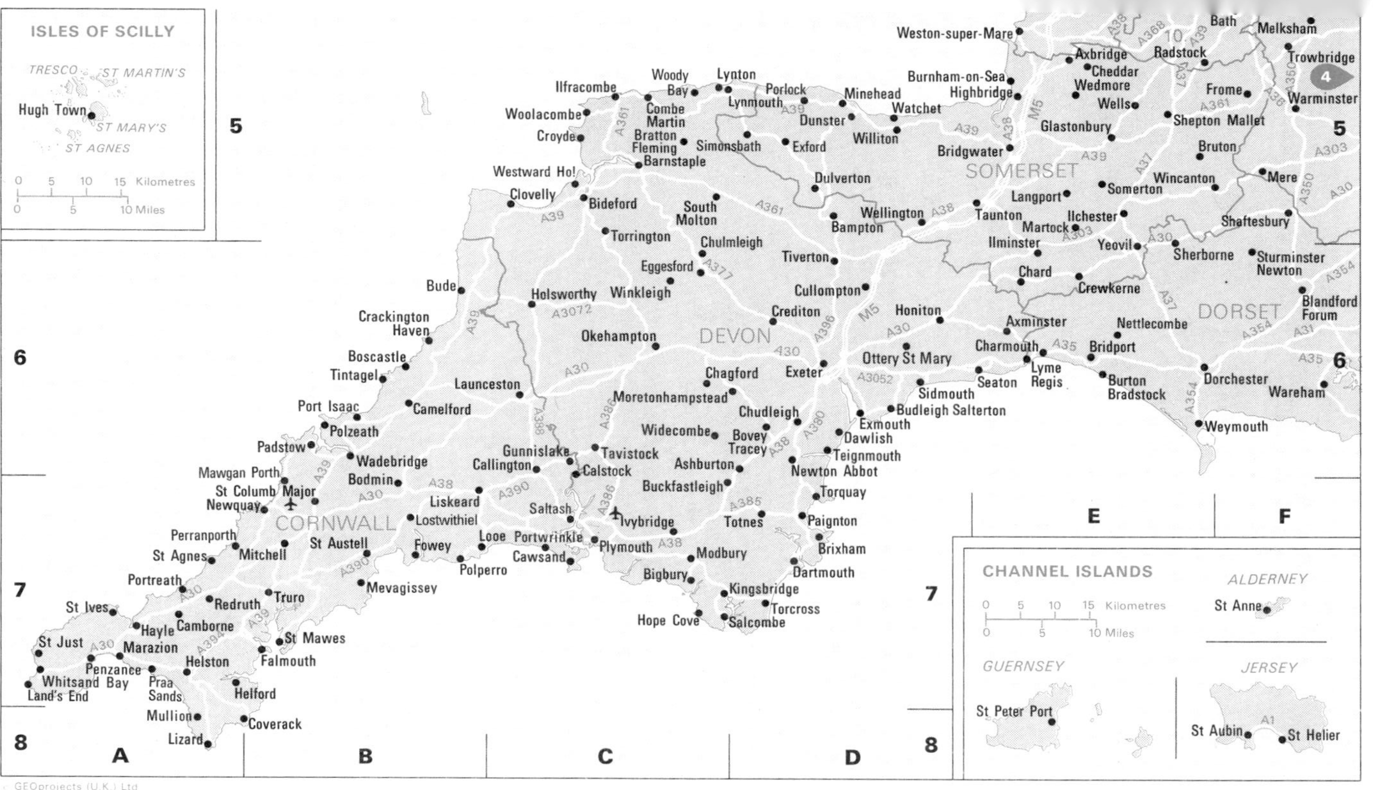

ISLES OF SCILLY
TRESCO
ST MARTIN'S
Hugh Town
ST MARY'S
ST AGNES
0 5 10 15 Kilometres
0 5 10 Miles
SOMERSET
DEVON
DORSET
CORNWALL
Weston-super-Mare
Bath
Melksham
Axbridge
Cheddar
Wedmore
Radstock
Trowbridge
Frome
Warminster
Wells
Shepton Mallet
Glastonbury
Bruton
Burnham-on-Sea
Highbridge
Bridgwater
Ilfracombe
Woody Bay
Lynton
Lynmouth
Porlock
Minehead
Watchet
Dunster
Williton
Woolacombe
Combe Martin
Bratton Fleming
Croyde
Simonsbath
Exford
Barnstaple
Westward Ho!
Clovelly
Bideford
Dulverton
South Molton
Wellington
Bampton
Taunton
Langport
Somerton
Wincanton
Mere
Martock
Ilchester
Ilminster
Yeovil
Shaftesbury
Sherborne
Sturminster Newton
Torrington
Chulmleigh
Tiverton
Eggesford
Chard
Crewkerne
Bude
Holsworthy
Winkleigh
Cullompton
Honiton
Crediton
Axminster
Nettlecombe
Blandford Forum
Crackington Haven
Okehampton
Charmouth
Bridport
Boscastle
Ottery St Mary
Lyme Regis
Tintagel
Launceston
Chagford
Exeter
Seaton
Burton Bradstock
Dorchester
Wareham
Sidmouth
Port Isaac
Camelford
Moretonhampstead
Budleigh Salterton
Weymouth
Polzeath
Chudleigh
Exmouth
Padstow
Widecombe
Bovey Tracey
Dawlish
Wadebridge
Gunnislake
Tavistock
Teignmouth
Callington
Ashburton
Mawgan Porth
Bodmin
Calstock
Newton Abbot
St Columb Major
Buckfastleigh
Torquay
Newquay
Liskeard
Saltash
Lostwithiel
Ivybridge
Totnes
Paignton
Perranporth
Looe
Portwrinkle
St Austell
Fowey
Plymouth
Brixham
St Agnes
Mitchell
Cawsand
Modbury
Polperro
Dartmouth
Portreath
Bigbury
Mevagissey
Kingsbridge
Truro
St Ives
Redruth
Torcross
Hope Cove
Salcombe
Hayle
Camborne
St Mawes
St Just
Marazion
Helston
Falmouth
Penzance
Whitsand Bay
Praa Sands
Land's End
Helford
Mullion
Coverack
Lizard
CHANNEL ISLANDS
0 5 10 15 Kilometres
0 5 10 Miles
ALDERNEY
St Anne
GUERNSEY
St Peter Port
JERSEY
St Aubin
St Helier

# Map 3

A
B
C
D
E
F
1
2
3
4
LINCOLNSHIRE
NOTTINGHAMSHIRE
DERBYSHIRE
STAFFS
LEICESTERSHIRE
NORTHAMPTONSHIRE
WARWICKSHIRE
WEST MIDLANDS
CAMBRIDGESHIRE
NORFOLK
SUFFOLK
ESSEX
HERTFORDSHIRE
BEDFORDSHIRE
BUCKS
GLOS
Skegness
Boston
Sleaford
Grantham
Spalding
Stamford
Peterborough
Hunstanton
King's Lynn
Downham Market
Wells-next-the-Sea
Blakeney
Sheringham
Cromer
Overstrand
Holt
Fakenham
Mundesley-on-Sea
North Walsham
Stalham
Winterton
Hemsby
Horning
Wroxham
Acle
Caister
Great Yarmouth
Norwich
East Dereham
Swaffham
Watton
Lowestoft
Beccles
Kessingland
Bungay
Harleston
Southwold
Halesworth
Diss
Thetford
Saxmundham
Aldeburgh
Framlingham
Woodbridge
Ipswich
Harwich
Walton-on-Naze
Clacton-on-Sea
Colchester
Dedham
Hadleigh
Sudbury
Lavenham
Stowmarket
Bury St Edmunds
Newmarket
Haverhill
Braintree
Stansted
Bishop's Stortford
Hertford
Ely
Cambridge
Huntingdon
Baldock
Hitchin
Luton
Dunstable
Bedford
Milton Keynes
Aylesbury
Buckingham
Bicester
Towcester
Brackley
Banbury
Northampton
Kettering
Daventry
Market Harborough
Uppingham
Oakham
Melton Mowbray
Leicester
Loughborough
Nottingham
Newark
Mansfield
East Midlands
Derby
Matlock
Bakewell
Ashbourne
Leek
Burton-upon-Trent
Stafford
Lichfield
Wolverhampton
Birmingham
National Exhibition Centre
Coventry
Rugby
Leamington Spa
Warwick
Stratford-upon-Avon
Chipping Norton
Kingham
Bourton-on-the-Water
Burford
Evesham
Broadway
Moreton-in-Marsh
Stow-on-the-Wold
Cheltenham

# Map 4

5
6
7
8
A
B
C
D
E
F
OXFORDSHIRE
BERKSHIRE
WILTSHIRE
HAMPSHIRE
SURREY
GREATER LONDON
KENT
EAST SUSSEX
WEST SUSSEX
ISLE OF WIGHT
LONDON
Cirencester
Malmesbury
Swindon
Chippenham
Melksham
Devizes
Marlborough
Hungerford
Oxford
Abingdon
Wantage
Wallingford
Henley-on-Thames
Reading
Newbury
Basingstoke
Andover
Amesbury
Salisbury
Winchester
Romsey
Southampton
Alton
Petersfield
Fordingbridge
Ringwood
Lyndhurst
Lymington
Wimborne
Christchurch
Bournemouth
Poole
Wareham
Studland
Swanage
Totland Bay
Yarmouth
Freshwater
Cowes
Newport
Ryde
Sandown
Shanklin
Ventnor
Chale
St Lawrence
Portsmouth
Gosport
Southsea
Hayling Island
Chichester
Selsey
Bognor Regis
Midhurst
Petworth
Pulborough
Arundel
Littlehampton
Worthing
Steyning
Shoreham-by-Sea
Hove
Brighton
Horsham
Crawley
Gatwick
Haywards Heath
East Grinstead
Uckfield
Lewes
Newhaven
Seaford
Eastbourne
Hailsham
Heathfield
Crowborough
Hawkhurst
Battle
Bexhill-on-Sea
Hastings
Rye
Winchelsea
New Romney
Dymchurch
Hythe
Folkestone
Dover
Deal
Sandwich
Ramsgate
Broadstairs
Margate
Herne Bay
Whitstable
Canterbury
Ashford
Tenterden
Tunbridge Wells
Tonbridge
Sevenoaks
Maidstone
Chatham
Rochester
Sheerness
Southend-on-Sea
Burnham-on-Crouch
Maldon
Chelmsford
Brentwood
Romford
Dartford
Bromley
Croydon
Epping
Hatfield
St Albans
Watford
Maidenhead
Windsor
Heathrow
Brentford
Richmond
Kingston Upon Thames
Weybridge
Epsom
Reigate
Dorking
Guildford
Haslemere
Hindhead
0 10 20 30 40 50 Kilometres
0 10 20 30 Miles
Grid interval is 30 miles
© GEOprojects (U.K.) Ltd
Crown Copyright Reserved

# Map 5

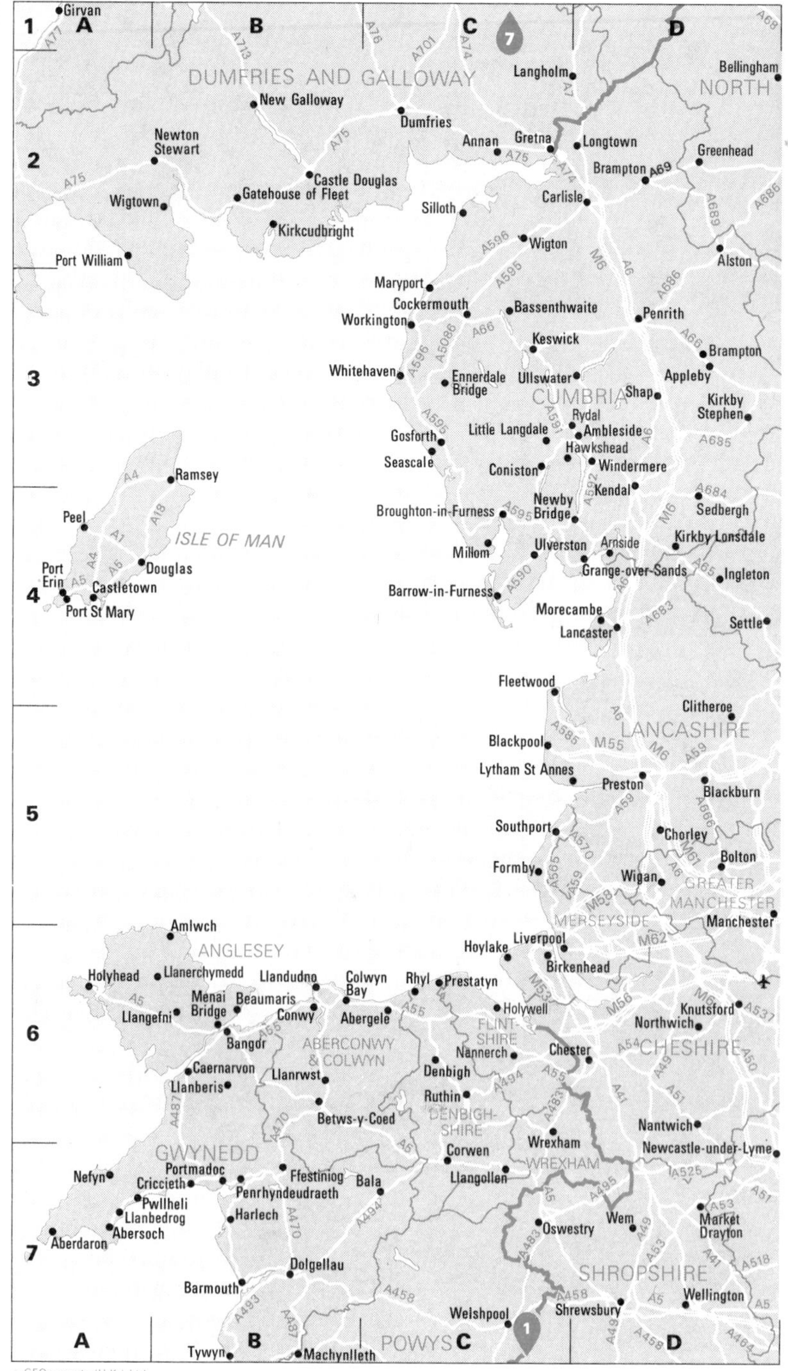

DUMFRIES AND GALLOWAY
Girvan
New Galloway
Dumfries
Newton Stewart
Castle Douglas
Gatehouse of Fleet
Wigtown
Kirkcudbright
Port William
Langholm
Annan
Gretna
Longtown
Brampton
Carlisle
Silloth
Wigton
Bellingham
NORTH
Greenhead
Alston
Maryport
Cockermouth
Workington
Bassenthwaite
Keswick
Penrith
Brampton
Whitehaven
Ennerdale Bridge
Ullswater
Appleby
CUMBRIA
Shap
Kirkby Stephen
Rydal
Little Langdale
Ambleside
Hawkshead
Gosforth
Seascale
Coniston
Windermere
Kendal
Sedbergh
Broughton-in-Furness
Newby Bridge
Millom
Ulverston
Arnside
Kirkby Lonsdale
Grange-over-Sands
Ingleton
Barrow-in-Furness
Morecambe
Lancaster
Settle
Ramsey
Peel
ISLE OF MAN
Douglas
Port Erin
Castletown
Port St Mary
Fleetwood
Clitheroe
LANCASHIRE
Blackpool
Lytham St Annes
Preston
Blackburn
Southport
Chorley
Bolton
Formby
Wigan
GREATER MANCHESTER
MERSEYSIDE
Manchester
Amlwch
ANGLESEY
Hoylake
Liverpool
Birkenhead
Holyhead
Llanerchymedd
Llandudno
Colwyn Bay
Rhyl
Prestatyn
Menai Bridge
Beaumaris
Llangefni
Conwy
Abergele
Holywell
Knutsford
Northwich
Bangor
FLINTSHIRE
Nannerch
Chester
CHESHIRE
ABERCONWY & COLWYN
Caernarvon
Denbigh
Llanberis
Llanrwst
Ruthin
Betws-y-Coed
DENBIGHSHIRE
Nantwich
Wrexham
WREXHAM
GWYNEDD
Corwen
Newcastle-under-Lyme
Nefyn
Portmadoc
Ffestiniog
Criccieth
Penrhyndeudraeth
Bala
Llangollen
Pwllheli
Llanbedrog
Harlech
Abersoch
Aberdaron
Oswestry
Wem
Market Drayton
Dolgellau
SHROPSHIRE
Barmouth
Wellington
Welshpool
Shrewsbury
POWYS
Tywyn
Machynlleth

# Map 6

E F G H
1 2 3 4 5 6 7

0 10 20 30 40 50 Kilometres
0 10 20 30 Miles
Grid interval is 30 miles

1. STOCKTON-ON-TEES
2. MIDDLESBROUGH
3. KINGSTON UPON HULL
4. NORTH EAST LINCOLNSHIRE

UMBERLAND
Morpeth
Whitley Bay
Tynemouth
South Shields
Corbridge
Hexham
Newcastle-upon-Tyne
TYNE AND WEAR
Sunderland
Durham
DURHAM
HARTLEPOOL
Bishop Auckland
Middleton-in-Teesdale
Redcar
Saltburn-by-the-Sea
Middlesbrough
REDCAR & CLEVELAND
Barnard Castle
Darlington
Guisborough
Whitby
Stokesley
Richmond
Hawes
Leyburn
Northallerton
Leeming Bar
Scarborough
Middleham
Thirsk
Helmsley
Pickering
Ayton
Cayton Bay
Filey
NORTH YORKSHIRE
Ripon
Castle Howard
Malton
Flamborough
Grassington
Huby
Sledmere
Bridlington
Driffield
Harrogate
York
Skipton
YORK
EAST RIDING OF YORKSHIRE
Hornsea
Keighley
Ilkley
Beverley
Bingley
Selby
Bradford
Leeds
WEST YORKSHIRE
Heptonstall
Hull
Withernsea
Halifax
Goole
NORTH LINCOLNSHIRE
Huddersfield
Scunthorpe
Grimsby
Cleethorpes
Barnsley
Doncaster
SOUTH YORKSHIRE
Glossop
Gainsborough
Louth
Sheffield
Mablethorpe
Worksop
Alford
Buxton
Macclesfield
Chesterfield
Lincoln
Horncastle
Bakewell
Skegness
Congleton
Matlock
Mansfield
Leek
DERBYSHIRE
NOTTINGHAMSHIRE
LINCOLNSHIRE
Newark
Ashbourne
Sleaford
Stoke-on-Trent
Boston
Nottingham
Grantham
Derby
STAFFORDSHIRE
East Midlands
Stafford
Burton-upon-Trent
Loughborough
Melton Mowbray
Spalding
LEICESTERSHIRE
Lichfield
Stamford
Oakham
Leicester
Uppingham
Peterborough

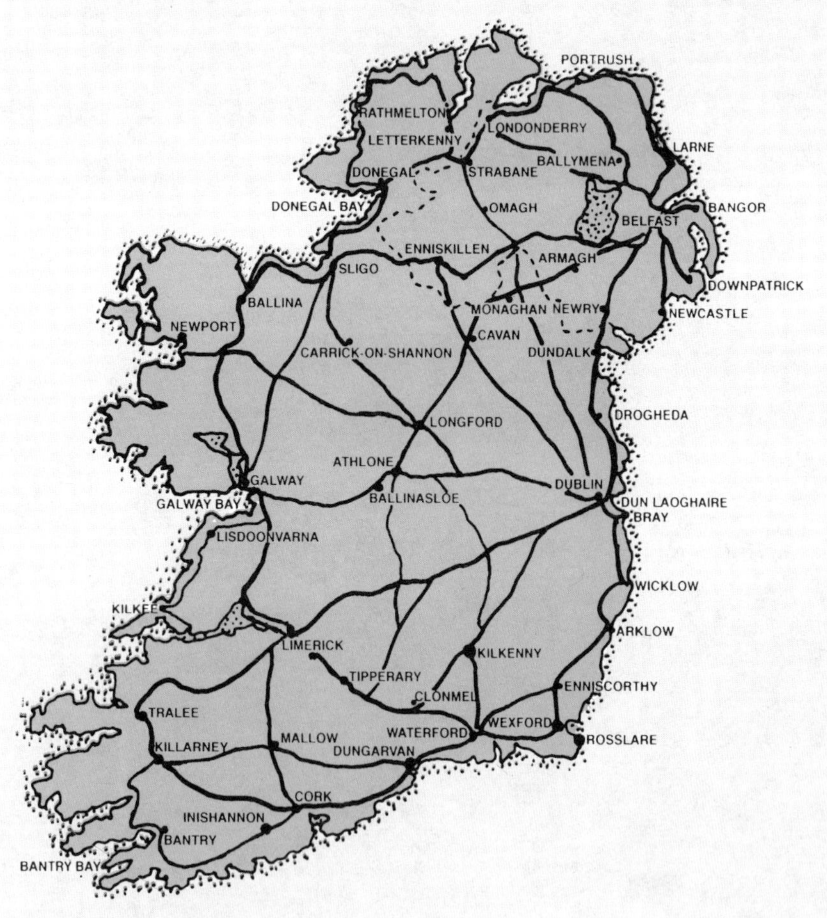
PORTRUSH
RATHMELTON
LONDONDERRY
LETTERKENNY
LARNE
BALLYMENA
DONEGAL
STRABANE
DONEGAL BAY
OMAGH
BANGOR
BELFAST
ENNISKILLEN
ARMAGH
SLIGO
DOWNPATRICK
BALLINA
MONAGHAN
NEWRY
NEWCASTLE
NEWPORT
CAVAN
CARRICK-ON-SHANNON
DUNDALK
DROGHEDA
LONGFORD
ATHLONE
GALWAY
DUBLIN
BALLINASLOE
GALWAY BAY
DUN LAOGHAIRE
BRAY
LISDOONVARNA
WICKLOW
KILKEE
ARKLOW
LIMERICK
KILKENNY
TIPPERARY
ENNISCORTHY
CLONMEL
TRALEE
WEXFORD
WATERFORD
MALLOW
ROSSLARE
KILLARNEY
DUNGARVAN
CORK
INISHANNON
BANTRY
BANTRY BAY